SOME SLAVES

OF

FREDERICK COUNTY, VIRGINIA

WILL BOOKS 1-28

1743–1868

COMPILED BY

Sandra Barlau

HERITAGE BOOKS
2024

HERITAGE BOOKS

AN IMPRINT OF HERITAGE BOOKS, INC.

Books, CDs, and more—Worldwide

For our listing of thousands of titles see our website
at
www.HeritageBooks.com

Published 2024 by
HERITAGE BOOKS, INC.
Publishing Division
5810 Ruatan Street
Berwyn Heights, MD 20740

Cover portrait: Mary Timbers Harrison

International Standard Book Number
Paperbound: 978-0-7884-3067-1

TABLE OF CONTENTS

PREFACE

The idea for the Slaves of Virginia series was conceived when I decided to find the mother of my enslaved 2nd gr-grandmother Mildred Timbers. How did Alexander Jeffries obtain her? She could have been willed (the reason for reading the Fauquier will books), deeded, gifted, or purchased.

After reading the Fauquier County, Virginia will books 1-31 from 1759 to 1869 I determined that she was not willed to him. That left the the deed books and tax records. I used the same format for the deed books as I had for the will books and set up a spreadsheet for the tax records. I included a column in the spreadsheet that added the number of slaves owned. That column was very useful because any changes in the number of slaves each year was obvious.

By comparing the will books, deed books, and tax records I came to the conclusion that Mildred Timbers was purchased from the Thomas Ingram estate. Estate sales were advertised in the local paper. I read the *Richmond Enquirer* from December 1837 to Dec 1838. There were only two notices. The only one that appeared relevant is found below. Note that it really doesn't give any helpful information. Hopefully something else will be found and complete the search.

FAMILY NEGROES FOR SALE

For sale 15 or 20 likely young Negroes, including men, women, boys and girls. Among them is one first rate seamstress, and one woman a good house servant. The above Servants are as likely as can be found anywhere, and can be recommended to any gentleman who wishes to purchase for his own use. Such a lot is seldom in the market.

Inquire at the office of the Enquirer March 20   102.4t[1]

---

[1] *Richmond Enquirer*, Volume 34, Number 102, 20 March 1838, pg 2, Library of Virginia

INTRODUCTION

Will books are a good source in the search for slaves only if the owner named the slave(s). Many times a will lists property without specifying if it includes slaves. For example: "I will and bequeath to my (wife, son, daughter, etc.) all my estate both real and personal of every sort." or "…the property I have already given to my (wife, son, daughter, etc.)…" The documents often do not include the slave's name, sometimes only girl, runaway, boy, etc.

The documents in this manuscript include wills, administrator's estate accounts, executor accounts, and inventories and appraisals which are found under Probate Records on the familysearch.org website.

Each slave owner is listed first followed by the page number, date and type of document. The list of slaves follows below. The new owner is listed if known. Surnames of the owner's children are indexed only if noted in the document.

Not included in this summary is a slave's monetary value, if the slave was sold, hired by the estate, hired out, or who hired the slave. The original text should be read to determine which occurred. Sometimes the estate or guardian account listed people paying money to the estate but not why the remittances were paid.

It is important to note the slave's age since the value of a slave increases or decreases with age and ability. It can also be used as a tracking tool. The ages are approximate.

When you read the digitized will books be aware that different spellings were used. Be creative in looking for first names: Seaser (Cesar), Ausker (Oscar), Cilvia (Silvia), Fillis, Phelice, Fillice, Philas, etc. Some names may be shortened, i.e. Cat could be Caty or Catherine or Cattrerine.

Handwriting is sometimes difficult to read. In some cases I placed an underscore between letters (e.g. Mi_n_a). Names beginning with an underscore are indexed first (e.g. __mia). Some letters can be mistaken for others: "L" and "S", "T" and "F", J" and "I". The letter "n" can look like "u", "nn" could be "rr".

There are question marks next to some of the names and places where the handwriting is too faint or difficult to read. Be sure to peruse the entire index and the original document to make your own decision regarding the spelling of the name, county or town. You may discover a name that has a similar spelling to the one you are researching. Names can also appear more than once on a page.

Some of the pages are very faint. The quality of the films varies and some digitized copies were difficult to read. There were many guesses as to the written names and I take full responsibility for any errors in transcription.

The documents read for this volume are on microfilm held by the Family History Library at Salt Lake City. They are available on-line through Family History Centers.

I hope this book helps you to locate a slave or an owner. Good luck in your search.

ABBREVIATIONS

Admin - Administrator

Admin Acct – Administration account

Co. - county

Comm Acct – Committee Account

con't - continued

dec'd – deceased

div - division

Estate Acct – Estate Account

Exec Acct – Executor Account

Inv & Appr – Inventory & Appraisal

Gdn Acct – Guardian Account

Jr. - Junior

KY – Kentucky

MD – Maryland

Sr. - Senior

TN - Tennessee

Trustee Acct – Trustee Account

yrs - years

WILL BOOK 1
1743-1751

Jonathan TEEMAN ....pg 10, 6 Dec 1743, estate acct

man to serve 2 3/4 years

Benjamin BORDON ....pg 39, 7 Mar 1744 in court, inv & appr

servant man

Leonard HEIM ....pg 62, 25 Sept 1745, will

Guy, servant woman to eldest son Meredith HELM

John SHEPHARD .... pg 76, 3 June 1746, will

old woman to John SMITH

David DAWSON...................................pg 134, 5 Aug 1847, inv & appr

servant man

Patrick GILLASPY ....pg 152, 11 Nov 1747, inv & appr

servant lad

Thomas ANDERSON ....pg 180, 24 Mar 1747, will

woman Kate, girl Rose, boys Harry, Jack to wife Elizabeth
ANDERSON & at her death to Winefred BAUGUS daughter of Robert
BAUGUS & to Richard BAUGUS son of Henry BAUGUS

.... pg 193, 6 Sept 1748 in court, inv & appr

woman Cate, girl Rose, boys Harry, Jack

Daniel HART ....pg 197, 25 Sept 1748, will

boy James Clerkson to be sold

William FERNLEY .... pg 211, 6 Dec 1748, inv & appr

old servant man Henry Booler

1

John ALFORD .... pg 231, 13 Nov 1748, will

    boy Cesar to son John ALFORD; girl Licia to daughter Priscilla
    ALFORD after the death of wife

.... Mar 1748 in court, inv & appr

girl List, young fellow

Baranaby McHENRY .... pg 357, 7 Dec 1749, will

orphan child living on the premises to James BAKER

William HEATH .... pg 389, 9 May 1750, inv & appr

orphan boy bound by order of P.? WILLIAM

Samuel ISAACS .... pg 396, 14 Aug 1750, inv & appr

servant man

Hugh FURGUISON .... pg 401, 15 Aug 1750, inv & appr

servant woman

Dorothy H. CARTMELL .... pg 412, 20 Apr 1749, will

    woman Peghe/Pegpee to grandson Edward CARTMELL for a term of
    5 years, also boy Jo

Israel FRIEND .... pg 418, 15 Nov 1750, inv & appr

woman & her daughter; old woman

Dorothy CARTMELL .... pg 434, 13 Feb 17__ in court, inv & appr

woman & child

John MUSGROVE .... pg 460, 12 Jan 1748, inv & appr

3 slaves

Ralph HUMPHREY .... pg 461, 17 May 1751 in court, inv & appr

    old man; servant girl Alice to serve 3 years; servant man Tom 1 year,
    8 months; girl Eliza Tibbs

WILL BOOK 2
1752-1761

4

Andrew CALDWALL......................pg 290, 29 Aug 1757, inv & appr

servant Richard Dean has about 4 years to serve

Nathan CARTMILL..................pg 299, 5 July 1758 in court, inv & appr

servant boy

Farrill RAILEY.........................pg 305, 29 July 1757, inv & appr

servant lad Richard Hamore

Joseph ROBERTS......................pg 351, 7 June 1759 in court, inv & appr

servant man Peter Hunter

Joseph MATHEWS of Albemarle Co.................pg 354, 1 Feb 1759, will

wench Sarah, boy William to sister's son John JONES

Thomas T. CHERRY, Sr.....................pg 364, 5 Oct 1759, will

girl Nell to wife Rachel & at her death Nell & her increase to 5 younger
sons William, John, Ralph, Moses, & Aaron

Elizabeth E. BROOKS..................... pg 368, 12 Dec 1759, will

man Major to son Joel BROOKS; girl Nancy to daughter Mary
THORNBACK

Samuel ISAAC.....................pg 376, 4 Mar 1760 in court, will

Ben to second son Elijah ISAAC; George to son Godfry ISAAC

Paul LONG.............................pg 391, 20 Aug 1759, inv & appr

negroes

Thomas SWEARINGEN..................... pg 402, 4 Apr 1760, will

girl Luse to wife Sarah SWEARINGEN & at her death to be divided
between daughters Drusilah MORGAN, Sarah SWEARINGEN, &
Eleonore SWEARINGEN

Thomas WATERS............................... pg 452, 14 Apr 1760, inv & appr

wench

WILL BOOK 3
1761 - 1770

(Note: The bottom portions of pages 6-9, 259 – 305, 346, 347, 362, 363, 370, 371, 376 – 379, 382, 383, 386, 387, and 401 - 406 were missed during filming but are intact on the microfilm roll. Pages 153-156 were not filmed.)

Elizabeth BROOKS...................................pg 15, 16 Feb 1760, inv & appr

man, woman

Philip BABB ....pg 42, 6 Mar 1762, will

girl Bet to wife Margaret BABB; Lynn to be sold & the money divided between daughters Jane & Margaret & son Mercer

Thomas REDMAN.................................pg 88, 17 Sept 1762, inv & appr

Dick, Pegg, Baker, Sly, Bess, Geffree

James STYNSON..................................pg 123, 5 July 1762, inv & appr

man

Elizabeth BROOKS............................... pg 134, Dec 1761, admin acct

2 negroes not sold which were appraised

Mathias CELZER................................pg 141, 8 Sept 1763, will

slaves to be valued; girl to daughter Christina; choice of a negro to wife

Matthias CELSER/SELSER....................pg 162, 7 Feb 17_4, inv & appr

woman Jem?, man Will, wenches Sal, Mol?, Nan, Jo? 8 years old

Frederick BEELER .... pg 182, 5 Feb 1764, will

man to sons George & Charles BEELER

Anthony TURNER................................. pg 198, 4 May 1764, inv & appr

girl Phillis

Thomas CHERRY ....pg 208, 24 Oct 176_, inv & appr

wench Nell

7

James CRUMBLEY .... pg 231, 1 Sept 1764, inv & appr

man, woman & child, girl

William BANE .... pg 287, 17 Apr 1765, inv & appr

servant maid

Richard STEPHENSON .... pg 288, 21 Mar 1765, will

woman Jean to wife Hena? STEPHENSON to nurse daughter Eleanor & after the death of the wife to John STEPHENSON, but if Eleanor dies during wife's lifetime Jean is to be sold

William HALL .... pg 302, 21 Mar 1766, inv & appr

servant maid to Mary McCRU__

Captain John DEVLON .... pg 317, 28 Sept 1765, inv & appr

man Samuel McCell_

Frederick BEELER .... pg 341, 3 June 1766, inv & appr

man

Jacob MILLER .... pg 347, 5 Aug 1766 in court, inv & appr

servant man to myself George DEACON; servant man to Elizabeth SMITH

Gershom KEYES .... pg 355, 8 Aug 1764, will

all slaves to wife Ruth KEYES & at her death to be emancipated

William STROUP .... pg 373, 10 Oct 1766, will

girl Bet to wife; remaining negroes to be divided between the children Mary, Elizabeth, Catherine, William, Barbara, George, Henry, Malagor, & James

William BROOKS .... pg 391, 7 Feb 1767, inv & appr

servant maid, woman & child, man Samuel, child

William ROBERTS, Sr .... pg 423, 9 Feb 1768, will

Harry to wife Elizabeth ROBERTS & at her death to be appraised & to choose his own master

Mary ULMAR.. pg 430, 28 Dec 1767, will

"...my oldest son Godlove...my will that he shall not be made a servant in any way...an apprentice learning the trade of a blacksmith." "...This is the Age of said three children in his Testament _ 1st Godlove born in Mar 1751, 2nd Barbara _ Mar 16th 1753, & 3rd Jacob _th Jan 1760."

George BOWMAN ....pg 431, 3 Nov 1764, will

fellow Harry & wench Esther & their increase to wife Mary BOWMAN & at her death to be sold

Richard THRASHER .... pg 436, 23 Mar 1768 inv & appr

man

David DEDERICK..pg 438, 10 Nov 1767, will

lad Tom to daughter Susannah DEDERICK & woman Sib to daughter Mary DEDERICK when each turns 20 years old; "...if the Negro Sib shall have any more increase than one child at the time of my said Daughter Mary's arriving to the full age of Twenty Years that then with a fewer increase is more than the one Child shall belong unto my youngest Daughter Elizabeth DEDERICK..."; boy Abraham to son David DEDERICK when he turns 21 years old; man Harry, woman Van to wife Susannah DEDERICK & sold at her death

Peter PAINTER.................................... pg 447, 28 May 1768, inv & appr

man James, woman Ja_ncy

John GARDENER..................................... pg 448, 6 May 1768, adm acct

"To boarding Elizabeth GARDENER before she was bound for seven years..."

William ROBERTS............................. pg 450, 29 June 1768, inv & appr

young fellow, old wench

Alexander STEPHEN.. pg 452, 12 Jan 1768, will

fellow Ambrose & all servants for the they have to serve to brother John

David DERICK .... pg 456, 5 July 1768, inv & appr

Harry & his wife Nan, boys Tom, Abraham, old woman Sib

9

WILL BOOK 4
Part 1
1770 - 1783

Joseph HAWKING .... pg 95, 8 May 1771, inv & appr

    servant man George Waley

George BOWMAN .... pg 120, 7 Aug 1771, inv & appr

    servant man, negro fellow

.... pg 121, 7 Oct 1769, sales

    servant man to David VANCE; negro fellow to Pater DEARLY

Charles BUCK .... pg 127, 4 Feb 1771, will

    a young negro, wench Pat to wife Lettice BUCK & at her death to sons
    John, Charles, & Thomas BUCK; lad James to son John BUCK; fellow
    Jeffery to son Charles BUCK; boy Moses to son Thomas BUCK

Henry BEDINGER .... pg 152, 18 Dec 1771, will

    wench Sina to wife Magdalen

John DAVIS .... pg 160, 5 Sept 1771, inv & appr

    servant girl

.... pg 162, 12 Sept 1771, sales

    servant girl to William WOODS

Joseph HAWKINS .... pg 179, 6 Aug 1772? in court, inv & appr

    servant man

Joseph HITE .... pg 203, 7 Oct 1772, inv & appr

    servant man Abraham Furey to serve 1 year 8 months, woman
    Elisabeth Ruston to serve 9 months

Christian BLANK .... pg 221, 2 Sept 1772, inv & appr

    servant girl

Joseph POLLARD .... pg 223, 11 Nov 1772, will

    Fanny to wife Frances & at her death to 5 children "William, Chattin
    Doggord, Joseph, Manna, & Elijah POLLARD"

Joseph POLLARD .... pg 233, 3 Mar 1773, inv & appr

    woman, boy

Robert HALFPENNY ....pg 256, 26 Nov 1773, inv & appr

servant woman to serve _ months

Thomas SWEARINGEN......................pg 257, 20 June 1760, inv & appr

girl Lucy, man

William CALMES..pg 262, 8 Sept 1773 will

man Bob, girl Milla to son Marquis CALMES; man London, girl Silvie to son George CALMES; wench Jude, boy Lemon to daughter Mariam CALMES; lad Tom, girl Jenny to son William CALMES; wench Peg, boy Charles to son Fielding Gibbs CALMES; girl Lett, boy Cato to daughter Isabella Elliche CALMES; wench Vole?, boy George to son Spencer Neavel CALMES; Will, Hannah, Sue to wife Lucy CALMES

William Frances POLLARD ....265, 6 Dec 1773, sales

wench to Frances POLLARD; boy the property of Samuel RICE

William ASHBY ....pg 266, 3 July 1773, inv & appr

fellow Daniel, girl Winney, boy James McIvoy, old woman

Isaac PARKINS.. 269, 9 May 1773, will

"...if my said wife do marry...the slaves...to be divided among my children...In case I dy without issue by my personal wife...my slaves and personal Estate to my said Daughters Leah Elizabeth and Ann after the decease of my said wife...to Daughters Hannah W. CLUN and Ruth CADWALLADER..."

William CALAMESE of Hampshire Co. pg 282, 2 May 1774, inv & appr

Bob, Peg

Mrs. William CALMES ....pg 284, 5 May 1774, inv & appr

girls Letice, Jude, boy George, James Virtue?, girl Jenny, woman Poll, man Will, man Tom, girl Silvia, boy Leman, child Charles, woman Hannah, old woman Sue, girl Milley, child Cato, man London

Isaac PARKINS..................................... pg 288, 20 Apr 1774, inv & appr

old woman & child, man

David WATTS ....pg 292, 12 Oct 1774, will

Esther to daughter Judith WATTS wife of Clibborn ROTHEL; Fanny to daughter Anne wife of Richard EASTON; Dinah to daughter Milley wife of Goodman BARKSDEL

Christian PLANK .... pg 302, 3 Apr 1775, inv & appr

girl hired; servant woman

David GLASS .... pg 302, 2 May 1775, inv & appr

servant boy Thomas Perkins, female Ealse

Taliaferro STRIBLING ....pg 306, 24 Apr 1775, inv & sales

Ned, Cato, Robin, Sarah, Milley, Lott?, David, Charles, George, Daniel, Pegg, Harry, Melford, Anthony, Joe, Hannah, Clary, Sampson, Jude, Lemon, Jacob, Lucy, Rose, Agg, Nann, Solomon, Aaron, Ben, Flora, Isaac

David WATTS ....pg 314, 6 Feb 1776, inv & appr

Humphrey, Will, Pegg, Bobb, Luce, Bill

Lewis NEILL.....................................pg 318, 10 Aug 1775, will

man Forester to son John NEILL; Harry & his son Samuel & his daughter Catherine with her 2 children to son Thomas NEILL

(End of reel, continues with WILL BOOK, 4 Part 2, 1770 – 1783)

16

WILL BOOK 4
Part 2
1770 - 1783

(Note: Will Book 4 Part 2 begins with page 320 and goes to page 360. It then starts using page 351 rather than continuing with page 362.)

17

John JOLLIFFE.. pg 355, 22 Mar 1776, will

boy ____ to son John JOLLIFFE; girl Phillis to unborn child of wife Mary JOLLIFFE; wench Gean to wife Mary JOLLIFFE

Edward REED.................................. pg 358, 20 May 1777, inv & appr

wench Luce, old woman, boy Rob, girl Judy

Samuel BLACKBURN....................... pg 352, 11 Dec 1776, inv & appr

white servant, negroes Yarrick, Will, woman & child Kate, Moll, woman Esther, boy

Robert HENNING............................... pg 356, 6 Apr 1777, will

girl Mime to wife Mary HANING; executors may dispose of slaves as necessary

James COVILL .... pg 357, , will

servants Davis and Philip Roberts to son John COVILL

James WILSON.................................. pg 361, 26 June 1777, inv & appr

men Peter, Bob, wench Winney

William RUSSELL .... pg 364, 9 May 1777, will

wench Agg to wife Mary & at her death to son Moses

Thomas HELM................................... pg 375, 16 Apr 1776, will

woman Hannah to wife Margaret HELM; Peter to youngest son Thomas HELM

Joshua DORSEY .... pg 380, 6 May 1778, inv & appr

5 years 6 months & 14 days of a servant man; wench Jean 35, wench Debborah 16, child Betsy, Nell 6, Luce 4, lad Tom 14, Moses 2

John LEHEN/LEHEW .... pg 387, 26 Jan 1777, will

fellow Will, Moll to brother Spencer LEHEN's son John LEHEN

William RUSSELL .... pg 388, 2 June 1778, inv & appr

girl

Margaret & Sarah WILSON.................pg 393, 5 June 1778, gdn acct

orphans of James WILSON

Bob & Winny hired to John TAYLOR till 1 Jan 1789; Peter hired to W. THROCKMORTON for the same time

John LEHEW.................pg 419, 27 Oct 1778, inv & appr

man Will

Angus McDONALD.................pg 419, 26 June 1775, will

servants & slaves to wife Anna

George HAMTON.................pg 421, 14 Aug 1778, will

woman Bett to son Thomas; man Charles, wench Dini to wife Mary HAMTON; boy Lewis to son Charles Chester Coulson HAMTON; "...to my son George HAMTON ...the above Negro man Charles after his mothers Deseast likewise if the wench Dini should have a nother living child my said Sone George to have it...to my sone Joseph HAMTON ...the negro wench Dini and her increase after my wifes Desese excepting the first living Child above mentioned and one negro boy called Daniel..."; girl Mill to daughter Margarett HAMTON; boy Sam to daughter Sary HAMTON; boy Moses to daughter Judith HAMTON; girl Fanny to daughter Frances HAMTON

George HAMPTON.................pg 425, 6 Apr 1779, inv & appr

woman Bett, girl Milley, boys Moses, Sam, Daniel, girl Fanny, man Charles, woman Dinah

John BELL.................pg 437, 24 Oct 1778, will

3 negroes to wife Ann BELL; remaining negroes to be divided among all children except daughter Mary CATTLET

Robert WILSON.................pg 444, Nov 1777, will

woman Rose & her increase & a small boy Jene? to daughter Elizabeth GLASS; man Ben to grandson Robert WILSON, son of James; Ben to be free if grandson Robert WILSON dies before the age of 21

William NEIL.................pg 455, Mar 1779, inv & appr

men David, George

John BELL .... pg 458, May 1779, inv & appr

women Pegg, Lucy, girl Hannah, boys Sam, Will, girls Frank, Amey, Sally, boy Ben, girl Phillis, woman Lydia

Peter CATTLETT Jr .... pg 460, 1 June 1779, inv & appr

woman Kate, girls Milly, Aggy, Jane

George KERFOOT .... pg 471, May 1779, inv & appr

fellow Ben, women Nan, Sarah

John HOWARD ....pg 478, Aug 1779, inv & appr

servant man with 2 years to serve

Mrs. Henry PEYTON .... pg 479, 10 Jan 1777, inv & appr

servant woman, woman Moll, lad Daniel

Robert WILSON ....pg 489, 2 Nov 1779, inv & appr

Benn, Rose & her child

William KERFOOT .... pg 495, 14 Mar 1779, will

boy Will to son Samuel KERFOOT

William CALMES .... pg 512, 27 Nov 1773 - 6 Sept 1777, estate acct

Bob, Milly to Samuel PRICE guardian to Marquis CALMES; Wiill, Hannah, Sue to George JUMP; London, Silvee to George CALMES; Tom, Jen to William CALMES; Jude, Lemon to Miriam CALMES

John JOLLIFFE .... pg 524, 26 May 1778, inv & appr

Jane 22, Phillis 5, Sam 2; 2 ½ years of servant William Allford

William HARFORD ....pg 528, 1 Aug 1780, inv & appr

boy

Isaac HICKMAN .... pg 565, 26 Nov 1777, will

"…if his wife should be with child of that a son he gave him all his land and one Negro Lad near his own age…at the age of Nineteen years…" ; boy Daniel to be sold if necessary for debts

George WILLIAM ....pg 567, 7 Aug 1781, inv & appr

    Harry, Reuben, Cate & child

Henry CHRISMAN ....pg 573, 7 Aug 1781, inv & appr

    fellow, wench

George ROSS .... pg 575, 25 Jan 1779, will

    man ___ to be maintained by wife Frances ROSS

Thomas Lord FAIRFAX ....pg 583, 8 Nov 1777, will

    full title: The Right Honorable Thomas Lord Fairfax Baron of
Cameron in that part of Great Brittain called Scotland and Proprietor
of the Northern neck of Virginia

    all slaves to nephews Donny MARTIN, Thomas Bryan MARTIN, &
Phillip MARTIN

.... pg 585, 27 Nov 1779, codicil

    slaves left to nephews to be divided into 4 parts, the 4th part to Bryan
FAIRFAX Esq

.... pg 589, 7 May 1782 in court, inv

    97 negroes

Ann REED .... pg 608, 11 May 1779, will

    woman Jane & her children wench Lucy & boy9Rob to Edward
FUGATE

Edward WHITHEAD .... pg 612, 5 Aug 1782 in court, inv & appr

    man Lemon/Simon

William JOLLIFFE .... pg 615, 5 Aug 1782 in court, estate acct

    Nero

Ann REED ....pg 626, 31 Aug 1782, inv & appr

    boy Rob, old woman Jane, wench Lucy

Hugh FERGUSON .... pg 629, 5 Nov 1782 in court, inv & appr

    man Dick, a man, boys Tom, Cuffe?, Bob, Dick

John BURNE...pg 643, 1780, estate acct

    hire of negro

Samuel Larue.....................................pg 651, May 1778, inv & appr

    wench Sarah

Maj. Morgan ALEXANDER .....pg 658, 6 May 1783 in court, inv & appr

    men Sye, Richmond, Sam, women Aggy, Milly

John HUMPHREY...................pg 659, 6 May 1784 in court, inv & appr

    men Gaby, Peter, women Daphney, Rou?

James HAGAN.................................pg 660, 15 Apr 1783, inv & appr

    old woman

Elizabeth JOLLIFE ....pg 668, 3 May 1779, will

    woman & daughter Ruth to be cared for by friends Rees
    CADWALLADER & David ROSS, Ruth to be free at age 18; man
    Crispon to be cared for by brother Lewis WALKER

Benjamin SEDWICK ....pg 672, 2 Mar 1782, will

    Nan to daughter Betty SEDWICK; girl Milly to daughter Christiana
    Mary SEDWICK; girl Henny to daughter Hannah Ann SEDWICK

John HUMPHREY ....pg 680, 3 Sept 1783, sales

    men Gaby, Peter, woman Daphney to Sary HUMPHREY; woman
    Rose to Benjamin BERRY

WILL BOOK 5
1783 - 1794

Benjamin HACKLEY ....pg 1, 16 Jan 1781, sales

a piece of girl Webb Michaell WHITE & Caper LARRICK

Jacob CRISM .... pg 10, 4 Nov 1783 in court, inv & appr

a wench

Meredith DARLINGTON ....pg 16, 27 Nov 1783, inv & appr

a man

Thomas EDMONDSON Jr....................... pg 28, 27 Apr 1784, inv & appr

girl Leah

Elizabeth ROBERTS.. pg 32, 8 Mar 1784, will

Hannah & her son Jacob to daughters Mary KNIGHT & Ann PETERS

Morgan ALEXANDER...........................pg 33, 25 Apr 1783, inv of sales

3 fellows, 2 women

William GIBBS..pg 41, no date, inv & appr

wenches Judy, Nann, man Hercules, boys Daniel, Sam, Charles, girls Suck, Nelly

HITE & GIBBS...................................... pg 42, 10 June 1779, inv & appr

the time of a servant man

Henry BOWEN .... pg 43, 8 May 1778, will

woman Hannah to son Henry BOWEN; boy Peter to son John BOWEN; boy Tom to son Jacob BOWEN; boy Ben to grandson Rees HILL; man Jack to be sold

Taliaferro STRIBLING .... pg 48, 28 Sept 1784, inv & appr

Flora, Robin, Mille, Lucy, Harry, Milford

Samuel CLAYTON.................................. pg 58, 14 Mar 1782, inv & appr

man Abraham

23

Samuel CLAYTON .... 58, 2 Nov 1784, sales

man sold to George THO_TAS?

Taliaferro STRIBLING ....pg 68, 15 May 1775, sales

girl to Morgan ALEXANDER; man Robin, boy Jacob to Edward SNICKERS

Mildred BUSHROD .... pg 85, 13 Mar 1785, will

Betty to nephew John LEWIS; Alice daughter of Brissa, Betty, Joe, Isaac, Tom, Daniel, & Harry children of the said Alice to niece Mildred WASHINGTON; Brissa, Judy, Venus, Phill Aga, & Maria children of Brissa, Juleous to niece Hannah WASHINGTON; Winnie, George, Bess, & Newman children of Winnie to niece Catherine WASHINGTON; Haney, Sarah, & Lutetia children of Haney to niece Elizabeth WASHINGTON; money to nephew Warner WASHINGTON from Col. Humphrey BROOKE for negroes hired in Gloucester County; "I request a favor of Mrs. John WASHINGTON to hire Issac as he is old and infirm to my Brother Warner WASHINGTON for I should be very ___ to think of his being a Second time Parted from his wife and children..."

.... pg 87, 30 July 1785, inv & appr

Winny, George, Ben, Newman, Brina, Judah, Alce?, Venus, Phil, Mariah, Aggy, Alec, Betty, Joe, Julius, Isaac, Tom, Daniel, Henry, Haney, Sarah, Laticia; Betty the property of John LEWIS

George BRINKER .... pg 93, 3 Aug 1785, inv & appr

women Easter, Jane

Joseph CARROL .... pg 94, 7 July 1758 – 20 Aug 1761, estate acct

negroes at Edward S__ERS

Benjamin SEDWICK .... pg 105, 7 Sept 1785 in court, inv & appr

fellows Tom, Bob, Davy, Harry, wenches Pat, Sue, Sarah, fellows Jim, Dick, Cuffee, Huton, Stephen, Mintee, Henry; Nan, Millee, Tom, William

Elizabeth VANCE .... pg 110, 12 Nov 1781, will

man Tom to son James David VANCE; wench Rose to daughter Sarah GILKESON

24

Elizabeth VANCE .... pg 116, 15 Oct 1785, inv & appr

man Tom, girl Rosannah

Henry WHITING .... pg 159, 27 Oct 1786, will

Moll & her 2 children Syrus & Luc to son Carlyle Fairfax WHITING; ¼ of all negroes to daughter Mary Blair WHITING; one other fourth of above negroes to wife Elizabeth; remaining ½ negroes to sons George Braxton WHITING & Francis Beverley WHITING

John LEITH .... pg 162, 17 May 1787 in court, inv & appr

servant boy to serve 5 years

Henry BOWEN .... pg 170, 5 Sept 1787 in court, inv & appr

old man; woman & child, 2 boys

John BATCHELOR .... pg 180, 19 Dec 1787, inv & appr

one man

James KNIGHT .... pg 183, 1 Apr 1788 in court, inv & appr

fellows Daniel, James, old Ben, wenches Sillah, Beck, old Judith, girl Frances

Francis H. CHRISTIAN .... pg 185, 18 Dec 1785, will

negroes to be divided among children Martin S. CHRISTIAN, Humphrey Francis CHRISTIAN, Edward CHRISTIAN, & Betsy CHRISTIAN after the death or marriage of wife Ann CHRISTIAN; negroes that wife Ann CHRISTIAN should get at the death of her mother should be her own

.... pg 186, 18 1785 Dec, codicil

"...at the time my son Tom CHRISTIAN arrive at the Age of sixteen or the death of my wife that my whole Estate Both real and personal be Sold..."

Samuel SAMPLE .... pg 198, 1 Mar 1788, will

negroes to wife Eloner; Hannah 50 & Jack 47 to be emancipated after the marriage or death of wife; "... the land willed to the negroes for life as above after their death be sold and the money be Equally Divided among the young negroes..."; Hannah 50, Jack 47, Hetty 15, Dan 13, Ben 9, Sall 4, Hannah 1 to be enfranchised

25

John KERCHEVAL ....pg 205, 4 Mar 1788, will

Joe, Solomon, Rose, Cate to wife Winnifred KERCHEVAL

Mary McDONALD ....pg 206, 18 Aug 1788, will

Cece to mother Eleanor HITE & at her death to brother Isaac HITE; man Toby to brother Isaac HITE; girl Milly together with her increase to Sophia BRE__ daughter of Archibald McDONALD

Philip SWANN ....pg 226, 25 Mar 1788, will

George, Sam to wife Mary; Agga & her increase to daughter Catharine SWANN

George BOWMAN ....pg 241, 3 Feb 1777, inv & appr

wench Nan, Phebe & child ___, girls Suckey, Jane, Katy, Milley, Easter & child Polly, boy Jim, girl Peg

....pg 244, 3 Feb 1777, sales

girls Nan, Milly, Phebe & child ___, Caty to Abraham BOWMAN; Easter, Peg, Polly to Isaac BOWMAN; boy James to Joseph BOWMAN; girl Suckey to Mary STEPHENS; girl Jane to George BRINKER

....pg 245, 17 Mar 1768, Vandue Bill of the Estate

woman & child, girl Winn; man; man & woman

Mrs. Mary MacDONALD ....pg 252, 11 Apr 1789, inv & appr

Bill, Tom, Fortune, Jack, Charles, Peggy & her 2 children; Lucy, Amy, Tamer, Caty & her child; Patience & her 4 children, Toby, Sall, Milly, Cece

....pg 255, 13 Apr 1789, sales

Fortune, Lucy to William A. BOOTH; girl Sall to Peter McDOUGLE; wench Amy, Patricia & 4 children; Charles, Peggy & 2 children to Arche McDONALD; wench Tamer to Francis GILDARD?; man Tom to John GILKESON; man Jack to L__ COLOEST?; Kate & child to Henry BUSH

William BOOTH Sr ....pg 262, 25 Sept 1789, will

negroes in his possession to son Mordechai BOOTH; negroes in his possession, & Rachel to son William A. BOOTH; Will, Suckey & all

26

her increase, Priscilla & her children, Hannah & her children to daughter Eliza WORTHINGTON

Mrs. Mary MacDONALD ... pg 263, Apr 1789 – 21 Nov 1790, estate acct

carriage of the ___ slaves? from Alexandria to Winchester

.... pg 265, Apr, Nov 1889, sales

hire of Tamer, Charles, Peggy

Francis Humphrey CHRISTIAN. pg 266, 3 Feb 1790 in court, inv & appr

Frank, Nan, Fan, Scissio?, Matilda, Winney, Rawleigh, Sinah, Betty

David DAVIS.. pg 270, 24 Dec 1789, will

Bob, age 18, to serve wife Margaret DAVIS & son Gabriel until age 30 and then be emancipated

Samuel BOYD.. pg 273, 15 Jan 1790, inv & appr

man Alleck, women Lette, Phillis, boy Phil

James SEDWICK..pg 284, 20 Feb 1790, will

man Davy to be emancipated provided he pay moather Christina SEDWICK 5 pounds yearly during her life; boy Baley to nephew Lewis Burwell WILLIS until he reaches age 21 & then to be emancipated

William GRAYSON ....pg 295, 11 Mar 1790, will

"...all my slaves born since the Independence of America Free..."

Edward SNICKERS .... pg 296, 18 June 1790, will

Jery? the ferryman, Sall & her 2 children Peg & Harry, Tom the ferryman, Flora, Dick, Bob, Tom the waggoner, Roben the blacksmith, Will, Sampson, Simon, Juliet, Jack, Walker, Jack, Peter, Nat, Ned, Sarah & her son Jerry, Cupid, Moses to son William SNICKERS & reserving a proportion thereof to daughter Catharine MACKIE; Sy, Milly, Richmond, Sam, Joe, Peg, Titus & son Titus, Betty, Sampson, Fortune, Jude & her 2 children Winny & Joe to daughter Sarah ALEXANDER; Tim, Winny, George, Lucy, Doll, Jim, Charles, Nan & her 6 children Jim, Charles, Matilda, Jo, Bill to daughters Sarah & Elizabeth; Ag & daughter Ag, Sam, Moll, Arthur, Patrick, Jacob, Francis & her child Jim of Prince William, Betty, Pallas' Jesse & son

Jerry, to daughter Elizabeth STRIBLING; girl Ag daughter of Ag, dec'd, Sall daughter of Pallas to granddaughter Elizabeth ALEXANDER; girl Kitty to granddaughter Polly MACKIE; boy Sam to grandson Edward MACKIE

David DAVIS...pg 299, 16 Oct 1790, inv & appr

Bob to serve to age 31

Peter CATTLETT ....pg 303, 22 Sept 178_, will

all slaves to wife Anny CATTLETT & to be emancipated with their increase at her death, those negroes under age to serve nephew Henry CATTLETT until they come of legal age

Robert ALLEN................................... pg 343, 10 Dec 1791, inv & appr

Patience & her child Milly, girl Susan, boys Harry, Peter, Moses, Tollifer

Thomas BRYERLY .... pg 350, 1 June 1791, will

Kate & her boy Dann (my negro boy) to son Richard BRYERLY; boy Sye to son Samuel BRYERLY; girl Conney, my negro boy Toulson to grandson Thomas BRYERLY son of Richard BRYERLY at the death or marriage of my wife; a girl of 50 pounds value to granddaughter Mary Tate KERFOTT when she turns 18; Jack, Dick, James, old Conney, young Conney, Toulson to wife Ann; at her descease Jack, Dick, James, old Conney to sons Richard, Robert, & Samuel BRYERLY

Robert ALDRIDGE.....................pg 389, 2 Oct 1792 in court, inv & appr

Jacob, Tom, Milly, Paisey?

William VANCE...............................pg 392, 25 Aug 1792, will

Anne to wife & her choice of the negro children until daughter Mary comes of age; the remaining negroes to be divided among the daughters

Robert WILSON ....pg 399, 3 Oct 1791, will

Benjamin to be emancipated

Robert WILSON orphan of James ....
....pg 408, May 1778 – 5 Oct 1791, gdn acct

Ben's wages from 1 Apr 1779 – 1 Feb 1789

William GRAYSON .... pg 417, 5 Feb 1798 in court, inv & appr

man Gloster, girl Jenny, boy Ned, woman Nancy, man Sam, Grace, Robert, Liticia, men Ben, Nace, Davy, Charles, woman Fida?, Mony, Joshua, Lucy, Dick, man Jim, women Hannah, Hager, Nanny, boy Bobb, girl Milly, boys Cato, Bill, Kate, Henry, men Cesar, Harry, Isaac

Joseph JONES .... pg 422, 18 June 1792, will

man Sam to wife Barbary JONES for 10 years if she continues a widow and sold or rented out & then to be emancipated after 10 years

Edward TALBOTT ....pg 426, 8 Feb 1778, will

man James to be sold; 4 negroes of her choice to wife Eleanor TALBOTT

.... pg 428, 6 May 1793, inv & appr

wenches big Nancy, little Nancy, Hannah, Minta & child, Betty, man Peter, wench Debby, man Hopewell, big Adam, old man James, men Jack, Abraham, Daniel, Joe, woman Eve, man Harry, woman Lydia, man Lymus

Henry RICHARDS... pg 432, 31 July 1793, will

(there are two pages numbered 432)

girls Sarah, Ledey to wife Jane until her marriage or death & then to sons John & Henry RICHARDS; Nanny, Philis, Fan, Rachal, Sam to sons; John to have first choice of Nanny, Philis, Fan, Rachel, Sam, the 5th to be by lot

William VANCE ....pg 439, 17 Oct 1792, inv & appr

Anne, Sall, Phillis, Thornton, Berkley

Joseph JONES .... pg 435, 31 May 1793, inv & appr

Sam to serve 10 years

Frederick CONRAD...pg 442, 28 Nov 1793, will

Grace & her child, Sal, old wench Pattis to wife Mary Clary CONRAD; George Sr, George Jr to sons John & Frederick; boy Tom to be sold

Edward WHITEHEAD...................................... pg 459, 9 Oct 1778, sales

man to Isaac LANE

Col. William GRAYSON .... pg 478, 5 Feb 1793 in court, sales

man James, women Hannah, Hagar, men Davy, Ben Sam, woman Fida?, Grace, Nancy, men Nace, Gloucester, woman Mary, men Charles, Peter, Isaac, old Caesar, old Harry; wench Kate & child Harry

.... pg 479, 1791, estate acct

negroes clothed for sale, inoculated for small pox; paid SO__ for taking charge of an old negro; Dr. MACKY attended one of the children of Kate; 4 negroes sold to John MILTON; William HELM kept 3 young negroes

William STRIBLING .... pg 484, 6 May 1793, inv & appr

men Peter, Gibb, woman & 3 children

Miss Elizabeth OSSIE .... pg 508, 7 Oct 1794 in court, inv & appr

man Charles, boys James, Solomon, Billy, Isaac, women Lucy, Sucky, Letty, Nancy, boys David, Jerry, Bob, girls Dorcas, Vanah, Janey, boy Presley

.... pg 508, 7 Oct 1794 in court, division

Isaac, Jane, David, Vanah to Thomas PARKER; Betty, Letty to Thomas OSSIE; James, Sucky to Susanna OSSIE; Lucy, Bob, Dorcus, Presley to Huroniah OSSIE; Nance, Jenny to Seray OSSIE; Charles to Ann OSSIE; Solomon to Janetta McAdam OSSIE

Capt. Henry RICHARDS .... pg 511, 15 Oct 1793, inv & appr

Nanny, Phillis, Fan, Rachel, Sam, Sal, Cid

Edward TALBOTT .... pg 513, 6 May 1793, inv & appr

wenches big Nanny, little Nanny, Hannah, Minta & child, Betty, man Peter, wench Debby, man Hopewell, boy Adam, old man James, men Jack, Aham?, Daniel, Joe, woman Eve, man Harry, woman Lydia, man Lymus

George MURRAY .... pg 516, 24 May 1794, will

girl Bet to daughter Jane MURRAY; girl Levinia to daughter Polly R. MURRAY

John MARQUIS..pg 519, 12 Nov 1794, will
girl Venus to daughter Elizabeth; 8 negroes to be divided among
children Elizabeth, Nancy, Priscilla, Peggy, Nelly, & Betsy

WILL BOOK 6
1795 - 1802

Joseph GLASS .... pg 2, 23 Jan 1792, will

Rosannah & her choice of one more femal5 negro to wife Elizabeth GLASS; remainder of negroes to be sold to children at public sale by Executors Samuel GLASS, Robert GLASS, & William VANCE

John ALLEN .... pg 13, 7 Feb 1795 in court, inv & appr

girl, boy

Jeremiah SMITH .... pg 20, 8 Apr 1795 in court, inv & appr

boy slave till thirty

John MARQUIS .... pg 24, 2 Jan 1795, inv & appr

women Phebe, Amy, Alley, Betty, boys Peter, James, girls Nancy, Jenny, woman Venus

Barnett WILLIAMS .... pg 26, 9 Mar 1775, will

boy Bob, girl Lindy to daughter Charlotte

Joseph GLASS .... pg 29, 17 Jan 1795, inv & appr

Garrow, Sye, Ben, Dianna, Ned, James

Barnett WILLIAMS .... pg 37, 10 Apr 1795, inv & appr

man William, wenches Winney, Cate & child, old Winney, lad Faddy,

Benjamin STUBBLEFIELD ....pg 39, 27 Feb 1795, inv

Daphney, Rose, David, Juddy, Charlotte, Rachel, Cynthia, Janney, James

James OLIVER .... pg 42, 13 Apr 1795, inv & appr

one slave

John GILKESON .... pg 45, 24 May 1794, inv & appr

wench & child, boy

33

Daniel ROBERDEAU ....pg 52, 1 May 1794, codicil

woman Sukey, William & his time to serve to wife Jane

Isaac HITE .... pg 55, 4 Jan 1794, will

Moses, Bob, Sib, Dinah, Jenny being them old & infirm to son Isaac HITE; lad James, girl Nancy to daughter Ann BUCHANNAN & at her death to be sold at public auction; "...women who have husbands belonging to me shall be sold with their Husbands and where any of the women have young children, that the child be sold with its mother."

.... pg 61, 16 Oct 1794, codicil

man Lewis, woman Molly, Daniel to son Isaac HITE Jr.; man Ash to daughter Rebecca

Nathaniel CARTMILL, Sr. ....pg 64, 7 Feb 1795, will

wench Sid to daughter Elizabeth ARCHDEACON wife of Dr. Michael ARCHDEACON; man Sam to son Solomon; remainder of slaves to remain on the lower part of the plantation to wife Sara & youngest son Martin; fellow Joe, Hester & her daughter Jude to wife

Gen. Daniel ROBERDEAU ....pg 69, 8 July 1795, inv & appr

woman Suckey

Jere SMITH...pg 76, 1 Dec 1795, sales

boy to Samuel SMITH

Col. Joseph HOLMES ....pg 79, 26 Sept 1794, div slaves

Silla, Esther, Jonathan, Lemmon, Aggy & her child Jack, Daniel, Nelly, Bob, Cornelius, Betty, Sambo, Levingston's Tom, Cupid to Mrs.? HOLMES; _on to Hugh HOLMES; Ned to David HOLMES; Sye?, Lucy & child to Mrs.? LEGRAND; Sam, Courtney to Eliza HOLMES; little Tom, Kitty to Rebecca HOLMES; Milly, Joseph to Nancy HOLMES; Cloe & 2 children to Gertrude HOLMES; big Tom to Joseph HOLMES; Harry, Lewis to Andrew? to Hunter HOLMES

John MARQUIS ....pg 81, 16 Apr 1895, div slaves

Lot 1) woman Phebe to Betty MARQUIS; Lot 2) Amey to William WYLEY; Lot 3) Ally & child to HUTCHINS; Lot 4) Betty to BLUNDELE; Lot 5) Peter, Nan to LIPSCOMB; Lot 6) Jenny, James to Nelly MARQUIS

Jane ROBERDEAU .... pg 84, 5 Nov 1795, renouncement

"...I will not take or accept the provision made for me by the will of the said Daniel ROBERDEAU...and do renounce all benefit which I might claim by the same will"

Edmund CLARE .... pg 84, 2 Oct 1795, will

boy John, Clarisa & her child Molly to son James CLARE; Mingo, Davy, woman Hanney to daughter Mary Helen; man Nathan, girls Frances, Janny to daughter Elisa Gibbs CLARE

James HOGE .... pg 90, 18 Mar 1793, will

Jude to wife Agnes HOGE

Robert CRAIGEN .... pg 97, 8 Oct 1785, will

Toby, Hanna to wife Susanna

Albion THROCKMORTON .... pg 103, 17 Aug 1795, will

boys Casas, Terry, Lewis, Robin, Harry to son Warner WASHINGTON and to be bound to a trade as is son Warner WASHINGTON; Betty & her son Billy, her daughter Alia? & her 2 other younger children, Esther & her 2 children to daughter Hannah FAIRFAX; "...In Case my wife Mildred who is now pregnant should bear a daughter I give the said daughter a negro woman named Alice with her Children Judy, Letty, and two other children that are twins. I Likewise give negro woman named Fanny with her Son Johnathan and her youngest child "

James OLIVER .... pg 106, 3 Feb 1796 in court, inv & appr

negro slave

John CONRAD .... pg 121, 24 Sept 1796, inv & appr

man Peter, woman Patty, man George

Joseph NEILL .... pg 151, 12 Feb 1796, will

Daniel, Sam to be emancipated at age 21; Lydia, girl Sarah to be emancipated at age 18

William STRIBLING .... pg 161, 6 Apr – 19 Dec 1893, adm acct

waggoner Peter

Isaac HITE ....pg 164, 5 Nov 1795, inv & appr

Charles Sr., James Jr., Sue, Nancy, Luck, Molly, Temp, Cate & 3 children Hannah, Providence, & Jack, Margory, Sy, Sylvy, Sall & her 4 children Isaac, Crete, Seaboy, & Poll, Charlotte & her 3 children Sarah, Joe, & Lyd, Reuben, Willoby, Jacob, Charles Jr., Bill, Rachael, Adam, Tom, Cato, Judy, Daniel, Simon, Joe, James Sr., Jack, Harry, Lewis; man Joe

Joseph HOLMES.............................. pg 176, 22 Jan 1793, inv & appr

Sambo, Sye, Daniel, little Tom, Harry, Levingston Tom, big Tom, Cupid, London, Lewis, Samuel, Joseph, Lemmon, Nelly & child, Cloe & child, Sylla & child, Betty, Katina, Milly, Agy & child, Courtney, Kitty, Lucy, Ned

James HOGE.............................. pg 200, 26 Sept 1795, inv & appr

woman

George MURRAY......................pg 207, 5 July 1796 in court, inv & appr

man Casar, Beck & 2 children Grey & Levinah, Nan & 3 children Nelson, Nathan, & Maryan, girl Sinah, boy Vincent, girl Bett; girl Winney is free

Edmund CLARE .... pg 211, 14 Dec 1795, inv & appr

men Mingo, Davy, Nathan, John, wenches Henny, Clarisa, girls Frank, Fanny, child Molly

William BALL .... pg 214, 14 May 1796, will

boy James to son William; boy Winchester to son Thomas, wench Milly to daughter Judith THROCKMORTON; wench Dinah to daughter Betsey HENRY; girl Winney to daughter Nancy

Samuel BAKER ....pg 223, 1 Sept 1796, will

negroes to young children Samuel & Elizabeth

William BALL & Ann GREEN orphans of Jesse BALL..........................
.... pg 245, 17 Jan 1797, inv & appr

Mima & her child Charles, Cyrus, James, boy Nelson

Robert GLASS .... pg 250, 13 July 1796, will

man Tom, woman Roze to wife & at her death to sons Robert & Joseph

John DONALDSON .... pg 259, 17 Jan 1797, will

negroes to be sold

Isaac HITE .... pg 267, 26 Mar 1796 - 7 Apr 1797, estate acct

....pg 274, 19 Nov 1795, inv & appr

men James Sr, black Joe, yellow Joe, Harry, Simon, Bill, Adam, Reuben, Suckey, Margery

John HATLEY ....pg 283, 19 Nov 1792, will

house servants to wife Catharine NORTON; Hannah to wife & at her death to her children

....pg 283, 6 Jan 1794, codicil

black Betty to wife Catharine & at her death to children George Hatley NORTON, Edmund Randolph NORTON, & Daniel Norborne NORTON

Robert GLASS .... pg 287, 4 Sept 1797 in court, inv & appr

man Tom, woman Rose, woman & young child Lucy, girls Cilla, Nancy, boy William

....pg 292, 4 Sept 1797 in court, sales

woman to Rutha GLASS; girl to Sally GLASS; girl to Susanna GLASS; boy to Peggy GLASS

James CATLETT Sr.. pg 296, 27 Mar 1797, will

negroes to children & now in their possession; Mary & her child Will to daughter Jane GOSNEY

Capt. Thomas CHAPMAN..................... pg 309, 1 Sept 1797, inv & appr

2 men, Filles, Frank, Loose, Easter, Reuben, Ben, Harry, Richard, Lot, Molly

Undril BARTON .... pg 320, 4 Dec 1797 in court, inv & appr

man Bob, woman & child, boy Save? girl Ann

Gen. Daniel ROBERDEAU .... pg 322, 5 Nov 1875, sales

woman to Mrs. ROBERDEAU

Frederick CONRAD .... pg 338, 16 June 1795, inv & appr

man George, boys George, Tom, wench Sall, Grace & her child

.... pg 345, 21 Jan 1794 – 8 Feb 1798, estate acct

HENING hired Harry; "to my 1/5 boy Tom"

.... pg 353, 7 Feb 1798 in court, sales

wench Sall to Frederick CONRAD; man Tom to Daniel CONRAD; Grace & her 2 children to William GROVERMAN; "The two negroes named Geo Sen & Jun being specific legacies the Executor is not to be charged with them here"

James DEALE .... pg 360, 15 Feb 1798, inv & appr

girl about 16 years old

.... pg 361, 17 Feb 1798, sales

girl to Jeremiah LEETCH

James HALL .... pg 367, 9 Jan 1798, will

boy Jim or called C_aal to daughter Elizabeth

William STRIBLING .... pg 368, 5 June 1793 – 7 Oct 1797, estate acct

Peter the waggoner

William BALL .... pg 385, 2 Jan 1798, div negroes

John, Adam, Hannah & her infant, Sally & Annaca, Nancy, Phil, Nelson, Andrew, Becky to widow Druscilla BALL; Lot 1) George, Mariah to William BALL; Lot 2) Bob, Jacob to Nancy BALL; Lot 3) Peter, Billey to Betsey BALL; Edmund, Harry to Mrs. Judith INGLETON?, Esther, Molly to Thomas BALL

.... pg 394, Feb 1797 – 7 July 1798, estate acct

negroes from Lancaster to Frederick; negroes hired from Winchester; Cyrus, Nelson hired

James SIMRALL..pg 395, 22 Aug 1797, will

man Harry to son William F. SIMRALL; Betty to son James SIMRALL; Frank to daughter Frances MEEM?; Nancy to wife Sarah SIMRALL; Jenny to son Alexander SIMRALL

John MARQUIS.. pg 397, 1795, estate acct

Free Jack

James SIMRALL.................................. pg 401, 12 Sept 1798, inv & appr

boy Frank, child Jane, girl Nancy, woman Betty, man Harry

Benjamin DRAGGO ....pg 418, 3 Mar 1798, will

woman Bett to nephew John JOLLIFFE

James CARTER ....pg 419, 5 Oct 1798, will

girl Lucy to wife Ann; Frank, Peter, Jane, Cezar, Harry to be divided between daughters Katharine, Mary, Sarah, & Rachel's (dec'd) children; negroes, if sold, to continue in the family & choose their masters

Thomas HELM................................. pg 421, 15 Oct 1778, sales

Moses, woman Dinah to Capt. William HELM for Meredith HELM Jr.; wench sold 15 Mar 1779; man La_ny, boy Tom sold 28 Nov 1778; girl Bett to Henry HUNTER; girl, woman to Jane LARUE on 28 Nov 1778

Cary MITCHELL .... pg 434, 24 July 1798, inv & appr

Doll, Gabriel, Jeff, Vilet, Easter, Christian, Abraham, Grace, Mill, Robbin, Betsey, Mime, Phill, Solomon, Dick, Jude, Dice, Alce, Jack, Gilbird, Nance, George, Ben, Delf, Sharlot, Harry, Daniel, Delf, Jerry, Seatin

Edward TALBOTT ....pg 439, 1793 – 21 Aug 1794, estate acct

Harry, cash paid for woman

Samuel BOYD..pg 445, 30 Nov 1798, estate acct

sale of negroes

William F. SYDNOR ....pg, 446, 17 Aug 1798, inv & appr

men Fortune, Peter, Dennis, Adam, old Dinis, Bayly, Joseph, George, Abraham, Solomon, Sam, little Dinces?, Betty, Sarah, Cate, Hannah, Ailee, Darkus, old Betty, Jemina, Esther, Jane, Jane younger, Sylvia, Dianna, Sally, Ann, Peggy, woman Sucky

James CARTER ....pg 452, 7 Dec, inv & appr

Peter, Cesar, Harry, Frances, Jane

John MOFFETT ....pg 461, Nov 1788, inv & appr

man Denis, woman Bina, girl Hanner, boys Richard, Dick, woman Philas, girl Nann

Henry WHITING ....pg 468, 25 June 1796, inv & appr

big Loue, little Loue, women Lucy, Alice, Hannah & child, girls Alice, Mary, boy Tom, man George

Moses GREEN ....pg 474, 31 May 1799, inv & appr

man Joe, lad Billy, boy Gilbert, girl Lilah

Edward WHITE..............................pg 494, 31 Mar 1800 in court, inv & appr

boy, girl

Timothy W. MAHAN ....pg 506, 8 Jan 1800, will

man Will to wife Sarah; woman & children to be sold & money used to purchase a girl 3 or 4 years old to go to daughter Mary Ann JULIET; wife Sarah may hire Nancy & her children if she wishes rather than selling them

Eleanor TALBOTT ....pg 520, 15 Apr 1800, will

woman Aminto to niece Ann NICHOLS wife of Samuel NICHOLS; woman Hannah to be emancipated

Isaac PARKINS..............................pg 526, 18 Oct 1793, inv & appr

boy

James WALKER ....pg 532, 5 July 1799, inv & appr

men Sye, Lewis, woman Aggy

James WALKER .... pg 540, 1 Dec 1800 in court, sales

Sye to Daniel OVERACKER?; Lewis to Robert VANCE; woman Aggy to William BALL

Carey MITCHELL .... pg 577, 24 July 1798, inv & appr

Doll, Gabriel, Jeff, Vilet, Easter, Christian, Abraham, Grace, Mill, Robbin, Betsy, Mime, Phill, Soloman, Dick, Jude, Dice, Alce, Jack, Gilbird, Nance, George, Ben, Delf, Sharlot, Harry, Daniel, Delf, Jerry, Seatin; in Aret__d BROWNLEY's possession: Delph 8, Seaton 2, Jerry 4

John DONALDSON .... pg 594, 20 Apr 1797, inv & appr

Peter, Joe, Nelly

William FROST .... pg 599, 16 Jun 1797, will

woman Judy to be emancipated; Tom & Jack to be bound out until the age of 21 & then emancipated

William BALL .... pg 634, 16 Dec 1796, inv & appr

men Bob, Peter, George, Adam, John, Jack (recorded in the Court of Frederick by Miss Sally KEMP), Edmond, women Nancy, Nelly, boy Andrew, girl Mariah, boys Nelson, Billy, woman Dinah, boy Harry, girl Beckey, women Molly, Hannah, girls Sally, Annaca, woman Easter, boys Jacob, Tom, Winchester, Phil, girl Winney

Elizabeth EVANS .... pg 649, 6 July 1801 in court, will

negroes to Robert ROACH

John DONALDSON .... pg 651, 1795 – 24 Sept 1798, estate acct

negro hired from William BOND

John MOFFETT .... pg 659, 6 Oct 1798 - 1 Jan 1801, estate acct

negroes belong to the estate hired at Front Royal; suit brought by SPENGLER over hire of negroes; Cap't LITTLE hired Daniel, Samuel CLEVINGER hired Binah, Maj. BEATTY hired Philis

Jacob WHITE .... pg 663, 9 Sept 1801, will

girl Sarah to be sold

Joseph MICHLIN .... pg 670, 1 Dec 180_, inv & appr

woman

Sarah KEMP ....pg 675, 18 Feb 1800, inv & appr

Jack

WILL BOOK 7
1802 - 1804

Joseph HOLMES Jr................pg 19, 12 Nov 1792 - 1 Oct 1797, gdn acct

    paid for attendance by an old woman; big Tom

Andrew Hunter HOLMES........pg 23, 16 Feb 1793 - 5 Jan 1798, gdn acct

    Louis, Harry

....pg 24, 20 Oct 179_ - 1 Jan 1801, gdn acct

    Harry, Louis

Benjamin TALBOTT................pg 30, 2 Feb 1802? in court, inv & appr

    old man Boson, Fanny 19, boys Mayor 9, Moses 5

Elizabeth HOLMES ....pg 1, 20 Oct 1792 - 1 Oct 1797, gdn acct

    Sam, Courtney; Sam hired to HUNTER

Rebecca HOLMES ....pg 6, 12 Nov 1792 - 1 Oct 1797, gdn acct

    little Tom, Kitty, Kit

Nancy HOLMES ....pg 11, 12 Nov 1792 – 1 Oct 1797, gdn acct

    midwife for woman; Milly

....pg 13, 20 Oct5 1798 – 3 Feb 1801, gdn acct

    servant

George NOBLE................pg 35, 17 Feb 1801, inv & appr

    men Bob, Jerry, James, Joe, George, boys Orange, Fairfax, Charles, women Amy, Libby, Phillis, Silvey, Hanny, Sophia, girls Sucky, Rachael, boys Peter, Isaac, Daniel, Reuben, girls Fanny, Nancy, Leticke, Letty, Hanah, women Jenny, Silvey, man Frederick

Jacob WHITE................pg 55, 4 Dec 1801, inv & appr

    girl

Jacob WHITE................pg 60, 10 Dec 1801, sales

    girl to Joseph SHULL

John BROWNLEY..........................pg 64, 15 Sept 1802, inv & appr

woman Dinah, girl Esther, Winney, Venus?, boy John, woman Nancy, girl Lucy, Betty, boy Ben, woman Judith, girl Amey, boy Nelson, girl Hannah, woman Thance?, girls Vena, Dolly, old woman Phebe, fellow Ralph, Will, Isaac, Peter, David, Allen, Toney, Harry, Armstead, Jack, Gilbert, fellow Phil

Outstanding Debt: George THENA runaway note; Abner LATHSOUR? runaway note

Philip ALLENSWORTH.......................... pg 83, 2 Apr 1801, inv & appr

James

Joseph HOLMES...............pg 87, 27 Sept 1792 – 25 Oct 1793, estate acct

to Daniel CONRAD's proportion of the slaves as for bill; Dr. BAMBRIDGE for attending the negroes

John COLVIL...pg 107, 2 Nov 1802, will

girl Mill 8, boy Griff 2 to sister Jennet until they are 30 years old, if she dies they are to be sold or hired out until they reach 30 & then be emancipated

John OBANION....................................pg 131, 25 July 1801, inv & appr

old man Tom

George CLOPTON..................... pg 134, 5 Sept 1809 in court, inv & appr

Julius, Ceasar, Henry, Caty & young child, Dolly, Hannah, Phill, Tulip, George, Ampy?

John COLVILLE.................................... pg 153, 27 Apr 1803, inv & appr

woman Sue

James CATLETT .... pg 162, 5 Dec 1803 in court, div of negroes

Dick 54, Prudence 40 & child about 15 days old, Isabella 20, Robert 18, David 15, Hampshire 13, Peter 11, William 8, Buckner 5, John 2

Lot 1) Dick, Prudence & child to Alexander BRADFORD; Lot 2) Robert to Thomas CATLETT; Lot 3) David, John to Nimrod CATLETT; Lot 4) Isabella, Buckner to George CATLETT; Hampshire, Peter, William to widow's dower

John COLVILLE......................................pg 164, 13 May 1803, sales

    Susan to Jane COLVILLE

Samuel LITTLE ....pg 171, 6 Dec 1803 in court, inv & appr

    man Faddy, woman Wenny, girl Clairy

Joseph POLLARD................................pg 180, 20 Oct 1803, inv & appr

    Ben, George, Sam Lee, Sam Coleman, Jim, Dick, Kate, Sarah, Winney,
    Dolley, Reuben, Archy, Molley, Purah, George, Zackery, Ben, Letty

William FROST ....pg 183, 14 Aug 1801, inv & appr

    man

.... pg 184, 18 Aug 1801, sales

    man

.....................................pg 187, 2 Jan 1804 in court, estate acct

    man hired

Robert CATLETT ....pg 191, 1803, inv & appr

    Isaac, Peter, Sylvia, Philis, Buckley, Sarah, Lyndia, Milley, William,
    George, Hampton, Henry

Barnet, Rebecca, Elizabeth, & Ann LITTLER...

....................................pg 193, 15 Apr 1802 – 9 Dec 1803, gdn acct

    2 slaves hired

Edward DOYLE................................pg 209, 15 Feb 1804, will

    Molley & young child to be freed; young Lionel, Moses to be freed at
    age 21

Casper RINKER.............................. pg 215, 22 Apr 1802, will

    girl Rachael now living with daughter Elizabeth wife of Jacob
    ALLEMAN & at Elizabeth's death to be set free with her children; girl
    Rachael now living with daughter Catharine wife of William
    CHENOWETH & at Catharine's death to be set free with her children;
    girl Fanny to wife Mary RINKER & at her death to serve daughter
    Mary the wife of John ROGERS & at her death to be free with her
    children

Phebe LARUE.............................pg 228, 30 Apr 1804 in court, sales

man Ellick, girl Mabriel, men Ned, Lott, woman Lucy

.... pg 229, 30 Apr 1804 in court, inv & appr

man Ellick, old Ned, Lucy, Lott, Ma__ch

Godfried MILLER..pg 237, 3 Feb 1804, inv

woman Molly

Hannah WASHINGTON .... pg 238, 14 May 1802, will

Mary & her children, boy Billy (son of black Milly) to daughter
Mildred THROCKMORTON; woman Nanny (daughter of Milly), boy
Ben (son of Edy) to daughter Hannah WHITING; Alice & her children
(daughter of Milly), boy Billy (son of Sally) to daughter Catharine
NELSON; girl Milly (daughter of Jenny) to granddaughter Lucinda
NELSON; woman Aggy to granddaughter Hannah
THROCKMORTON; girl Fanny bought at a sale of negroes belonging
to the estate of __ Albion THROCKMORTON to granddaughter
Catharine THROCKMORTON; girl Judy (daughter of Amey) to
granddaughter Louisa WHITING; girl Kitty (daughter of Jenny) to
granddaughter Hannah NELSON; girl Becky (daughter of Amey) to
granddaughter Hannah WHITING; old Charles, Dick, Tom, Bristol,
Bill?, Charles, Scipio, Ben, Hitt, Lewis, Nepney?, Green__, Charles,
Dick, James, Harry, Bob?, Dick, Godfrey, Miles, Phill, Billy, old
Nanny, Amey, Jenny, Sally, Sarah, Maria, girl Polly, to sons Fairfax
WASHINGTON & Whiting WASHINGTON; woman Cynthia, who
was given to her by her husband, to be emancipated

John POWERS ....pg 240, 12 Jan 1804, sales

woman to widow

WILL BOOK 8
1804 - 1810

Alexander WHITE .... pg 1, 6 May 1804, will

boy Abel to nephew John WHITE; men Amos, Harry to nephew Alexander WHITE; girl Flora to Claraline LEE after the death of her grandmother; girl Pleasants to niece Margaret WHITE; Jude to niece Margery BEALL; Kitty to niece Mary WHITE; Esther to niece Sarah MIDDLETON; wife Sarah WHITE's male slaves to be emancipated at age 25 & female slaves at age 21, includes Flora; girl Milly, born 1 Feb 1795? to be free at the age of 18; remainder of slaves to nephew Robert WHITE to be emancipated as above; slaves devised to wife from former husband to go to his children

Meredith HELM .... pg 23, 29 Sept 1804, will

Pat with her 3 children to son Strother after the death of his mother

.... pg 51, 5 Feb 1805, inv & appr

Benjamin, Davy, Ned, Squire, Moses, Daniel, Wallis alias Neel, Cesar, Ham alias Abraham, Jerry, Abel, Edmond, Nancy, Chris, Kate?, Delia, Sidney, Matilda, Leona, Jude, Charlotte; Pat & her children Lewis, Willis, & Henry bequeathed to son Strother HELM

Jacob MOYERS .... pg 59, 13 Feb 1805, inv & appr

woman & child, small girl

John OBANON .... pg 61, 25 July1801, estate acct 40

negro

.... pg 62, 14 July 1801, sales

man Tom

Enoch FENTON .... pg 73, 23 Mar 1789, will

Peg, Jul?, Philis, Jacob, Jonah to wife

Enoch FENTON...pg 75, 21 Jan 1805, codicil

Jul? to be free; Peg, Philis, Jacob, Jonathan, William, Sam, Bets, Sam, Hanson to wife until they reach 30 years of age & with their offspring be emancipated; if his wife dies before Jacob & William are 30 Jacob to go to daughter Rebeckah & William to son John

Matthew WRIGHT, SR.................pg 81, 6 Apr 1805 in court, inv & appr

Jesse 25, Frank 65

John PEYTON.......................................pg 93, 13 Apr 1805, inv & appr

boy Jack, man Dennis, boys Burdet?, Daniel, woman Jane, boy Ned, women Winney, Sinah, old man Jack, man William, woman Nelly, girls Hannah, Milly, Clio, boy Charles, girl Lucy

....pg 96, 1 July 1805 by court, sales

John, man William, Winney & child to Mrs. PEYTON; "...a Suit in the Superior Court of Chancery...improper to proceed with the Sale of the Slaves as advertised except Jack Winney & Child and William the title of Whom Cannot be effected by Said Suit)..."

Philip EARHART ....pg 101, 26 Apr 1805, inv & appr

man, boy

David ROSS.......................................pg 113, 14 Dec 1804, sales

old Jacks _____? to David ROSS

Alexander WHITE ....pg 116, 6 Dec 1804, inv & appr

Amos, Henry, David, Jack, Abel, Sal & her child Lucy, Pleasants, Judy, Flora & her child Darius 6 months old, Kitty, Dave, Edmund, John, Ruthy

Enoch FENTON...............................pg 128, 16 May 1805, inv & appr

bequeathed to the widow: old woman Peg, woman Fillis; the following to be free at the age of 30 years of age: Jacob born 22 Jan 1787, Jonathan born 24 Oct 1788, William born 11 June 1789, Thomas born 14 May 1792, Betz? born 29 Sept 1795, Samuel born 1 July 1798, Henson born 13 Oct 1800, Isaac born 22 Apr 1805

49

Robert CATLETT ....pg 189, 16 Jan 1804, sales

Peter to Mary CATLETT, Rebeckah, Henny, Hampton to David CATLETT, Lindy to Henny CATLETT, Milly to Robert O. RISER, Billy to Robert CATLETT, Phillis to Jesse CATLETT, George to George CATLETT; Isaac, Silvah, old woman Sarah taken by Mrs. Mary CATLETT at the appraisement

John BROWNLEY........... pg 191, 31 Oct 1805 – 29 Jan 1806, estate acct

dower in the personal estate exclusive of the slaves

John CONRAD ....pg 192, 1794 – 18 July 1802, estate acct

George KIZER for 2 year hire of Ben

Joseph KING.............. pg 203, 2 Apr 1806 in court, inv & appr

Milly, Will, Sylvester, Sall, Isaac, Enoch

Philip EARHART ....pg 206, 1 Jan 1806, sales

man Simon to Griffin TAYLOR; man Samuel to Marg EARHART

John TAYLOR ....pg 207, 15 Nov 1805, inv & appr

man Dick, women Lucy, Mary, girl Milly alias Poll

Joseph FRYE........................... pg 232, 21 Jan 1806, inv & appr

Dave, Pat, Hanah, Abel, Harry

Lewis ASHBY................................ pg 251, 20 May 1806, will

Hannah's daughter Polly to daughter Judy ASHBY; Hannah's son George Brock to son Buckner ASHBY; negro stock to children Judy, Alfred, Mildred, Jinny, John, Buckner, Sidney, & Lewis

Peter LUKE .... pg 262, 25 Sept 1806, inv & appr

boys Rawley, Nelson, women Let, Netah?, girl Lucy, man Fortune? Thortum?

Isaac LITTLER .... pg 264, 20 June 1806, will

men Bob, Glascoe to wife Barbara; man Glascoe to son Daniel after her death, Bob to be emancipated after her death

Edward McGUIRE, Sr .... pg 272, 19 July 1806, codicil

man Phill to wife Milicent McGUIRE & 3 daughters Elizabeth, Ann, & Susannah

Rebecca HOLMES .... pg 273, 10 Oct 1806, inv & appr

Nelly & child Daniel, Robert, Cornelius, Milly, Cleo, Judy, Nelson, Aggy, Jack, William, George, Tom, Celia, Lemmon, Easter, Silvy, Kitty, Cupid

.... pg 274, 5 Jan 1807 in court, allotment of dower slaves

Lot 1) Nelly & child, Celia to Judge HOLMES; Lot 2) Robert, Judy to Rebecca CONRAD; Lot 3) Cornelius, Cloe to Gertrude HOLMES; Lot 4) Milly, George to Nancy BOYD; Lot 5) Nelson, Sylvy to David HOLMES; Lot 6) Lemon, Cupid to Joseph HOLMES; Lot 7) Easter, Aggy to Nash LEGRAND; Lot 8) Jack, Kitty to Hunter HOLMES; Lot 9) William, Tom to Edward McGUIRE

Samuel TURNER .... pg 281, 29 Dec 1806, sales

Old Nelly to Benjamin TUTT; Mary & her 2 children Cinthia & Gabriel to Samuel ASHBY

Orphans of George MURRAY .... pg 282, 2 Jan 1799 - 1806, gdn acct

Reuben MOORE balance in division of his lot in dower slaves; Cesar, Cyrus, Nanny, Sinah; "By John RUST bond for Cesar sold him Runaway…"

.... pg 283, 1 Jan 1807, subscriber's report

"…due to Jane MURRAY nee BRYARLY for the hire of her Negro Girl Bet, a Specific legacy left to her by her father's will…"; fellow Cesar; 15 slaves were divided: woman Nancy, Nelson, Nathan, Mary, Juliss, Sippio, Ellen, Kitty, Sinah & child Jacob, Anna, Fanny, Billey, John, Lewis

Lot 1) Nanny, Juliss, Billey, Anna to George MURRAY; Lot 2) Sinah & child Jacob, Tom, John, Lewis to David BRYARLY who married Jane MURRAY one of the orphans; Lot 3) Nelson, Mary, Kitty to Polly MURRAY; Lot 4) Nathan, Ellen, Sippio to Cyrus W. MURRAY

Peter LUKE .... pg 283, 20 Nov 1803, will

all negroes to wife Elizabeth & to be sold at her death

Robert WOOD.................... pg 284, 13 Jan 1807, inv & appr

man Lewis with about 6 years to serve; man Frank with 5 years & a few months to serve; boy Joe, a slave for life; woman whose child is Alfred; Emily, John; boy Davy, a slave for life; women Pheby, Margaret?, Jenny slaves for life

Abraham ANDERSON.............. pg 289, 2 Feb 1807 in court, inv & appr

women Tildy, Philis, Margaret

Lewis ASHBY........................... pg 289, _ Dec 1806, inv & appr

men Abraham, David, Solomon, Andrew, Harriet & child Daniel?, women Hannah, Emily, Lucy, Eliza, Winny, Harry, Pat, White?, boy Bob, girls Maria, Rachel, Milly, boys Ned, Andrew, Reuben, man Phill, women Pez, Charity, boy George

Lewis YOUNG.......................... pg 294, 7 Apr 1807 in court, inv & appr

woman

Samuel IRELAND ....pg 303, 25 Mar 1807, negroes hired

woman Oris to Frances IRELAND; Milly, Tandy, Tammy to Mrs. IRELAND; Tom to George COOPER; Daniel to Elijah POLLARD

Negro John ....pg 315, 2_ Apr 1807?, will

children of 1st wife: Benjamin, Abram, Henry, & Jane;

wife Nancy, daughter Minta & her 2 boys Harry & Daniel

Adam ALBERT.................................. pg 317, 5 May 1807, will

woman Pegg to wife Flora

Joseph KING.......................... pg 325, Oct 1803, sales

Negro Peter bought corn & 2 mares; Sally, Tom, Enoch, boy Isaac to Butler ALLENSWORTH; man Will, to Amilia KIZER; man Silvester to George LAUDER; woman Milley to Elijah KERCHWOOD

Adam ALBERT......................pg 333, 24 Oct 1807, inv & appr

Peggy & child ___, boys Sampson, Bill

Peter LUKE .... pg 333, 20 Apr 1807, sales

woman Fortune, Let & child to John LUKE; boy Rawdy, in account of? his bid for Let & child to Amos CLAYTON; Netah? & 2 children to Lewis NEAL

James IRELAND .... pg 337, 31 Dec 1806, bonds

amount of bonds taken for the hire of the estate slaves

John WILSON .... pg 340, 4 Jan 1808 in court, inv & appr

Peter, Adam, Ben, Fanny, Flora

Jacob MADDEN .... pg 344, 1 Feb 1808 in court, inv & appr

men Randel, Robert, woman Rachel, girls Lindy, Abby, boy Tom, girl Fanny, boys Isaak

John STRIBLING .... pg 345, 22 July 1802 – 29 Jan 1808, estate acct

Mariah, Masia, Meg, London, young negroes, 4 men 3 women hired; paid Gramah Amah for 2 visits

John MOFFETT .... pg 349, 1 Jan 1801 - 1 Jan 1807, negroes hired

Daniel, Binah, Phillis hired out to Benjamin JOHN, Samuel BELL, Major BETTY, Peter ROMINE, Jacob BEARD, Mrs. BRESKIRLL?, Peter HAM; Mrs. ROWSEY, Mr.? CARSON, Nathen SMITH

.... pg 350, 1 Feb 1808 in court, estate acct

negroes hired

John CAMPBELL .... pg 354, 2 Feb 1808 in court, inv & appr

woman Lucy

Joseph CORDER .... pg 358, 12 Oct 1807, will

girl Hannah to Lucy CORDER

Strother G. SETTLE .... pg 362, 12 Feb 1808, inv & appr

men Sam, Planter? women Mary, Hanner, boys George, David, women Peg, Lynis, girl Charlott

Dr. Daniel CONRAD .... pg 365, 24 Oct 1806, inv & appr

Thomas, Molly, Sally; Louis 19, to be free at age 20; Harry

Jasper BALL .... pg 374, July 1807, inv & appr

man Ned, his wife Rachel & 2 daughters Lucy & Rachel, Lewis, Isaac, Joseph, Polly, John, Judy

William GLENN .... pg 383, 8 Apr 1808, estate acct

"By one Negro man mentioned in the Will Sold by the Exc for 133.39"

Daniel HENRY .... pg 387, 5 Sept 1808 in court, inv & appr

boy George to serve 8 ½ years, girl Lucy to serve 2 years & 8 months, boy Solomon, girl Sidney, woman Fanny, girl Mima

Jacob CRYZER .... pg 395, 5 Sept 1808, inv & appr

man Harry

Jasper BALL .... pg 397, 5 Dec 1807 in court, div of slaves

Lewis to George SMITH; Joseph to Edward BALL; Judy to William FOLEY; Isaac, Rachel, Lucy to Samuel CONNER; John, Polly to Jasper BALL

Presley HAYNIE .... pg 405, 4 Aug 1807, inv & appr

men Jim, little Jim, woman Easter, children Phillis, Eadine to the widow

Stephen JONES .... pg 415, 7 Feb 1809, inv & appr

man James, Lettie & child?, boys Ned, Sawny, girls Mary, Jane, Ester

Cyrus W. MURRAY .... pg 422, 1 Jan 1807 - 1 Jan 1809, gdn acct

negroes hired

George MURRAY .... pg 423, 1 Jan 1807 – 2 Jan 1809, gdn acct

paid sister Jane her due in division of negroes; negroes hired

Polly MURRAY .... pg 424, 1 Jan 1807 – 2 Jan 1809, gdn acct

paid sister Jane her due in division of negroes; negroes hired

Stephen JONES .... pg 427, 20 Dec 1808, sales

boy Ned hired by D. SAWERS; boy Sawney by Thomas LINDSEY; man Sam, Letty & 4 children for upkeep by C. JONES

Charles HAMMOND ....pg 433, 3 June 180_, est acct

    Bob sold

Sarah JACKSON late of MD ....pg 436, 3 Feb 1809, will

    boy Tom, who has lived with her for several years, to daughter Elizabeth the wife of Joseph LONGACRE

John SCARFF ....pg 437, 1 May 1809 in court, inv & appr

    man Parker

Daniel HENRY ....pg 439, 29 Mar 1808, estate acct

    negro hired

Moses PAYNE ....pg 441, 30 May 1809, inv & appr

    boy Sam

Charles HAMMAND ....pg 442, 5 June 1809 in court, inv & appr

    Andrew, Jim, old Sue

John LARRICK ....pg 445, 5 June 1809, inv & appr 230

    Joseph

....pg 446, 24 May 1804, sales

    Joe to Margaret LARRICK

Molly HANEY ....pg 450, 30 May 1809, inv & appr

    Hannah 20 & child Fillis? 3, girl Sharlotte 11

....pg 451, 6 June 1809 in court, sales

    Hannah to Griffin HAYNIE; Fillis to Presley HAYNIE; girl Charlotte to John RAMY

Cyrus & George MURRAY ....

................................pg 455, 2 Jan 1809 – 20 May 1809, gdn acct

    by the hire of Cyrus W. MURRAY's negroes, by the hire of George. MURRAY's negroes

Hugh Henry McKEARN ....pg 459, 9 June 1809, inv & appr

    man Smith, woman

Alexander WHITE .... pg 461, 27 Dec 1804 – 27 Sept 1805, estate acct

slaves left by the will delivered to Robert, John, Margaret, & Alexander WHITE; Flora & child in possession of Mrs. WHITE to Caroline; Nelly to Polly WHITE

Isaac SETTLER .... pg 464, 24 Apr 1809, inv & appr

Bob 42, Glasgow 45

Sarah JACKSON .... pg 480, 4 Sept 1809 in court, inv & appr

Hannah 36, girl Ann

Strother G. SETTLE .... pg 485, 23 Aug 1809, div of slaves

Sam 27, Planter 30, Mary 57, Sharlotte 12, George 11, Hannah 21, Alfred 6 months, Daniel 2, Peggy 40, Mariah 1, Linny 45

Lot 1) Planter, Daniel to Welford G. SETTLE; Lot 2) Mariah, Peggy, Charlotte to George BERRY; Lot 3) Hannah, Linny to John HAMPTON; Lot 4) Samuel, Alfred to Mansfield SETTLE; Lot 5) Mary, George, to Larkin SETTLE

Charlotte MARTIN .... pg 496, 7 Mar 1806, inv & appr

women Harriett, Dinah, girls Levina, Darcus, man Manuel; Emanuel belonging to Francis TOLLASTIN?

John CAMPBELL .... pg 499, 4 Dec 1809 in court, sales

woman to Thomas CAMPBELL

Ignatius PERRY .... pg 501, 30 Nov 1809, inv & appr

Jansy (old Peter wife), Jany (Nancy's sister), Polly, Beck, Sillah, Sall, Sophy, Betty, Charity, Patt (or Matt), Peggy, Hannah, Lidia, _aly, Sall, Cassa, Drury, Matilda, Mosy, old Peter, Jack, Jacob, Andrew, Anthony, David, George, Aron, little Lewis, Daniel, Wall, Bob, little Peter, Nancy, Harry, Berkeley, Sam (Rachel's son), boy Moses bound until 21 years of age, Ben, Pompey, Joshua, Jim, William, Samuel (Cassy's son)

James LARNE .... pg 505, 7 July 1804, will

negroes, to wife Clary, to be emancipated at age 30

Sally POWERS .... pg 510, 1 Nov 1805 - 25 Dec 1807, gdn acct

the proportion of the division of the negroes; woman

James LARNE .... pg 531, 4 June 1810 in court, inv & appr

man Peter, Elick, Silvester, Nelson, John, Edward, Anthony, Beverly, Moses, Rachel & her 2 children, Lucy, Liddy

Thomas B. WALTERS .... pg 536, 1 June 1800, will

girl Jane to be hired ou andt then sold once youngest WALTERS' daughter, Susannah, comes of age

WILL BOOK 9
Part I
1810 - 1816

Thomas CAMPBELL .... pg 1, 10 June 1810, will

Lewis, Winny, Robert, Bill son of Winny, Benjamin, Daniel to son Thomas CAMPBELL; Hampton, Harry, Rodger, Plummer, Bill purchased of Joseph VANMETRE to son John CAMPBELL; girl Fanny to granddaughter Elizabeth CAMPBELL

George LOUTHAN .... pg 9, 13 Dec 1809, inv & inv & appr

children ages 2?, 4, 6, woman aged 26?, woman aged 30, man age 30; man hired from Mrs. HAMPTON

Joseph BEALOR/BEELER .... pg 12, 3 Feb 1808 - 18 Apr 1810 , gdn acct

WHITING's Tom

Polly BEALOR/BEELER .... pg 13, 3 Feb 1807 – Dec 1809, gdn acct

Richard Glover, Barney Fagan, William, Samuel, Peter, George

Lucretia BEALOR/BEELER . pg 14, 23 Jan 1808 – 1 Sept 1810, gdn acct

Lewis, James, George, Harry

John TAYLOR .... pg 29, 15 Nov 1805, sales
.... pg 30, 23 May 1809, sales

Dick hired till Christmas to John PITMAN Jr; Mary hired till Christmas to Mrs. WELLS; Lucy & her child Edwin sold to Mary H. TAYLOR; Milly hired till Christmas to Bryan M. STEPHENS

William KERFOOT .... pg 38, 9 Apr 1805, will

1/3 slaves to wife & at her death to son William KERFOOT

.... pg 39, 7 Mar 1811 in court, inv & appr

Charles, Margaret, Washington, Abraham, Job, Soul, Milly, Lucy Ann, Jacob, Mary Ann, Charlotte, William, Winney, Fanny

Lionel BRANSON .... pg 41, 6 Mar 1811 in court, inv & appr

girl

Urial ASH.................pg 42, 26 July 1798 – 28 Apr 1807, estate acct

boy sold to S.G. SETTLE; "…we the subscribers after dividing the negroes (five in number)…17 Mar 1811"; Siller to Pamely ASH; Lucy to Littleton ASH; Sampson to Peggy ASH; Polly to Urial ASH; Winny to Dolly ASH

Lawrence BUTLER..............................pg 44, 4 May 1811, will

negroes excepting Tom & Betty to Richard M. BECKWITH son of Jennings BECKWITH; Tom, Betty to remain on the lands bequeathed to Richard M. BECKWITH

William VANCE.....................pg 45, 1793 - Jan 1810, estate acct

negroes, girl, Jenkins, Sall & child, Dinah, overpayment in division of negroes

William CHIPLEY..............................pg 48, 18 Aug 1808, will

slaves to son James CHIPLEY; one slave to be purchased by "…daughter Polly HARDESTY… she shall not lay any claim to my negro man Ben who was once in her possession…" "…if any slaves desire to become free under the restrictions of the laws of my Country they may do so on the following terms…"

.... pg 52, 27 Mar 1809, codicil

Hannah was purchased for Mary HARDESTY

.... pg 52, 1 Feb 1809, codicil

"…except she lays claim to Ben & if she does nothing it is my will that Polly HARDESTY shall have and hold…"

Abraham TAYLOR..............................pg 56, 30 July 1811, inv & appr

man Peter

.... pg 56, 31 July 1811, sales

man Peter to Mary TAYLOR

Thomas POWERS.....................pg 68, 31 Aug 1811, inv & appr

girl Milly; balance due from the negro estate of his father

Thomas POWERS .... pg 68, 2 Sept 1811, estate acct

woman Sillow & girl Milly sold; balance due from the negro estate of his father

John CONRAD's heirs .... pg 73, 16 Oct 1805 - 17 Jan 1811, gdn acct

"...cash sent by a mulatto boy of Mrs. PEYTON..."

Robert WOOD .... pg 78, 12 Dec 1806 – 31 May 1811, estate acct

Milly & child sold to Mrs. C. WOOD...by Mrs. F. HELM; Lewis to James TIDBALL; small girl Emily sold to Mr. R.? HETRICK

Peter DERMAN .... pg 88, 5 June 1811, will

woman Tama, boy Joseph, girl Charlet to John, Mary, Ann, & Betsy DERMAN

Richard RIDGWAY .... pg 92, 4 Mar 1806, will

girl Esther to either of the children

William THROCKMORTON .... pg 94, 6 Jan 1812 in court, will

slaves to wife

John READ .... pg 105, 12 Nov 1809, will

Harry to son Samuel READ; Silva? to brother James of Loudoun Co.

Enoch BERRY .... pg 110, 28 Dec 1811, div of negroes

Lot 1) Abby & child Peter, Reuben, Silva to Lettia N. HOGAN; Lot 2) Sally & child Lewis, Eliza, Harriet to Edwin BERRY; Lot 3) Harry, Lurany? to Maria BERRY; Lot 4) Abram, Lydia, Salena to Matilda BERRY; Lot 5) Nelly & child Moses, Mary to Winney BERRY

Nathaniel McPHERSON .... pg 111, 6 Apr 1812 in court, inv & appr

woman, 2 girls

John REED .... pg 113, 6 Apr 1812 in court, inv & appr

man Harry, boy Lewis

Samuel B. SYDNOR............ pg 120, 1 Jan 1805 – 20 Nov 1811, gdn acct

keeping woman & 3 children at lowest bidder; keeping a crippled woman; girl age 4; boy Abram; man Peter; woman & child; woman Darcus; girl Silva; man Adam

Nancy TOLOVER......................................pg 131, 17 Feb 1812, will

Moses to Jesse HENDERSON

Mary WOOD.....................................pg 139, 20 Sept 1790, will

Sarah & her infant son, Robin, Anne, Charlotte to granddaughter Mary Anne HARRISON; Jude, Solomon to granddaughter Elizabeth HARRISON; Charles, Rachell to granddaughter Mary HARRISON after my death; Butt, Ned, Thorn to son James WOOD; George, Jack, Lewis, Frank, John to son Robert; all slaves when reaching the age of 36 to be emancipated; Sy to be emancipated after my death

....pg 141, 5 Feb 1811, in court

"...Sarah who claimed her freedom under the will of Mary WOOD dec'd produced the same in Court and offered it for probate which the Court refused. the same being opposed by Peter LAUCK who claims said Sarah as a slave..."

Abraham FURR....................... pg 147, 3 Aug 1812 in court, inv & appr

woman

....pg 148, 3 Aug 1812 in court, sales

woman to John FEGINS

Major Lawrence BUTLER...................pg 150, 26 Aug 1811, inv & appr

big John, little John, Phill, Ben, Jack?, Harvy, Daniel, old Charles

Daniel POOL.................. pg 166, 23 Feb 1808 - 27 Feb 1812 estate acct

negroes kept by B. BERKELY; Harry sold to Daniel ANNIN; Sal to James V. GLASS; Betty to James H. LOWERY; Lucy & child to James BEAN; Cinthea to Reuben BERKLEY; Esther to James RILEY

Sampson BABB ....pg 172, 18 Feb 1812, inv & appr

boy, girl

Peter DERMAN ....pg 174, 7 Aug 1812, inv & appr

woman Fanny, boy Joe, girl Sharlet

Nathaniel McPHERSON .... pg 176, 3 Nov 1812, sales

Doll & 2 children to Edward TURNER

Jacob MADDEN .... pg 181, 30 Nov 1812 in court, estate acct

Lynda sold

John MUSE ....pg 182, 25 Aug 1810, will

Hannah 8 to nephew John ARMSTRONG son of George
ARMSTRONG

Philip BUSH...pg 189, 4 Sept 1810, will

Becky to choose either son or daughter as master/mistress; Sally & her
daughter Louisa to daughter Polly BUSH & at her death to be sold

....pg 191, 27Feb 1811, codicil

"to daughter Polly...the house and Lott Slaves and personal estate..."

John TAYLOR .... pg 193, 10 Jan 1812, estate acct

Mary, Molly, Dick; man Tom sold to Septimus TAYLOR

....pg 195, 25 Nov 1811, inv & appr

Dick, Mary, Milly

Barnet, Rebecca, & Betsey LITTLER...
....pg 197, 1 Apr 1804 - 3 June 1813, gdn acct

old woman Winna, girl, man, Faddy

Philip BUSH... pg 207, 6 Jan 1813, inv & appr

Sam, Anthony, boy Nelson, girl Betsey, Daphny

Sarah WIGGINTON ....pg 227, 31 Aug 1811, will

Davy, Bett & her 3 children Patty, Ellick, & Harriet, Anna alias Kip &
her child Jenny, Judah & her 2 children Mary & her youngest not yet
named, Isabella, boy Charles, girl Silva to daughter Nancy MITCHEL
& at her death to be divided among her children except son William
MITCHEL & grandson William MITCHEL; man Mos, girl Frank,

Dick, Adam to son Benjamin WIGGINTON; Bob, John, Moses, Sue, Jenny to son James WIGGINTON; girl Amy to daughter Betsy LITTLE wife of Edward LITTLE; boy Lewis to grandson William Pendleton WIGGINTON when he turns 21; boy Robin to grandson James Bott WIGGINTON when he turns 21; son James to have Lewis & Robin until his sons come of age

George SOUTHARN ....pg 235, 18 Jan 1810 – 10 Dec 1811, estate acct

Kalph

Sarah WIGGINTON, Culpeper Co. ...... pg 236, 10 June 1813, inv & appr

man Richard, women Betty, Ann, Judah, girl Amy, boy Charles, girls Jinney, Harriett, Mary, boy Lewis, old woman Isabella, boy Ellick, girl Patty

.... pg 237, 2 Aug 1813 in court, inv & appr

men Adam, Moses, Robert, John, boys Lewis, Robin, woman Suck, Ginny & 2 children Fanny & Judy, girl Cilvia

Hannah THROCKMORTON..

.... pg 246, Apr 1805 – 1 Jan 1812, gdn acct 426

Esther, Sarah 12, John 10, Mary 6

Kitty THROCKMORTON .... pg 247, Apr 1805 – 1 Jan 1812, gdn acct

Judah 14, Letty 12, Bryna 10, Maria 8, Cyrus 6, Molly 6, Anna 2; they could not be hired for anything until the year 1807; Judah had a young child in 1812

Mary MEADE .... pg 251, 7 Sept 1813 in court, will

negroes are to choose their masters

Ann BONHAM ....pg 252, 23 Mar 1813, inv & appr

man Fortune

Samuel LITTLER.................................pg 254, 30 Oct 1813, inv & appr

old woman, man, girl

James POWERS .... pg 256, 29 Sept 1813, gdn acct

girl Louisa by allotment; Louisa to Lynn; proportion of value of negroes

WILL BOOK 9
Part 2
1810 - 1816

Robert C. BURWELL .... pg 278, 9 Dec 1813, inv & appr

Sam White, Charles, Harry, Bob, Isaac, Godfrey, John, little John, Katy, Rosella and child, little Jenny, Fanny, Ben, Nat, Sam, Ben, Archy, Cobler, Frederick, Molly, Tenar, Dercas, Nelly, Jack, Lucy

Richard B. BECKWITH...... pg 283, 26 Jun 1812 – 13 Oct 1813, gdn acct

Betty & Tom's legacy; Phil, Daniel, Harry, Ben Jr., Charles, Dick, John Park

Henry MOORE .... pg, 287, 8 Jan 1812, estate acct

woman Betty

Sarah CHURCHILL .... pg 292, 26 May 1814, will

"...woman Cross...to my children or that one unto whose hand she may fall that she maybe tenderly used and permitted to be hired out to some person in Winchester so that she may not to be separated from her husband."

John MUSE .... pg 293, 15 Jan 1813, inv & appr

West, Adam, Phill, George, Natt, Sarah, Fick, Hannah

Margaret HELM .... pg 294, 27 May 1814, inv & appr

man Sam

James POLLARD .... pg 302, 4 June 1813, will

negroes in her possession & holds as her dower, boy Archy to mother Nancy POLLARD

Orphans of Thomas B. WALTER ....
.... pg 312, 1 Aug 1810 - 1 Jan 1814, gdn acct

girl Gin

William HURST .... pg 319, 30 Sept 1814 in court, estate acct

slaves from 7 Mar to 31 Dec 1812

67

Mordicai BEAN .... pg 331, 19 Aug 1814, will

woman Nell to wife Juda; man Tom to be sold; boys Jem?, Thornton to son Isaac; boy Charles to son James

George DENEALE Jr. .... pg 335, 9 Nov 1814, inv

man Joe, woman Sarah, girls Lucy, Phillis, boys Lewis, Frank, women Nelly, True Love, boys Jesse, Antony, Betty & child Libby, boy Harry, man Sampson, girl Lucy

John SOWERS .... pg 337, 17 Jan 1815, will

Daniel, Siller, Nero to daughter Polly HEISKELL

Alexander MELTON .... pg 342, 8 Dec 1814, inv & appr

women Nancy, Dorcas, boys Armstead, Nelson, George

John SOWERS .... pg 343, 9 __ 1815, inv & appr

Nero?, Daniel, Siller

negro Free John .... pg 346, 13 Nov 1807 – Feb 1815, estate acct

son Benjamin a legacy; Minty's deed of emancipation recorded

Henry HOOVER .... pg 347, 19 Jan 1813, will

girl Caty, boy Sam to son John HOOVER after his mother, Charity HOOVER's, death; boy James, girl Hannah to son Phillip HOOVER after Charity HOOVER's death; girls Fanny, Nancy to daughter Catherine HEILSEL after Charity HOOVER's death; wench Jude, girl Milly to be sold after Charity HOOVER's death

Catherine JONES .... pg 359, 4 Jan 1809 – 16 Mar 1815, estate acct

paid for negroes' clothes

John HOOVER .... pg 362, 1 Mar 1815, will

woman Caty to wife

John ROUT .... pg 365, 15 Jan 1815, inv & appr

Shenandoah River:

John, Benjamin, Moses, Thomas, Joseph, Hannah, __ & child, Nancy, Rachel, Lucretia

John ROUT .... pg 367, 21 Mar 1815, inv & appr

Timber Ridge:

man ___, girl Betsy, Nancy & child, boys Nero, Daniel

Sarah CARTMELL .... pg 377, 20 Mar 1815, will

Het, Tilden, Sarah, Gilbert, Peggy, Elijah to be sold

John CHURCHILL .... pg, 5 Jan 1815, div dower slaves

Mary & her son David to Philip CLAYTON; Hannah, Cilir to Richard CHURCHILL; Moses, Jacob, Criss to John R. HEDGES; Armisted, Bet to Mary CHURCHILL

Sarah CARTMELL .... pg 394, 20 May 1815, inv & appr

woman Hetty, girls Matildia, Sally, Peggy, boy Gilbert

Joseph SAVAGE .... pg 406, 6 June 1815 in court, inv & appr

girls Lucy, Sarah, Maria, Mina

Frances Howden BURWELL .... pg 434, 24 Mar 1815, will

maid Caty, after sister Anna BURWELL's death, & when she becomes 24 years of age to hire? herself or choose her mistress/master; all servants except Ben & Jim to nephews Thomas & William NELSON; "...I wish to be Bought for Rachel a Servant woman of W.? NELSON..."; Ben * Jim to W. Philip NELSON

Henry HOOVER .... pg 444, 13 Apr 1815, inv & appr

Juda & infant, Milly, Catherine, boy James, girls Hannah, Nancy, boy Samuel, girl Jane

William T. COLSTON .... pg 447, 4 Sept 1815 in court, inv & appr

James, George, Robert, Janny, Gincy? Tom

Charles GRAVES .... pg 450, 15 Dec 1812, will

choice of 2 slaves to wife Elizabeth; slaves to be hired out

Daniel SOWERS .... pg 453, 14 Mar 1815, inv & appr

Billy & his wife Beck, Rob, Aggy & her child, Hood, Aron, Joannah, Billy, Mike, Jessy, Jeanny, Patsy, Shederick, Mary, Joce, General

John S. WILLIAMS ....pg 459, 17 Mar 1815, inv & appr

men John, Phil, Gabriel Green, woman Nelly, girl Betsey

Thomas BELL Jr. .... pg 466, 20 June 1815, inv & appr

girl age 14

John MUSE .... pg 469, 15 July 1813, sales

hired out: males - West, Philip, Adam, females – Fick?, Sarah, Hannah

Bennett TAYLOR ....pg 474, 11 Aug 1815, inv & appr

men Nathan, Peter, William, boys Ben, Isham, women Suckey, Nancy, Priscella, girls Mary, Suckey, Nancy

John TALBOTT ....pg 490, 1 Apr 1791 – 7 Dec 1810, gdn acct

hired man

Benjamin TALBOTT .... pg 495, 6 __ 1813 in court, estate acct

Harry's emancipation recorded

Walker Y. PAGE ....pg 505, 9 July 1813, will

boy Ned to sisters Sarah W. BROOK, Judith R. PAGE, Catherine PAGE, & Molly PAGE

Robert GLASS .... pg 506, 6 Jan 181_, inv & appr

man Tom

Adam ALDRIDGE ....pg 540, 10 Mar 1815, inv & appr

man Tom, girl Cleo, men Liberty, York, boy Sam, girl Easther, men Abraham, Jim, boy Reubin, Patty & her child Marie, girls Jude, Flora, Harriet, Charity, Faithey, boys Hiram?, Bob, D_mmo_d, Fielding, girl Caroline?, boys Randle?, Charles, girls Emily, Drucelia, boy Alfred, girl Lucy, boy Tofer, Blake, James, Tom

Richard BECKWORTH ....pg 559, 1 Jan – 28 Dec 1814, gdn acct

Phil, Daniel, John, Ben, Harry

WILL BOOK 10
1816 - 1820

William TAYLOR Sr. .... pg 6, 10 Jan 1816, will

negroes, except Tony to son Benjamin TAYLOR, to be divided into equal lots

.... pg 11, 21 Feb 1816, codicil

old man James to be emancipated; old Kate to choose her master

John SINGLETON .... pg 13, 10 Nov 1815, inv & appr

women Sarah, Syller, Dice, boy Lewis, girl Daffney, boys Bob, Dennis, girls Peg, Hanner

Samuel KERFOOT .... pg 24, 3 June 1816 in court, inv & appr

Ailly? & her child, Reeth, Henory?, John, Nelson, Harry, Harriett, Daniel, Sirus?, Pomp

Charles GRAVES .... pg 40, 18 Sept 1815, inv & appr

Mary, Sonny, Dick, George, Nace, Ally & her 4 children Mely, Sofy, Eddy, & Henry, Jinny & her 4 children Matildy, Mariah, Harriett, & Harrison

Leannah ASHBY .... pg 59, 26 June 1809, inv & sales

family of negroes, 3 negroes, 1 woman, 2 negroes to Alfred D. ASHBY

John D. ORR .... pg 64 29 May 1816, codicil

woman Jenny, man Jack legacies

Bennett TAYLOR .... pg 84, 2 Sept 1816 in court, inv & appr

Pompy, Charles, Simon, Arch, Phill, Adam, Jacob, Harey, Sam, William

Orphans of Dr. Solomon CARTMELL ....
.... pg 90, 1805 – Oct 1809, gdn acct

Sam, Hester, Ames

William PASH...pg 97, 1 Nov 1815, inv & appr

old woman

William PASH... pg 98, 2 Nov 1816, sales

negroes hired by Thomas JORDAN

John MUSE..pg 104, 1812 – Jan 1813, estate acct

to Susannah MUSE for use of Famy?, negroes

Nathaniel McPHERSON............................... pg 105, 22 Nov 1810, sales

woman & 2 children to Edward TURNER

James BENNETT........................ pg 108, 5 Nov 1816 in court, inv & appr

woman & child, Bill 15, Daniel 4

Frances WOODCOCK.....................................pg 112, 17 Mar 1816, will

"Elizabeth RUST daughter of my brother Benedict and now the wife of Peter RUST...to make a purchase of Julian the child of Liddy and at a proper lawful age to manumit her..."

Margery BEALL ....pg 116, 11 Dec 1805, will

all slaves & servants to daughter Mazy VANCE & at her death to her children

Elisha PHELPS ....pg 130, 6 Nov 1815, inv & appr

Catherine 70, Solomon 44, Ruben called Pero 7, George 5, Mary 3; "...James and Patty the Executors are of opinion ought not to be appraised but are entitled to their freedom"

William PASH..............................pg 136, 1 Mar 1817 in court, estate acct

man hired by PASH in his lifetime

John S. McNAMARA .... pg 147, 14 Apr 1817, inv & appr

Bill

Daniel SOWERS Jr. ....pg 152, 19 Jan 1815 - 23 Jan 1817, adm acct

man hired

Jacob ROSENBURGER............ pg 161, 7 Apr 1815, inv & appr

girl Elby, Absalom

Jacob ROSENBURGER............... pg 166, 26 Apr 1815, sales

Absalom to Jacob SAVICK; Elby to Henry SAVICK

Mordecai BEAN............ pg 174, 14 Dec 1814, inv & appr

man

Mordecai BEAN...............pg 179, 4 Jan 1815, sales

man to Henry WISECOMBER

Margaret KERFOOT............ pg 188, 27 Dec 1816, inv & appr

Becky, Clary, Will, Jake

Catherine ALLENSWORTH..... pg 192, 4 June 1817 in court, inv & appr

boy James

William HURST............ pg 198, 17 June 1817, inv & appr

man Lewis, Adam, Sam, Eleck, Punch, woman & child, boys Ruben, Willis

Rebecca HURST............ pg 200, 30 Dec 1812, dower

Elick, Punch

Robert DUNBAR............ pg 204, 16 May 1817, inv & appr

men Frank, Moses, boy John, man Peyton, woman Sarah, girl Florinda, boy Lindsey, old woman Frances; Harry a free black man

Orphans of Daniel SOWERS ....
.... pg 240, 26 Mar 1815 – Mar 1817, gdn acct

man Ned; balance due Mrs. CHUNN late Mrs. SOWERS on the division of slaves; negroes sold; Owing, Mary kept by Andrew CHUNN; Billy hired by David BROWN; Flood hired by James BELL

Joseph FAUNTLROY............... pg 242, 1 Sept 1817 in court, inv & appr

Moses, Sinah, Moses Jr., Isaac, Peter, Rebecca, Lucy, George, Leah, Humphrey, Lewis, Winny, Betsy & child, Aaron, Polly, Michael, Jack, Jenny, Richard, Louisa, Sarah, Nelly, David, Betty, Dick, Humphry,

Dinah, Nat, Jane, Isaac, Phillis, Samantha & child, Letty, Fanny, Agnes, Robin, Edmund

James D. NANCE .... pg 252, 22 Apr 1817, inv & appr

Lucy 27, Clary 10, Milly 8

Adam ALDRIDGE .... pg 262, 6 Mar 1815 – 3 Sept 1817, estate acct

23 negroes appraised, 34 negroes delivered to the legatees

George DENEALE, Jr .... pg 267, 5 Nov 1817 in court, sales

Joseph, Harry, Sampson, Milly, Betty & children, True Love & child Sarah, 2 children to Mrs. DENEALE; 20 Nov 1816 payment secured by Deed of Trust on said negroes

John S. WILLIAMS .... pg 270, Mar 1815 – 6 Sept 1817, estate acct

Mrs. WILLIAMS hired negroes; Gabriel, Nelly, John, Phil, Betty; Mead BOWEN hired negroes

John CARTER .... pg 276, 4 Apr 1817, inv & appr

women Amy, Cass, Laney, boy Andrew, girl Mary, boy Ned, man Chube?

Lewis RODES .... pg 288, 2 Mar 1818 in court, inv & appr

Peter

Ariana BURWELL .... pg 293, 21 Dec 1816, will

½ servants to nephew Thomas NELSON; remaining servants to nephew William NELSON

Thomas B. WALKER .... pg 313, 2 June 1818 in court, estate acct

woman hired

John CATLETT .... pg 318, Mar 1814, will

Jerey, David, Charlotte, Cate & her offspring to wife Rachel CATLETT; Sam to son Peter CATLETT; Clifton, Lucy, Libby to daughter Winnifred GREEN; Frederick, Bill, Mary to son Robert CATLETT

William TAYLOR .... pg 322, 7 May 1818, inv & appr

man Harry, boy Reuben, girl Sarah, boys Charles, Moses

Griffin TAYLOR.. pg 324, 20 June 1818, will

Dinah's son Jacob, Jeny? or Jerry?, Adam & his wife Hannah & their son James, Dinah, Grace's daughter Mary, Joan's? daughter Mary to wife Mary TAYLOR; remaining negroes excepting those to Mary TAYLOR & those already given to daughter Sarah G. ALLEN to be divided among sons David H. ALLEN, John B. TAYLOR, & daughter Catherine G. TAYLOR; old Ned requires support; Adam, his wife, & children to choose their master after the death of Mary TAYLOR

Orphans of Daniel SOWERS Jr. ....
.... pg 331, 8 Sept 1817 – 1 May 1818 , gdn acct

two small negroes kept by Andrew CHUNN; hires of old Billy, Flood, Mike of Stephen DAVIS; Ned, Aaron, Bill of Thomas CASTLEMAN; old Beck, Jonah & child

Elizabeth WRIGHT.................pg 339, Mar 1811 – May 1818, estate acct

man from March 1811 till May 1818 when he died; man sold

James LINDSEY.. pg 341, 26 Apr 1818, will

man London & woman Letty to be sold; remainder negroes except those chosen by wife Sarah LINDSEY to be hired out until youngest child arrives of age; each child upon marriage or arriving of age to receive one negro

.... pg 362, 1 Feb 1819 in court, inv & appr

men James, Moses, women Dinah, Letty, Mary, men London, George, boys Jacob, Matthew, Richard, Alfred, Barnett, Israel

John POLAND ....pg 365, 1 Mar 1819 in court, inv & appr

Ben 14, Agnes 10

Bartholomew SMITH...................................... pg 372, 29 Dec 1818, will

woman Fanny to wife Margaret; female negroes to be liberated at age 21, males at age 25 after wife's death; female hired to Mrs. KYGER

Henry CRUM ....pg 375, 20 Nov 1818, inv & appr

boy, his time valued; girl

Catharine ALLENSWORTH .... pg 387, 3 Mar 1819 in court, sales

Jim to John ALLENSWORTH

75

John C. MITCHELL .... pg 390, 12 Feb 1813 – 20 Jan 1819, estate acct

Robin sold to John S. THORNTON; Ben, Christian, George, Jesse, Elijah, Jess, Peggy, Frederick; George sold; jail fee for George; Tom, child, woman Nancy kept by James SOWERS; George ran away twice; girl

Thomas BERRY .... pg 393, 20 Feb 1806, will

boy Milfred, girl Milly gifted to daughter Peggy RANKINS wife of Col. Robert RANKINS & now in her posession; boy Moses now in her posession, girl Mariah to daughter Betsey CALMES; men Moses, Wilmore to son Joseph BERRY's sons Joseph & Samuel BERRY to be held in trust reserving the use of Joseph BERRY's wife during her life; girl Patience to daughter Jane KERCHEVAL to be held in trust by grandson Thomas B. KERCHEVAL for the use of their mother during her life; man Ambrose now in his posession, girl Mary to son William BERRY & land in Mason, KY; girl Lucy to daughter Sally KERMAN wife of William KERMAN to be emancipated at age 25; boy Nelson, girl Delphia now in her posession to daughter Sally KERMAN; boy Hampton gifted to son Samuel BERRY; boy Juboy, girl Clary to daughter Caty BERRY; girl Charity gifted to granddaughter Matilda KERCHEVAL daughter of Jane KERCHEVAL

Benjamin WROE .... pg 399, 7 Oct 1811, will

woman Judath to daughter Salley C. WROE; woman Susannah to daughter Jane SETTLE; Fanny to daughter Rebecca WROE; first choice of a negro to son Chancellor WROE; next choice of a negro to son Benjamin WROE; "…if Daniel SETTLE should incline to hold negro Grace from the devision then…value the said negro…and deduct from my daughter Janes SUTTLE's part of my estate…"

John CAMPBELL .... pg 406, 28 Mar 1819, will

all slaves to be liberated, men at age 21, women at age 18; young slaves to be apprenticed; Alfred to be bound to the shoe making trade until he is 21; "…William Martan an orphan boy now under my protection…"

Sarah CARTMELL .... pg 421, 15 Nov 1815, sales

Hetty, Pegg to Martin CARTMELL; Matilda, Gilbert to Nathaniel CARTMELL; Sally to Stephen PRICHARD

Bartholomew SMITH .... pg 429, 26 Mar 1819, inv & appr

girl Luisa to serve 7 years

James DAVIS ....pg 430, 16 Feb 1819, will

slaves may be sold by the executors with consent of wife Sally I. DAVIS

Stephen PRITCHARD ....pg 432, 17 Nov 1818, will

Jacob, Richard, Mary to daughter Margaret Eskridge PRICHARD; Young Amos, William, Caroline to daughter Susannah James PRITCHARD; Anthony to daughter Mary Ann FAW wife of Samuel FAW; John, Robert, Nelly to daughter Betsy Kanner PRITCHARD; Barbara, Kitty, Paton, Jonathan, Emely to daughter Judith Kanner PRITCHARD

John SENSENEY ....pg 438, 15 May 1819, will

boy Phill, girl Fann to wife Nancy

Cassandra PURVIS ....pg 444, 22 June 1819, will

men at age 25, women at age 21 to be free; those under age to be sold to masters of their parent's choice for a term of years until they reach the ages above; Patty, over 45, to have the benefit of her labors, her son Ben to pay her support after his liberation

Stephen PRITCHARD ....pg 445, 11 June 1819, inv & appr

men Jacob, Dick, girl Mary bequeathed to Miss Margaret; men Amos, William, girl Caroline to Miss Susan; man John, boy Bob, girl Nelly to Miss Betsey; man Anthony to Mrs. FAW; man Amos to Stephen PRITCHARD; woman Barbara, girl Hetty, boys Jonathan, Peyton, child Amelia Susan to Miss Judith

Hugh H. McKEARN .... pg 453, 22 July 1809 - 1 Jan 1812, estate acct

Smith, Judy hired

Daniel SOWERS ....pg 464, Mar 1817 – 1 Sept 1819, estate acct

child Orange 1 year old; Beck, old Billy, Baron, Ned, Aaron, Bill, Mima, Flood, Joannah

Daniel CRUM ....pg 465, 4 Oct 1819 in court, sales

boy, girl to Mrs. CRUM

William ELLZEY ....pg 479, 10 Mar 1819, will memorandum

girl Hannah to James HUME?

William DAVIS.................pg 485, 6 Dec 1819 in court, inv & appr

Henry, Judy, Betty, Patrick, Susan, Richard, David, Reuben, Gil, Sam, Nelson, Mariah

Capt. James DAVIS .... pg 487, 10 June 1819, inv & appr

girl Kitty, Rose, Ally, Fanny

Elijah LITTLER .... pg 495, 3 Nov 1817, sales

Grace & her 5 children Nelson, Thornton, Alexander, William, & Harriet, man Jacob, boys Lewis, Isaac, Henry, man William, old woman Jane to Charles W. LITTLER; Betsy & 5 children George, Jane, Evelina, Rebecca & Sarah Ann to Francis STRIBLING for the heirs; man Solomon to Sigismund STRIBLING; boy William to Robert HAMILTON; girl Fanny to John HOFF; negroes Thomas & Simon both bought heifers

Walter DENNY .... pg 522, 31 Jan 1820 in court, inv & appr

old woman

Robert GLASS .... pg 523, 1797 – 10 May 1798, estate acct

Tom

Elizabeth BROWN .... pg 527, 31 Jan 1820 in court, inv & appr

man Reuben, boy George, woman Aggy, girl Harriet, boy Sam?, woman Easter, girls Sarah, Areanna, Patty, Louisa

Cassandra PURVIS .... pg 531, 5 Mar 1820 in court, inv & appr

Patty 20 to serve until 7 Oct 1820; Agga 2 yrs & 6 months to serve until 7 July 1838; John 4 months to serve until 7 June 1844; Maria 4 yrs & 4 months to serve until 7 June 1836; Sam 4 yrs 4 months to serve until 7 June 1840; David 10 to serve until 7 Oct 1834; Molly 13 yrs & 6 months to serve until 7 Apr 1827; Adline 15 to serve until 7 Oct 1825; Bobb 15 to serve until 7 Oct 1829; Milly 16 to serve until 7 Oct 1824

Thomas PARKER .... pg 537, 22 Dec 1817, will

Amos to Armistead T. MASON after the death of my wife; negroes to my wife

Cassandra PURVIS .... pg 538, 7 Oct 1819, sales

Patty 20 to serve until 7 Oct 1820 to Richard MORGAN; Agga 2 yrs & 3? months to serve until 7 July 1838, John 4 months to serve until 7 June 1844, David 10 to serve until 7 Oct 1834 to George D. HARRISON; Maria 4 yrs & 4 months to serve until 7 June 1836 to Ann WINDLE; Sam 4 yrs 4 months to serve until 7 June 1840 to Thomas DENT; Molly 13 yrs & 6 months to serve until 7 Apr 1827 to Walter TANQUARY; Adline 15 to serve until 7 Oct 1825 to Levi A. WICKHAM; Bobb 15 to serve until 7 Oct 1829 to James CLARE; Milly 16 to serve until 7 Oct 1824 to Jacob EVERHART

Mary STEPHENS ....pg 544, 23 Feb 1820, inv & appr

Sukey 50, Rachel & her 2 children a female 8/9 & David 6; William 8/9, John 18, Daniel 13/14

David STIGLER...............................pg 545, 14 Feb 1820, inv & appr

woman Rose

Catharine MOORE..............................pg 569, 14 Sept 1818, will

Betty and her 4 children sold to daughter Betsy

Thomas RUST.............................pg 573, 20 Oct 1819, inv & appr

Bandy?, Abraham, Reuben, Rebecca, Elizabeth, Henny, Lyley?, Anna, Jack, John, James, Jenny, Sylla, Sam, Rose, Sarah, George, Jefferson, Eliza, old woman Jenny

Richard MASTIN..................................... pg 588, 9 June 1819, estate acct

Kate, Sam sold; Sam hired from B. ELLIOTT

Dr. Robert BERKELEY .... pg 594, 5 June 1818, inv & inv & appr

men Ralph, Harry, Sam, boy Godfrey, men George, Jacob, Sam, Solomon, Beverly, Carter, Simon, Jack (or Jacob), woman Jane, George, Sam, Peter, Polly, William, Betty, Eady, Thornton, woman Fa_me_, Betsy, Henry, Milly, Phebe, Molly, Daniel, Billy, Fanny, John, Lidia

David WILSON.................................pg 606, 4 Feb 1818, will

children Mary & Martha to wife Mary WILSON

Ephraim GARRISON.............................pg 610, 20 Sept 1816, will

fellow Jacob, his wife Grace & children Charles & Arenia? to wife;
"...the Death of my son my estate and his was joint...no alternative
has ben made...Phoebe negro woman...Tom, Peter, Rachel, Antzelly?,
Jack."

WILL BOOK 11
1820 - 1823

William BOND .... pg 103, 10 Nov 1818, will

Cynthia, Tabetha, Bill to grandchildren Elizabeth Susan & Martha SWEARINGEN daughters of dec'd daughter Elizabeth SWEARINGEN, wife of John SWEARINGEN

Archibald MAGILL .... pg 105, 11 Feb 1821, will

all slaves to be emancipated; "...I wish Pleasant, her husband and children to live on the place they now live on as long as they can be permitted by the Court."

Whitson GREEN .... pg 108, 27 Feb 1821, inv & appr

woman Winney?, girls Mary, Priscilla, Hannah, Ceally, child Milly

Jane MADDEN .... pg 110, __ , inv & appr

girl Lucy

Thomas BERRY .... pg 123, _ June 1821 in court, sales

Poll, Henry to Thomas MURPHEY

Charles HAMILTON .... pg 132, 2 Apr 1821, will

man Benjamin to brothers Thomas HAMILTON & John HAMILTON, & sister Ruth HAMILTON

Thomas MARSHALL .... pg 134, 4 March 1817, will

town of Washington, Mason County, KY

boy Alfred to son Thomas; boys Armstead, Frederick to son Charles; boy little Reuben, Harriet to daughter Mary Keith MARSHALL; Jacob, Charlotte, Milly to daughter Elizabeth; girls Nancy, Rachel to daughter Lucy; boy Henry to son James MARSHALL; boys Martin?, Davy? to son Charles after the death of his mother; negroes not specifically devised to wife Fanny MARSHALL

Edmund PENDLETON .... pg 139, 6 Oct 1820, inv & appr

Mimy, Tony, Mimy, Nelly

.... pg 141, 23 Mar 1821, sales

Mima 26, man Toney, Nelly to R.G. WARD; old woman Mima to Elizabeth PENDLETON

Benjamin WROE .... pg 148, 2 July 1821 in court, sales

man David to William HOPEWELL; girl Rachael to John SCROGGIN; girls Nancy to William WROE; girl Eliza to Daniel LITTLES; boy Daniel to Richard HALL; Lucy & child Henry, girl Maria to Benjamin WROE; girl Susan to Alexander COOK

David WILSON .... pg 152, 11 June 1821, inv & appr

Fanny, Lavina, Samuel, Milly, Louisa, Lewis, Patsy, Mary, infant Harriet, Mimery

Rev. Alexander BALMAIN .... pg 157, 22 May 1821, will

"...after the decease of my said wife, I devise & bequeath...my slaves...to be divided in such a manner among her brothers & sisters, children...she shall have the power of imancipating them..."

Michael DORMISE .... pg 169, 9 Aug 1821, estate acct

old man & old woman died

Richard P. BARTON .... pg 179, 7 June 1821, inv & appr

Phil, John, Alick, Jesse, Isaac, Frank, Moll, Hannah, Charity & her child Isabell, Polly, Letty, Bella, Evelina, Sally, Lucy, Tom, Geleka?

James WARE .... pg 183, 10 May 1821, will

children Sarah Elizabeth Taliaferro STRIBLING, Charles Alexander WARE, & Josiah William WARE to choose 1 negro each that live at Spring Field; Emily to said daughter; boy Peter son of Billy to son James William WARE; boy Albert Harley son of Billy to son Thomas Marshall WARE; Mary Ann daughter of Billy to daughter Lucy Catharine WARE; girl Juliet Ann daughter of Billy to daughter Harriet Mary Tod WARE

Sarah PARKER ....pg 186, 2 Feb 1821, will

big Janey, her children & grandchildren, General, Joe to Richard C. PARKER; Emile? to Polly CLA__LTON & at her death to brother H. OPIE; Nancy to be free with her daughter's services; Marcia to be free; Dina & her children to Margaret Sarah OPIE; "...to the said H. OPIE all the lands slaves and other property...not disposed of..."; "...the Negroes hereby willed...shall be kept toegether..."; the will was signed by Sally PARKER

Joseph GLASS .... pg 190, 26 Oct 1821, will

servants to wife Ann; girl Mary Ann daughter of Cassee to daughter Eliza Willson GLASS; girl Chloe the daughter of Cassee to daughter Sarah Ann GLASS; Betsy the daughter of Abraham to daughter Mary; boy David the son of Abraham to daughter Hester Sophia GLASS; girl Sally the daughter of Molly to daughter Susan Emily GLASS; boy John the son of Abraham to daughter Sidney _inesby GLASS; Mingo the son of Abraham to daughter Emmeline Marshall GLASS; boy Robert son of Abraham to daughter Ann McCalister GLASS; Abraham to be cared for by son James McCalister GLASS; men James, Joseph to son Joseph GLASS; men Cuffee, Frank to son James; woman Rachel, wife of Cuffee, to wife Ann; woman Nancy to her own proper___; woman Molly to daughter Eliza Willson GLASS; remaining servants & increase may be sold or divided among the above children

William RICHARDSON .... pg 203, 13 Dec 1821 in court, inv & appr

2 men

Rev. Alexander BALMAIN .... pg 220, 5 Nov 1821, inv & appr

Sarah 54, Phillis 43, William 24, David 21, John 19, Kitty 17 & her child Cleo? Poindexter 2, Julia 12, Robert 14, Alexander 10, Frank 8, Sally 4

James CARTER .... pg 226, 4 Feb 1822, will

boy Nead to brother William CARTER

John WILSON .... pg 228, 8 Sept 1807 – 1819, estate acct

Mrs. WILSON kept young negroes 11 years; Flora, Fanny, Ben, Adam, Peter; Ephraim, Ben sold

Sarah WILSON widow .... pg 231, 5 Mar 1822, adm acct

kept young negroes

Mrs. C.M.B.DAINGERFIELD .... pg 238, 2 Jan 1822, inv & appr

man Cesar, Isaac, James, Ambrose, Caty, Betsey, Patty

Casper SEEVERS .... pg 241, 27 Apr 1816, will

girl Henrietta to wife; girl Phebe? to daughter Catharine; girl Fanny to daughter Rebecca; girl Eliza to daughter Amelia

Isaac LUPTON .... pg 244, 1 May 1822, inv & appr

boy Sam

James CARTER .... pg 258, 18 Mar 1822, inv & appr

boy

.... pg 259, 18 Mar 1822, sales

boy to William CARTER

George COPENHAVER .... pg 264, 20 Apr 1822, inv & appr

James

John & Charlotte TAYLOR ....pg 266, 1 Nov 1821, gdn acct

men Pompey, Charles, Phil, Archy, Adam, Jacob, Simon, Sam, boys
William, Ned, William, women Celia, Nancy, children James,
Pompey, Harriet, Ben, David, Eliza, Joshua, Sam

William T. THROCKMORTON............pg 267, 14 Aug 1816, inv & appr

old Nanny, Violet

.... pg 272, 17 Aug 1816, sales

woman to Joseph HOOPER; woman to Amelia THROCKMORTON

Mary BARTON.................................pg 287, 19 Nov 1820, will

Fanny & her daughter Kitty, Lucy & her children to be sold; man
George to son James G. BARTON

....pg 287, 10 May 1822, codicil

Lucy, Vind, Sarah to son James G. BARTON

Richard & Ann MARTIN....................... pg 290, 1 July 1822, inv & appr

man Sam, woman Cate

Frances HELM .... pg 290, 6 Dec 1820, inv & appr

man Frederick, boys Henry, Reuben, woman Sarah, men Sam, Dennis,
woman Letitia, girls Easter, Ann, Polly & 2 children Mariah & Evelina

Casper SEEVERS ....pg 294, 16 Mar 1822, inv & appr

girls Henrietta, Phebe, Fanny, Eliza, man Lewis, boy Peter

William T. THROCKMORTON...
.... pg 295, 23 July 1816 0- 1 Apr 1822, estate acct

man hired by Benjamin HARVY

Samuel McCOMRICK .... pg 296, 24 Dec 1816, will

negroes may be sold if necessary otherwise to wife Margaret McCOMRICK

Elizabeth M. GLASS..pg 297, 10 July 1819, will

Hannah & her child Lucinda to daughter Elizabeth GLASS; boy Harrison, a child of Hannah, to son Thomas GLASS

George DENEALE Jr.......pg 301, 14 June 1816 - 28 Jan 1822, estate acct

Betty & child sold to Willis UTTERBACK; girl Lucy & child boy Jack, man Sampson to Walter A. SMITH; boy Anthony to John PADGETT; woman Truelove, girl Phillis, boy Frank to William R. SMITH; boy Jesse by Joseph D. SMITH to Elvin TAYLOR; girl Harriett, boy Lewis, old woman Sarah & her 2 children Jane & Unity, child Sibby to Walter A. SMITH; woman Nelly to William R. Smith

Mary HAMPTON ....pg 306, 20 July 1818, will

Pompay, Dinah to be free at the end of 31 Dec after my decease

Peter Ransone....................................pg 307, 12 Sept 1822, will

a free negro man, wife Charlotte Ransone

Elizabeth GLASS ....pg 308, 6 Sept 1822, inv & appr

woman Hannah, girl Lucinda, boys Harrison, Horace

John TRIPCOTT ....pg 313, 7 Oct 1822, inv & appr

man Oliver, woman Letty, boy Lewis, girl Jane

Jacob SOWERS................................ pg 320, 20 Apr 1822, will

man Roger to son-in-law James GLASS; Titus, Dinah given their freedom

Daniel, Catharina, & Eliza A. SOWERS..
.... pg 326, 30 Dec 1820 - 14 Oct 1822, gdn acct

Mike, Aaron, old Billy, Bill, Flood, Ned, James, Joanna, Shedarick, old Becky

Bennett HALL....................................pg 336, 25 Sept 1822, will

Sam, Bob, Juda, Joseph to son James Bennett HALL; Duke, Jefferson, Abby, Charlotte to daughter Hannah BEAN; Harry, Rachel, Jacob, Lewis, Emaly to daughter Sally HALL; girl Ruth to wife Nancy HALL

Thomas BERRY.................... pg 341, 16 Dec 1820, inv & appr

Willoughby & Sinah his wife, boy Bailer, woman Hannah

....................................pg 341, 1819 - 12 Dec 1822, estate acct

negroes

....................................pg 343, 16 Dec 1820 in court, inv & appr

man Ambrose

Thomas CAMPBELL....................pg 346, 15 Aug 1810, inv & appr

men Lue, Roger, woman & child, boys Bill, Hotten, Daniel, Ben, girl Fanny, boy Hampton, Plummer, Lucy, Bob

Thomas WARE .... pg 348, 29 Nov 1821, inv & appr

men Spencer, Jacob, Billy, Sam, Sawney, Joseph, Presly, Jim, boys Jerry, Henry, Lewis, Susan & 2 children, woman Rachel, girl Milly, Mary & child Evelina, girls Amy, Fanny, boy Mortimer, old man Dick, man Tom Bundy since dead, woman Betty a runaway

William N. BURWELL.................... pg 352, 7 Jan 1823, inv & appr

Charles, Mars?, Tom, Daniel, James, Jack, Miles, Frank, Sam, Billy Kennedy, Senaca, Andrew, Robbin, Wat, Harry, George, Betty, Eve, Suckey Liberty, Maria, Betsy, Jenny, Nancy, Suckey, Chancey, Nelly, Priscilla, Emily, Rachel, Lill, Jenny, Liz, Georgianna, Beck

William CONRAD ....pg 358, 13 Nov 1822, inv & appr

man Perry, woman Letty, boys Alped, Juber

Josiah CRAIG ...... pg 369, 2 Oct, 1819, will

girl Maria to son Josiah CRAIG; man Joe, girl Evelina to son Samuel CRAIG; woman Matilda to granddaughter Polly the wife of Samuel PECK; girl Sarah to grandson Samuel PECK

Christopher GRIGLAR ...... pg 372, 18 Mar 1822, inv & appr

men Dick, Bob, Lyda & child, girl Mary, boy Henry, Frederick, boy John, girl Hester, woman & child Ann, boy John, Rachael & child, boy Jerry, girl Harriet, boy Ralph, Nicy & child, Betsy, men Isaac, James, woman Cleary

LeRoy DANGERFIELD ...... pg 381, 13 Jan 1816, will

men John, Henry, boy Ambrose, girl Lizzy, woman Caty & her child Pretty, child Patty already received by son William DANGERFIELD; man Robin already received by son LeRoy P. DANGERFIELD; boy Davy, girl Patty already received by daughter Elizabeth F. DEADRICK; woman Caty already received by daughter Mary B. BELFIELD

Jacob SOWERS ...... pg 383, 13 Sept 1822, inv & appr

man Titus, woman Dinah, man George

James WILLIAMS ...... pg 386, 13 Feb 1823, inv & appr

girl Jane

Sigismund STRIBLING ...... pg 409, 11 Nov 1822, inv & appr

man Bob, girl Emily, Jack 15

Hulda BERRY ...... pg 415, 29 Aug 1822, inv & appr

old Reuben, old George, old Cate, Aggy, young Reuben, Elias, Daniel, Clary, Nancy, Dick, Emily, Aranah, Alped, Alexander, John, Juliet, Eliza, Nill, Laura

Innis BRENT ...... pg 440, 25 Oct 1822, inv & appr

boy Cornelius

Isiah CRAIG..pg 452, 20 Mar 1823, inv & appr

man Joe, girl Eveline, Malinda & 3 children Sarah, Adam, & Mary, girl Maria

Archibald MAGILL ....pg 456, 11 Feb 1821, will

all slaves to be emancipated; Pleasants, her husband & children to live on the place they now live

George ASH.. pg 461, 23 Jan 1823, inv & appr

Isaac, Peter, Mary & her infant child Mary James, Sarah & her infant son James, Hannah, Milly, Maria, Sally, Henry, Gabriel, Ellick, Stape, Cornelius, Lewis, Isaac Jr. Eliza, Henrietta & her infant child Catherine

Orphans of Samuel McCORMICK ....pg 466, 14 July 1823, gdn acct

men Tom, Harry, boy Solomon, girl Nancy, Maria and her 5 children Ariana, Juliet, Maria, Emily, & Sarah

Francis HUTCHIN ....pg 471, 21 Nov 1822, inv & appr

woman Nancy

Alexander CLEVELAND ....pg 489, 15 Aug 1823, will

woman Daphney to daughter-in-law Selah CLEVELAND wife of Elijah CLEVELAND

Francis STRIBLING Sr..................................... pg 490, 4 June 1823, will

wife to choose slaves & at her death to be divided among the heirs; the remaining slaves to be sold

Casper CLINE ....pg 495, 17 Feb 1821, inv & appr

man

Walter DENNEY................................pg 511, 11 Mar 1822, estate acct

Milly kept by William ADAMS

WILL BOOK 12
1824 - 1825

Harriet M. WARE .... pg 3, 9 Dec 1822, inv & appr

Lucy & 2 children William Henry & Fairfax

Orphans of Daniel SOWERS Jr ....pg 7, Nov 1822 – 4 Feb 1823, gdn acct

Orange, Flood, Aaron, Mike, Bill, Joanna, Ned, James, Shredrech, old Bill,

Sarah THOMAS .... pg 13, 13 Jan 1824, inv & appr

boy, girl

William ABBOTT .... pg 18, 2 Feb 1824 in court, inv & appr

Jenny & her 6 children Emily, Dolly, Morgan, Fanny, Armstead, & Reuben

Alexander CLEVELAND .... pg 29, 17 Dec 1823, inv & appr

Moses 20, Washington 12, Augustin 13, Beverly 8

Joseph GLASS .... pg 30, 24 Jan 1824, inv & appr

Cuffce, Frank, James, Joseph, Old Abraham, Young Abraham, Molly, Nancy, Sarah, Fillah, Rachael, Mingo, John, Robert, Louisa, Mary Ann, Betsey, Chloe, boy David, girls Sally, Chloe

Philip BUSH, Jr. .... pg 32, 31 Dec 1823, additional estate acct

woman Beck kept by John BUSH

.... pg 34, 1815 – 1822, estate acct

old woman Beck

Maria MOORE late HANY .... pg 47, 1822 – Dec 1824, gdn acct

Esther, Jim, Eveline, Davy

William CARNEGY .... pg 51, 28 Jan 1823, will

old woman Hannah, fellow Glasgow to Nancy POWERS, widow of Yancy POWERS, and in her possession for many years; girl Margery, man Gloston? to the children of dec'd sister, late wife of John

POWERS, Gloston? being in the possession of John & his mother; child Jasper to Daniel POWERS; child Grace to the children of Polly WAGGONER daughter of Nancy POWERS & wife of William WAGGONER; young child to Thomas POWERS, youngest son of Nancy, 2 years after my decease; young woman Nancy, Emely with her child Thornton to sister Mary; "...negroes to be hired out for benefit of daughter Ann wife of Thomas KENNERLY...for and during the term of fifty years then as many as think proper and all their Descendants to go to the American Coloney in Affocea..."

French GLASCOCK .... pg 53, 29 Apr 1824, inv & appr

girl

Richard S. REDMAN .... pg 56, 12 Dec 1823, inv & appr

man George, woman Ashalinda, girl Lucy, boys Mingo, Bill, Joseph, Major Kudgoe, Mansfield, girl Mina, boy Robert, girls Sarah, Louisa, boy Benjamin, woman Alice, boy James, girls Jane, Cashanner, Elizabeth

Elizabeth FAUNTLEROY .... pg 58, 3 May 1824 in court, inv & appr

Amy & her child Daniel, Maria, Richard, Joshua

Dr. Robert DUNBAR .... pg 62, 30 May 1815 – 1 Jan 1821, estate acct

men Frank, Moses, Peyton, boys John, Lindsey, women Sarah, Frances, girl Florinda

.... pg 68, 4 Aug 1815 – 1 Jan 1821, estate acct

boy John

.... pg 71, 1815 - 1 Jan 1821, estate acct

Mary, Payton, Frank, Sarah, John

Jacob SOWERS .... pg 82, 13 Sept 1822 - 10 Jan 1824, estate acct

Titus, Dinah, a special legacy of freedom

Elizabeth MARSHALL .... pg 84, 19 Jan 1824, inv & appr

girl Jane?

.... pg 84, 4 June 1824, sales

girl to John RUST

Francis STRIBLING ....pg 95, 25 Oct 1823, inv & appr

Joe, Charles, Harry, Frederick, Jake, Sam, Bill, Dick, Cyrus, Aaron, Ralph, Doll, Hannah, Flora, Clara, Moses, Rachael & 2 children, Dan, Dinah & child, Aggy & child, Sall & 3 children

....pg 96, 24 Nov 1823, sales

Ralph to Robert McCANDLESS; Jake, Dick to Francis STRIBLING; Sally & 3 children to John MACKY

Henry MITCHELL .... pg 100, 15 June 1824, inv & appr

Frederick County:

man Jacob 60, Rachel 50, Lec 4, Susan 12, Fanny 9

....pg 102, 22 July 1824, inv & appr

Augusta County:

Dick 20, George 10, Washington 10, Lucy 25, Daniel 35, Levin 50

James BERNETT .... pg 109, 15 Sept 1816 – 1822, estate acct

woman & child, boy Daniel appraised but not sold; Bill sold

John ELLSEA ....pg 111, 27 June 1820 – 14 Dec 1822, estate acct

boy boarded by Isaac B. ELLSEA, Jack, Kit; hire & sale of negroes

William CARNEGYpg 126, 28 July 1724; 4 Oct 1824 in court, inv & appr

43 slaves, young & old

Mary STEPHENS .... pg 131, 7 Feb 1822 - 20 Oct 1824, estate acct

sold: Sukey & her children Rachael & David, John, Billey, Daniel

Meredith HELM ....pg 136, 10 Jan 1821, sales

Benjamin to Catharine HELM; Davey, Squire, Caesar to Philagathus ROBERTS; Ned, Emma to Maria HELM; Daniel, Rachel, Judy & her child, Davey to Robert SANFORD; Wallace, Milly, Aggy, Charlotte to Helen M. HELM; Ham alias Abraham to Charles W. LITTLER; Jerry, Delia & her child William, Sydney to Harriet S. CORBIN; Nancy, John to John JOLLIFFE; Chris to John VONREIZEN; Leana to Isaac BAKER; Cate & her child Solomon, George, Deborah, Araminta to Catharine HELM; Charles to Elisha W. WILLIAMS

Jacob MADDEN .... pg 143, 2 Nov 1824 in court, inv & appr

man Robert

James WALKER .... pg 148, Aug 1799 – 2 July 1808, estate acct

tax on 3 slaves

John RAMEY .... pg 153, 25 Nov 1822, inv & appr

man Thornton, women Pricilla, Sharlotte, boy Henry, girls Comfort, Mariah, Berthe__, boy Jacob

Frederick FLORES .... pg 157, 23 Oct 1823, inv & appr

Molly

Elizabeth MARSHALL .... pg 161, 4 Dec 1824, estate acct

girl Lucy sold

John D. ORR .... pg 162, 24 Aug 1816, inv & appr

men Essea?, Samuel, Jessy, Abraham, Nelson, Daniel, William Mumpha?, Jack, William, woman Janny, child Alice, woman Susana

Mary BYRD .... pg 175, 6 Mar 1824, will

Daniel Williams to son Francis Otway BYRD; Jenny was gifted to Francis OTWAY by his father in the summer of 1817; Betsey Potter to daughter Elizabeth Hill BYRD; Susan's son William to daughter Maria Carter NICHOLAS; Gabriel Williams to son Thomas Taylor BYRD; Jack Williams to son Charles Carter BYRD; young Christopher Williams to Richard Evelyn BYRD; remaining slaves to be divided into 7 equal parts – 2 shares to son Francis Otway BYRD; 1 share to each of my other children Elizabeth Hill BYRD, Maria Carter NICHOLAS, Thomas Taylor BYRD, Charles Carter BYRD, & Richard Evelyn BYRD; Randolph, Ralph, John now in possession of son Charles to be divided among my 4 sons; daughter Elizabeth Hill BYRD may take Ralph Williams is she wishes; daughter Maria Carter NICHOLAS may take Susan's fdaughter Phillis; son Charles Carter BYRD may take Nancy's son Thomas; son Richard Evelyn may take Nancy's daughter Nancy

Thomas SMITH .... pg 178, 8 Oct 1824, will

family of negroes as yet undivided to brother Paul SMITH

Charles A. WARE .... pg 191, 13 Jan 1824, inv & appr

men Newman, Bob, boys Jerry, Frederick, Sally & her child Miles

Jacob MADDEN .... pg 193, 23 Nov 1812 – 9 Dec 1824, estate acct

man Bob

John MILTON .... pg 197, 24 Mar 1818 – 2 Feb 1824, estate acct

women; old man Daniel died; Isaac sold for robbing

James WARE .... pg 200, 1 Oct 1821 – 24 Nov 1824, estate acct

jailer's fees for Sam, Betty; Billy, Milley

Harriet M. WARE .... pg 203, 10 Nov 1822 – 2 Dec 1824, estate acct

negroes7Taliaferro M. McILHANY

....pg 208, 1 Mar 1813 – 27 Dec 1824, gdn acct

Virgil

Marquis Q. BLAKEMORE .... pg 214, 24 Nov 1824, inv & appr

men William, Lowcy? George, lad John, boy Thomas, Fathy & 2
children, Kittey & 1 child, old woman Rose

John CARTER .... pg 217, 1817 – 1824, estate acct

negro tax

John BOWEN .... pg 221, 14 Aug 1823, inv & appr

men Mat, John, William, Rhody, Mariah, Peter

Thomas BROWN .... pg 227, 5 Jan 1825 in court, inv & appr

woman & 2 children

Maxwell DOWDALL ....

.... pg 234, 29 Mar 1821 - 20 Mar 1824, comm report

man Gilbert, old Tom

Jane DOWDALL ....

.... pg 236, 20 Mar 1821 - 20 Mar 1824, comm report

Essex, Winney

John HOLKER ....pg 238, 16 Apr 1822 – 1 Jan 1825, estate acct

negroes

William RICHARDSON ....

....pg 240, 6 July 1821- 1 Jan 1825, estate acct

Roger, Harry; Roger sold; Harry died

Joseph GLASS ....pg 244, 21 Dec 1821 – 1 Jan 1825, estate acct

Abraham

Jacob CRYSER ....pg 263, 29 Jan 1825, estate acct

Harry sold

John C. & Charlotte B. TAYLOR ....

.................................pg 267, 1 Jan 1822 – 31 Dec 1824, gdn acct

servants; Fanny Sweeney paid wages

William N. BURWELL...

..................................pg 271, 16 Sept 1822 – 22 Nov 1824, estate acct

Jim to John BAKER

Casper CLINE ....pg 296, 22 Nov 1824, estate acct

Christmas

Nancy SENSENEY ....pg 298, 26 Oct 1820, inv & appr

girl named Fan free at age 30 years, boy named Fill free at age 30 years

John SENSENEY .... pg 308, 12 June 1819, inv & appr

old Charley?, Evelina

....pg 310, 14 June 1819, sales

girl Evelina to John SENSENEY; old man? ___ to Widow SENSENEY

John GOLD, Sr...................................pg 320, 13 Mar 1823, inv & appr

Betty, boy Godfrey, girls Charity, Ellen, boy Daniel, old man Jim

John GOLD, Sr. ....pg 329, Mar 1823 - 27 Feb 1825, estate acct

woman sold in Battletown; slaves advertised; girl Ellen sold by James GOLD to Thomas SHEPHERD; Godfrey, Daniel purchased by Stephen PRITCHARD from Daniel GOLD

James RICHARDSON .... pg 336, 2 June 1824, inv & appr

old man Richard, Aaron, Solomon, Phillip, boy Robert

Jesse O'REAR ....pg 343, 15 Feb 1825, inv & appr

Harry, Hayes, Stephen, Jacob, Willis, Nelson, Eveline, Nelly, Susan, child Richard, Fanny, Kizzey, Emma, Ruth

Hannah FENTON ....pg 347, 26 Oct 1816, will

Phillis to be free & her children Hence, Isaac, Joshua, & Poll be hired out until they are 21 & then be free; Bets to serve Sally DAVIS until she is 25 & then be free; "...that Polls children if any she should have be born free that Jonathan be hired out until he is entitled to freedom by the last will and testament of my husband Enoch FENTON, and that Tom be hired out until he arrives to the age of twenty five years and that he shall be free, and that Sam be hired out until he arrives to the age of twenty five years and that he shall be free..."; if Bets has any children they shall be free born

Francis HUTCHINGS .... pg 355, 28 Nov 1822, sales

Nancy hired to Mrs. HUTCHINGS

David GROVE .... pg 357, 24 Nov 1824, appr 189

boy

Richard P. BARTON........ pg 364, 23 May 1821 - 2 Mar 1825, estate acct

Phillis, Frank, Jesse, Harry; woman in labor; Kate's value transferred to Mr. GRAMMER; hire of girl

John NOBLE .... pg 378, 23 Mar 1807, sales

Cyntha, Mary to DIXSON, Lemon to DOVEY, Daniel to E. SWEARINGEN; Lucy & 2 children Jerry & Washington to Mrs. NOBLE

John NOBLE .... pg 379, 23 Mar 1807 – 23 July 1810, estate acct

Lemmon, Syntha, Mary, Daniel, Lucy & 2 children sold; Lee, Sue

Peter BABB..............pg 391, 2 May 1825 in court, inv & appr

    boy Steve

John SENSENEY.................. pg 395, 18 Apr 1825, estate acct

    Fanny, Phillip hire ends 1 Jan 1825 "...left by will of said SENSENEY to his wife Nancy the boy to serve & stay with her 15 years and the girl to stay & serve with her...till she arrives at the age of 30, at that age they are both to be free..."

Orphans of Samuel McCORMICK..
....pg 405, 1 Jan 1824 – 10 Mar 1825 , estate acct

    2 children boarded by Isaac McCORMICK; Tom, Harry, Saul

John RAMEY.................................. pg 408, 26 Nov 1822, sales

    man Thornton, woman Sillah, Charlotte & children, small girl, small boy

Laurence B. FAUNTLEROY..
....pg 414, 1 Jan 1822 – 11 Mar 1825, gdn acct

    Polly, Michael

Robert H. FAUNTLEROY...
....pg 414, 1 Jan 1822 – 11 Mar 1825, gdn acct

    Agnes, Dinah, David?

John FAUNTLEROY..
....pg 415, 1 Jan 1822 – 11 Mar 1825, gdn acct

    Edmund; "...supporting negro Samantha for 2 yrs with 4 children 1 year & 6 children the next year and 1 child the third year."

Sophia Carter BERKELY ....pg 435, 1 Jan 1820 - 1 June 1824, gdn acct

    2 negroes sold in Hanover

Julia BERKELY......................pg 436, 1 June 1821 - Jan 1825, gdn acct

    2 negroes sold in Hanover

Elizabeth W. BERKELY...... pg 437, 1 June 1821 – 1 June 1824, gdn acct

    2 negroes sold in Hanover

Sarah ALEXANDER ....pg 474, 5 July 1824, will

negroes to be divided between grandchildren Sarah E.T. STRIBLING & Josiah William WARE children of the late James WARE

Henry FRANKS ....pg 476, 21 Feb 1825, inv & appr

man Jesse, Jane & her 5 chldren Emily, George, Hariett, Sarah, & Coulston, Celah & her child James

....pg 479, 19 July 1825, div of slaves

Lot 1) Jesse & Colston to Strauther FRANKS; Lot 2) Jane, Sarah to Henry FRANKS; Lot 3) Sehelah & child James to July Ann FRANKS; Lot 4) Emily to George O'REAR; Lot 5) George, Harriett to Edward FRANKS

Peter McMURRAY ....pg 482, 28 May 1825, will

boy Barney to son John McMURRAY; Harriet, Sarah to daughter Elizabeth; Bristo, Joanna to daughter Mary; Charles to Peter McMURRAY; boy Alfred to grandson Peter M. PIERCE

Susannah OVERACRE ....pg 483, 30 Apr 1805, will

man Jack (or John) to be free

WILL BOOK 13
1825 - 1827

William CHIPLEY .... pg 3, 5 Sept 1825, inv & appr

Charles, Robert, Ben, Caty, Doll

Joseph SNAPP .... pg 7, 18 July 1825, will

Lettie, John to wife Magdalene; man John to daughter Christiana after her mother's death

John HAMILTON .... pg 10, 12 Aug 1825, will

slaves to be sold

.... pg 12, 12 Aug 1825, codicil

woman Flora to Mrs. Sarah WILSON

Catherine PAGE .... pg 13, 19 Mar 1820, will

Harry to niece Mary P. BROOKE

Thomas KENNON, Sr .... pg 19, 30 Oct 1824, inv & appr

Angellah 60, Enock 50, Edmond 30, Tillah 35 & child, Alse 30 & child, Milley 25 & child, Sam 20, London 15, Rachel 15, Sharlotte 13, Charles 10, Jack 8, Janney 6, Dilley 4, John 7, Richard 3, Mary 6, Sarah 5, George 3, Henry 15

Sigismund STRIBLING ...... pg 21, 23 Apr 1822 - 2 July 1825, estate acct

midwife for woman, Solomon, Betsey died, man Bob sold, boy George sold; Betsey's daughter age 5 sold; man Jim sold to J.W. WARE, Betsey's son age 3 sold to George BARNHART; Betsey's daughter age 7 sold to William MILLER; Betsey's child age 5 sold to Taliaferro STRIBLING; Emily, boy Jack to Mrs. Sally STRIBLING; Solomon to Thomas STRIBLING

James S. MARTIN .... pg 27, 20 Feb 1815 - 6 Apr 1824, estate acct

Ambrose a man of color proved acct; Mary, Sarah, Rebecca, Harriet, Joseph, Christopher; Angelina age 2 kept by Mrs. WOLFE,

James SINGLETON .... pg 30, 23 Mar 1815, inv & appr

Ephraim, London, Cook, Solomon, Bill, Fanny, Franky, Winney

101

Gen. James SINGLETON ....pg 32, 4 Oct 1825 in court, inv & appr

Estate at Paxton & in Winchester:

Tom & Hannah his wife, Nathan, Eliza, Sarah, Andrew, Hannah & her child Daniel, Cloe, Franky, Peggy, Nancy, Patty, John, Mingo, James, Richard, Esther, Adam, Sarah, Hannah, George, Aaron, Charlotte, Winney, Zachary, child Adam, Susan, Willis, Milly, Pegg, Sally

....pg 39, 1 Jan 1823, sales

Andrew to James V. GLASS; Cook to Isaiah HOLLINGSWORTH; George to Bushrod TAYLOR; Aaron to George PELTER; Tom to Edward PENDLETON; Tom's wife Hannah to Moses NEWBANKS; Charlotte to John HEISKELL; Willis to Wilson HAMILTON; Jim, John to Dr. Robert O. GRAYSON; Nancy to Madison HITE; Peg to Dr. Robert BALDWIN; Hannah to John M. BROOM?; Hannah's daughter Sally to Thomas BALL; Hannah's daughter Sukey to Bushrod TAYLOR & John BIRCHELL; Adam, Dan to John B. TAYLOR, Richard to James B. HALL; Sally & child to Samuel LARUE; Fanny & child, Solomon to James G. FICKLIN; Winney, Cloe to Martin CURTWELL; Easter to John SUNSON; Patsey to Samuel LARUE; Zachria to John BIRCHELL; Frankey to Thomas BAYLIS; Eliza to Isaac BESLIN; Hannah & 3 children, Peggy & 2 children, Molly to Thomas K. BALL; Charles to Henry CLOWSER; Mingo to John RICHARDSON

Joseph TULEY ....pg 43, 26 Feb 1823, will

Phil & his family, Peter & his family, Molley to wife Nancy; Billy Bowen, Tamer & children, Rose & her children, Frank to daughter Mary; Suitha, Jula & 3? children, Jeffery, little Peg, Jacob, Rachel to daughter Belinda; Bob, Mary & her children Sarah, Cealey & her children to daughter Sarah; Hannah to be free

Charles BECKLEY ....pg 45, 31 Oct 1825 in court, inv & appr

man Ned, woman Pheby & child, girls Ann, Fan, boy John, girls Sally Ann, Eliza, Dice, old woman Judy

.... pg 46, 31 Oct 1825 in court, sales 289

man Ned to Elizabeth BECKLEY; Pheby & child to David POWERS; Ann to Susan BENCKLEY; Fanny to Esais EARLE; John to John JOHNSTON; Sally Ann, Eliza, Dice to Daniel POWERS; Judy to Ivan _ARE_ORNT

102

Jabez LARUE.......................... pg 49, 1 Nov 1825 in court, inv & appr

Jack Cook, John Weaver, Isaac, Cyrus, Ceaser, Anthony, Levy, Toliver, Ned, John, little John, Polly & 2 children, Sarah & 2 children, Maria & her infant child, Alice & 1 child, little Alice, Sarah, Hannah, Billy, Daniel, Joseph, Judea & 1 child, Aby & 1 child, Philis & 3 children, Mary, Eveline, Leah, Sophah, Richard, July Ann & 1 child, Anne, Benjamin, William, Simeon, Beggy & 2 sons, Emmy Liza

Hugh KENNEDY of Burbon Co., KY.................. pg 65, 3 Apr 1821, will

negroes to Nicholas TALBOT, Washington KENNEDY, & Jesse KENNEDY in trust for daughter Susan STEEL & if she is a widow to her children

Thomas McCOWAN..pg 66, 17 Sept 1811, will

"...man named Jonas be and he is hereby declared to be set free aat the expiration of eight years from and after the 15th day of December in the year 1806 (being the time I bought him)."

....pg 67, __, codicil

man Abraham to be free after 8 years from the 1st of Jan 1816

Richard S. REDMAN..pg 71, 13 Dec 1825, sales

boy Bill to J. SHIVELY; boy Mingo to B. TAYLOR; girl Lucy to G.S. LANE; boy Joe to L. NEILL, boy Major to I. ISLER; boy Mansfield to T. SMITH

R.S. REDMAN......................pg 80, 1 Dec 1824 – 1 Dec 1825, estate acct

midwife for Isaac Ethalinda? & Alice; boys Bill, Mingo, girl Lucy, boys Joe, Major, Mansfield sold

Henry GROVE ....pg 82, 3 Sept 1825, will

slaves to be divided among sons Isaac, James, Abraham, & David; woman in son Isaac's possession

William HELM ....pg 83, 11 Feb 1815, will

negroes on land on which she lives to daughter-in-law Nancy HELM widow of son Meredith HELM; Leanah & all her children, now in possession of son-in-law Samuel BRYARLEY, to grandson Tate BRYARLEY; remaining negroes to son William HELM

Daniel SOWERS ....pg 86, 3 Oct 1825 – 2 Nov 1825, estate acct

negroes sold to James BROWN?; Billy

Francis HUTCHINGS ....pg 93, 6 Dec 1825, estate acct

Nancy

Mary A. BYRD ....pg 95, 2 Jan 1826 in court, inv & appr

old men Samuel, Nathan, old woman Susan, old man Edward Niell, boy William, girl Philis, Molly & child, Ariana & 2 children, Nancy & 3 children, girl Letitia, Gabriel, Ralph, Daniel, Christopher, John, George, Nathan, Hampton, William, Solomon, Harry, old man Humphrey, Robert, Thomas Cooper, Thomas Potter, William Law?, Richard Potter, Betsey Potter, Courtney & 3 children, Abby, Kitty, Molly

....pg 96, 10 Dec 1824, inv & appr

old Samuel, old Nathaniel, old Susan, William 9, Phillis 5, Molly 36 & child 3, Arianna & 2 children, Nancy & 3 chldren, Letticia 10, Gabriel Williams 25, Ralph Williams 15, Daniel Williams 13, Edward Neill 65, Frank 54, George White 43, Nathan White 32, William White 20, Hampton White 30, Solomon Black 62, Humphrey Cooper 65, Robert Cooper 32, Thomas Cooper 28, Thomas Potter 18, William Law? 15, Richard Potter 41, Henry Barnett 64, Courtney Mackey & 4 children, Abbey Cooper 26, Kitty Potter 13, Molly Potter 55, Christopher Williams Jr, John Williams

William ABBOTT ....pg 106, 18 July 1823 – 6 June 1824, estate acct

girl Eveline & boy Beverly sold

Vance BUSH ....pg 114, 16 May 1820, will

all negroes to be manumitted at age 21 except woman Henny

Thomas McCOWIN ....pg 117, 4 Feb 1826, inv & appr

Abraham, Jonah

Maria HELM ....pg 131, 26 Oct 1825, inv & appr

Ned 45, Emma 16

.... pg 132 Dec 1825, 7 Jan 1826, sales

man Ned to Allen WILLIAMS; girl Emma to Ph. ROBERTS

John CATTLETT .... pg 156, 30 Jan 1826, will

Randall, Levi to daughter Mary F. CATTLETT; Samuel, Judy to son John CATTLETT; remaining slaves to be sold

Margaret DAVIS ....pg 160, 27 Jan 1826, sales

old Molly to S. DAVIS for Elizabeth BARTLETT; Emily & child to James S. BROWN; "The above property was acquired by Margaret DAVIS after the death of her husband the following that which she by virtue of her husbands will the late William DAVIS.": Richard to William DAVIS; Reubin to Thomas CASTLEMAN; David to Joseph TULEY; Gabriel to Charles STROTHER; Samuel, Robert, John, Harry, Judy to D. TIMBERLAKE; Nelson to Andrew CHUNN; Patrick wife & child to S. DAVIS for Elizabeth BARTLETT; Mariah to John GILKESON

Baalis DAVIS ....pg 167, 10 Mar 1826 in court, inv & appr

David, Zenah, Jack, David

Mrs. Margaret DAVIS ....pg 168, 11 Dan 1826, inv & appr

old Molly, Emily & child

.... pg 169, 10 Mar 1826 in court, acquired from husband's will

old man Harry, old woman Judy, Patrick, Sucky & child, Richard, David, Reuben, Gabriel, Samuel, Nelson, Mariah, Robert, John

Sarah ALEXANDER .... pg 175, 27 Apr 1826, inv & appr

old Sie, Milly, Sampson, James, Winny, Judy, Joseph, Haynie, Mary, Anthony, Jenny, Henry, Alfred, Fanny, Florinda since dead, Louisa

John CATTELL....................................pg 182, 27 Mar 1828, inv & appr

Kit, George, Lewis, John, Marge, infant Mariah

Elijah WAY..pg 206, 27 Oct 1823, inv & appr

George, Nathaniel, Charles, Peter, Philip, Frances, Wesley, William, Alfred, Susanna, Aggy, Martha, Milley, Jane & children Mildred & Jane, Winney, Alfred

Francis STRIBLING ....pg 210, 4 Nov 1823 - 6 May 1826, estate acct

distribution of slave valuation among the legatees; old Hannah

John DRAKE.............................pg 215, 26 May 1826, inv & appr

woman

John HADDON.........................pg 217, 17 Mar 1826, inv & appr

Janney, Salley, Ailsey, Meriah, Anna, Mary, Eliza

Elizabeth B. FISHER .... pg 219, 25 May 1825, will

Sidney & her children to half-sister Mary WRIGHT, wife of Jonathan WRIGHT; woman Emily to Mary, Louisa, & Betsey SHANK children of half- sister Lucy SHANK; boy Alfred, now in possession of David CLOUD, to niece Catharine NEWMAN; boy Marshall, now in possession of William MONROE Jr. to John NEWMAN son of niece Catharine NEWMAN; Phebe, now in possession of nehew John MONROE to niece Eliza MONROE; Phebe's daughter Sidney to Catharine MONROE, daughter of nephew Thomas MONROE; Phebe's son Fielding to William BROWN, the grandson of niece Catherine NEWMAN; Phebe's son Alfred to William MONROE son of nephew Thomas MONROE

....pg 219, 3 Apr 1826, codicil

Phebe, Sidney, Alfred, Fielding have been sold

James BAKER Jr.....................pg 233, 31 July 1826 in court, inv & appr

girl Hannah, boy Edmon, Winny & 3 children

John BURCHELL ....pg 235, 29 July 1826, inv & appr

man Emanuel

Henry MITCHELL,...........................pg 237, 17 Dec 1824, sales

Augusta Co:

man Daniel, boys George, Washington to Joseph TULEY

.... pg 238, 13 Nov 1824, sales

Frederick Co:

Jacob, Rachel, Lee, old Jacob, girls Susan, Fanny, Lucy to Joseph TULY

Henry MITCHELL............ pg 242, 4 Oct 1824 – 25 July 1826, estate acct

Rose & her children sold; Bill of Sale by Nathaniel BURWELL for Dick, Leven?; Jacob, Rachel, Lee, Susan, Fanny, Lucy, Daniel, George, Washington purchased by Joseph TULY

Thomas BROWN Jr .... pg 244, 5 Nov 1823, sales

woman & 2 children to John RICHARDSON

Reuben ALLENSWORTH.................... pg 250, 11 June 1825, inv & appr

Sarah, Julia

John SELF... pg 252, 5 Apr 1825, will

Frederick, James, Alfred, Loo?, Pat, Sofy to wife Sarah SELF & at her death 3 slaves each to children John SELF, Harris SELF, Sally CONRAD wife of Joseph CONRAD, Fanny EL___?, Henry SELF, & Elizabeth OLIVER, the remaining slaves to be sold; a negro each to sons John SELF & Henry SELF; Fanny, Peg now in her posession to daughter Sally CONRAD

Nathaniel CARTMELL.................................. pg 254, 10 Apr 1825, will

negroes, James, the son of Barbarah, to wife Sarah CARTMELL

Robert BOYD..pg 256, 20 Aug 1825, will

man Frank to sons Abraham & John BOYD

James MOORE...pg 257, 13 Feb 1826, will

Bob 19, purchased from Mrs.? Ben DAWSON to be free at age 35

Elizabeth HOLME...pg 258, 14 Sept 1825, will

Louisa, granddaughter of George, to be free after 7 years, George to be free; Beckey free at age 21

....pg 260, 1 Sept 1824, inv & appr

Peter, George, Jack, Solomon, Brister, Davy, Esther, Aggy, Phillip

William McCORMICK ....pg 271, 10 Aug 1824 – 1 Sept 1826, estate acct

negroes

Oliver FUNSTON ....pg 276, 18 Sept 1826, will

Hannah & child to daughter Fanny WITHERS; wife Margaret FUNSTON to emancipate 10 negroes as she sees fit

Vincent SERVINER...................pg 278, 2 Oct 1826 in court, inv & appr

men James, Neale, woman Lucy, old woman

Vincent SERVINER............................ pg 279, 2 Sept, 18 Nov 1825, sales

private sale of men James, Neale, woman Lucy

Dr. Lewis BURWELL............................pg 283, 12 Aug 1826, inv & appr

Phil, boy George, girl Hannah, woman Maria, girls Betsey, Lucy, Henney, boy Watt, girl Flora?, old man Arthur, woman Venus, man John, boy Henry, girls Sally, Hannah, boys Isaac, Scy, Jim, Charles, girl Jinney Ann, woman Priscilla, boy Ellick, girls Sally, Louisa, Judy & child, boy Zachariah, woman Fanny, boy Andrew, girl Fanny, Tenar & child, boys Robert, Daniel, Harry, Hannibal, girls Lucy, Betsey, man John, Franke & child, boy James, Daniel, man Scy, men Billy Draper, Sam Grason, old Rose, old Cragar?

Robert GRAY... pg 289, 20 May 1826, will

woman to wife Anna GRAY; Thornton from the plantation willed by her former husband to her 2 sons James VANCE & William VANCE; Georgeylina & her offspring to wife's daughter Mary VANCE until they are of age to be free; Lotty not to be sold out of the family

Matthew PAGE ....pg 291, 14 Aug 1826, will

Ruth & all her children, young Gilbert his wife & children, the children of Anna (dec'd) to wife Ann R. PAGE; Anthony's wife Patty & all her children except the 2 eldest to sister Sarah PAGE; Israel his wife & all their children, old Frankey's daughter Milly & her children, Gilbert's daughter Penny? & her children to nephew John W. PAGE; old Milly's daughter Fanney & all her children to niece Mrs. Sarah W. BROOKE;

.... pg 292, 14 Aug 1826, codicil

2 boys & a girl to nephew William B. PAGE

Benjamin HARRIS..pg 293, 5 Aug 1823, will

Samuel to son Fulton I. HARRIS, Sarah to son John B. HARRIS; Matthew to son Franklin; Kitty to son Benjamin; Tom to son William H. HARRIS; Milly to daughter Rebecca WHARTON

Susan MUSE...pg 294, 5 Mar 1825, will

negroes to sons Warner & John MUSE

Baalis DAVIS....................................pg 304, 8 Nov 1826 in court, sales

man Jack to Henry S. LONGHORN; woman Zena, man David to Francis B. WHITING; man Daniel to James CASTLEMAN

Nathaniel CARTMELL............................pg 310, 25 Oct 1826, inv & appr

men Jacob, Gilbert, Matilda & her 3 children, Barbarah

William HAND ....pg 311, Oct 1825, will

Kitty, Jack, Frank to grandson Thomas HAND alias WAY at age 21, child of Elias WAY dec'd; Providence, Maria, Thornton, Michael, Kate, children Cy, Elias to daughter Sarah HENDREN wife of Robert HENDREN; Alice, Harry, Lucy, little Esther now in her possession to daughter-in-law Sarah HAND widow of Robert HAND; slaves given to sons-in-law Francis ASHE & James SILVER; Sy & Esther to choose their master

Esaias EARLE..................................pg 315, 23 Aug 1826, will

slaves to be valued & divided among children John B. EARLE, Archibald EARLE, Miriam HAMILTON wife of William HAMILTON, Matilda DENEALE wife of John E. DENEALE, Lucinda CARTER wife of James CARTER, Nancy, Elias, & Sally Ann; small girl Milly to daughter Sally Ann

.... pg 319, 16 Oct 1826, codicil

"...the dower negroes are to be divided in like manner after the death of my wife..."; girl Hannah to daughter Nancy; girl Evelina to daughter Matilda DENEALE

Robert BOYD.....................................pg 323, 30 Sept 1826, inv & appr

Frank 44

109

Henry HOOVER ....pg 325, 1 Jan 1827, sales

girl Mill to Isaac BAKER; woman & child Jude to John SUTHERLIN

Cornelius BALDWIN..............................pg 328, 17 Nov 1826, will

3 negroes to be sold

Jesse O'REAR..................pg 331, 1 Nov 1825 – 29 Nov 1826, estate acct

"...part of Mildred O'REAR's third of the slaves gave up to the administrator...including the slaves divided amongst the legatees of J. O'REAR..."

John CATLETT.. pg 340, 29/30 Mar 1826, sales

man Kit to Catlett LEHEW; man Lewis to William F. NORTHCRAFT; man George, boy John to John A. CATLETT; woman Margaret, infant to Alexander CATLETT

Benjamin HARRIS...................... pg 347, 4 Jan 1827, inv & appr

woman Rose, man Aguilla, woman Susan

Thomas K. BALL................................. pg 347, 11 Jan 1827, will

Mrs. SINGLETON's daughters to have a girl each; girl Nancy & his choice of men to Joseph H. SHARRARD; Peggy & her children shall not be separated & to be divided between brother William P. BALL of KY & sister Mrs. SINGLETON

Edward SMITH.................................. pg 348, 2 Apr 1823, will

Sue, John, Charles & any 4 more to daughter Mary; Matilda & her children, Henry, Robert, James, Rebecca to daughter Eliza; Isabel, Martha to daughter Emily; Ben to daughter Sidney; Charlotte, Maria to daughter Arianna; James, Courtney to son Philip; remaining slaves to wife Elizabeth & at her death to be divided among the children Kitty, Edward, Jacquelin, Eliza, Philip, Emily, Sidney, Arianna, & Mary; 2 slaves each to children Kitty, Edward, & Jacquelin

Benjamin McDONALD ....pg 350, 7 Feb 1825, will

man Ned to wife Massey McDONALD & at her death to be sold

John McALLISTER .... pg 362, 2 Jan 1826, will

"...all my slaves (except Dick, who I bought of John SOWERS now living in Stanton in Virginia)...are emancipated..."; Dick ran away; all the slaves in Tennessee to be free the first day of Jan after his death: Pona?, Bill, Blackwell, Robert, John; land in TN to be set aside for freed slaves

Benedict RUST Sr .... pg 365, 6 Feb 1827 in court, inv & appr

Thornton, Sidney, boys David, Dennis

Baalis DAVIS .... pg 365, 21 Dec 1825 – 5 Oct 1826, estate acct

old man Daniel sold; 3 negroes sold to William LANGHORN

William HAND ....pg 370, 5 Mar 1827 in court, inv & appr

old women Esther, Rachel, men Charles, Cyrus, Providence & 3 children Thornton, Michel, & Catherine; boys Frank, Jack, girl Kitty, boy Harry, Alice & 2 chldren Lucinda & Hester

Benjamin O'REAR .... pg 372, 25 Jan 1827, inv & appr

men big Daniel, Noah, Robert, Elie, boys Jary, David, Talor, Henry, John, women Bety, Catey, Pru, Lorande?, girls Harriet, Sharlotte, woman Celia

William HAND ....,,,,......pg 382, 5 Mar 1827 in court, sale

Charles, Rachel delivered to Capt. Francis ASH

Thomas McCOWAN.........pg 384, 12 May 1825 - 1 Jan 1827, estate acct

Johah, paid Free Jane for cooking, Doyle

Thomas KENNON .... pg 394, 1823 – 1 Feb 1825, estate acct

man sold

Orphans of William N. BURWELL ....
.... pg 397, 11 Oct 1824 – 30 Dec 1826, gdn acct

servants

Children of Strother M. HELM ....pg 400, 5 Mar 1827, gdn acct

Sylvia & her children

111

Benjamin HARRIS.................pg 402, 4 Jan 1827, sales

Aguilla to John B. HARRIS; Rose to William H. HARRIS; Susan to Solomon CUMBLETON?

Benedict RUST.............pg 418, 21 Sept 1824 – 8 Mar 1827, estate acct

boy David sold; Thornton, Denny

Francis STRIBLING...... pg 475, 18 Aug 1826 – 27 Apr 1827, estate acct

fee for division of slaves

Thomas T. BYRD............. pg 476, 4 Aug 1825 - 6 Aug 1826, estate acct

negroes

Mary A. BYRD.............pg 477, 8 Oct 1824 - 27 Dec 1826, estate acct

negro

Charles MAGILL.............................pg 493, 21 Mar 1827, will

slaves of her choice to wife Mary; girl Rebecca to son John; boy Edward to son Alfred; girl Rose to daughter Mary; girl Caroline to daughter Frances

Vance BUSH.................pg 502, 27 Feb 1826, sales

woman Henny to Joseph LONG on 1 May, boy Moses to Lewis MAHANEY, girl Maria to Thornton McLEOD, boys George, Joseph to Samuel SIMPSON, girl Harriet, boy Harrison to Joseph KEELER, girl Mary to Randolph CLINE, girl Milly to Jacob REED, boy Phil, girl Sarah to Lewis B. MARTIN; all hired, terms of service noted

Daniel SOWERS............... pg 516, 28 Dec 1825 – Nov 1826, estate acct

Ned, Mike, Jones, Joanna, Orange, Bill

James WILLIAMS.............pg 518, 5 Oct 1822 – 1 Apr 1827, estate acct

Jane

Thomas McCORMICK Jr. .... pg 1, 27 Dec 1824, inv & appr

man Daniel

....pg 1, 27 Dec 1824, sales

man Daniel to Samuel McCORMICK

Orphans of Samuel McCORMICK ....
.... pg 3, 1 June 1825 – 5 May 1827, gdn acct

Tom; 3 children kept by Isaac McCORMICK; girl; Juliet?, Maria, Solomon, Harry

Susan MEADE .... pg 5, 3 July 1820, will

"...uncle FITZHUGH...the slaves left by him to his son William H. FITZHUGH..."; Lucy & her 2 children Lucy & Alice to be free; "I would suggest the advantage of purchasing Andrew the husband of the elder Lucy..."

Joseph ANDERSON ....pg 7, 6 Aug 1825, inv & appr

the half of one negro man called Ampel?

William JACKSON........................pg 9, 2 July 1827 in court, inv & appr

boys Robbin, Daniel to serve terms of service noted; man Milford for a limited bill of sale

Ephraim GARRISON.........pg 14, 15 Dec 1820 – 26 Jan 1827, estate acct

Negro Jacob; boy Charles sold to Jesse HARRIS

John MACKY .... pg 25, Apr 1825 – 22 June 1827, estate acct

negroes

James RITTER .... pg 36, 30 July 1827, inv & appr

girl

Joseph TULEY .... pg 52, 22 Dec 1825, inv & appr

Bill 27, John Armstead 30, George Armstead 32, John Brown? 27, Seipio? 58, Boatswain 16, Molly & 2 children, Winney, Hitty?, old ___, Pleasants, Robert, boy Thornton, Julia & child, girls Sarah, Rachael, woman Hannah, man Bob, old man Peter, old man Jeffry, Bill Brown, boy Elisha, old Boatswain, boy Armanias?, Franky & child, young Pegg, Mary & 4 children, Lucy & 2 children, old Nan, old Peg, boys Gabriel, Jacob, _anone? & child, man Jack, old Phil, woman Betty, Lucy & child, girls Maria, Ellen, Lydia, Jane, Jim, old Sarah

John TRIPLETT .... pg 56, 12 Feb 1827, sales

woman to Samuel SIMPSON; 3 girls, 1 boy to Hedgman TRIPLETT

Sigismund STRIBLING .... pg 61, 2 July 1825 – 6 Aug 1827, estate acct

Anthony sold to William STEPHENSON

Maria HELM .... pg 64, 24 Nov 1825 – 8 Aug 1827, estate acct

Ned

Peter McMURRY .... pg 66, Aug 1825 - 8 Aug 1827, estate acct

negroes

Charles BEKCLEY .... pg 80, 3 Sept 1827 in court, comm acct

"...pd Thomas KENNERLY for provisions furnished BECKLEY & family..."

.... pg 80, 29 Nov 1825 – 15 Dec 1826, estate acct

"paid Lemmon a black man who furnished the family of Mr. BECKLEY with necessary articles..."

Vincent SERVINER .... pg 85, 26 Aug 1825 – 19 Apr 1827, estate acct

James, Neale, Lucy to Lewis __TTS

Thomas McCORMICK .... pg 88, 14 Nov 1823, inv & appr

old man Thomas, men Joseph, Daniel, Bob, Jack, Pompey, old woman Molly, Patty & her children boy Bob, girl Frances?, boy William, boy child, women Delphy, Lucy

Thomas McCORMICK ...... pg 94, 1 Dec 1823 – 31 July 1826, estate acct

"...Molly & child they being divided with the negroes belonging to this estate (the said Molley & child belonged to the estate of Abraham _T

Samuel McCORMICK .... pg 96, 1_ Oct 1822, inv & appr

men Harry, Tom, woman & 8 children, man Natt, boy Solomon

William McCORMICK .... pg 101, 17 Aug 1819, inv & appr

boy Charles

Charles GIBBS .... pg 104, 11 Oct 1824, inv & appr

man Peter, Jarret, old woman, girl

.... pg 120, 15 Oct 1824, sales

boy Jarret to D. SNYDER; man Peter to William D. NORTH

Bartholomew SMITH .... pg 141, 24 Mar 1825 - 28 Jan 1827, estate acct

2 children kept by E. SMITH; 2 children kept by Fanny BAKER; 4 negroes; 5 negroes

Edward SMITH .... pg 150, 28 July 1827, inv & appr

Sam 60, Richard 30, Reubin 28, Ned 45, Patty 40 & sons Richard 8 & Sam 6, Elizabeth 66

"The slaves specifically devised by the testator, had been previously given by him to the legatee, and in their possession before the will was made, and were not considered as any part of his estate, but were bequeathed in confirmation of the previous donations consequently they were not appraised..." Elizabeth SMITH

Sampson BABB .... pg 154, 1812 – 1813, estate acct

hire of negroes

John CATLETT .... pg 189, 30 June 1827 - 1 Feb 1828, estate acct

small boy, Randall, Sam

Thomas McCORWAN .... pg 204, 1 Jan 1927 – 1 Jan 1828, estate acct

paid Alfred H. POWELL, Eben MITTON "Depy Shff" for costs fee at the suit of negroes; Jonas, Abraham

Thomas B. WALTER........pg 205, 1 Aug 1812 - 25 Dec 1827, estate acct

"...paid Alfred H. POWELL for fees defending the suits brought by negroes Jane & Kitty..."

Orphans of Daniel SOWERS Jr ....
....pg 208, Jan 1826 – 23 Jan 1828, gdn acct

division of negroes; Bishop?, Ned, Janey, Flood, Orange, Mary, Jonnah, Bill, James, Jonna

Benjamin GLASSCOCK...................... pg 211, 26 June 1827, inv & appr

men William, James, Darkey & child Jane, woman _ppy, Linda & child Thomas, Milly & child Minty, Sibby & child Mary, girls Harriet, Lucy Ellen, Pricilla, boy Daniel/David, girls ___, G___, Louisa, girl __ Jane, woman __by, girl Joseine?, boys Jack, John Washington

Vance BUSH....................pg 215, Feb 1826 – 20 Aug 1827, estate acct

slaves emancipated; woman sold; support of Joe Taper?

Bartholomew SMITH...................... pg 221, 29 Dec 1826, appr of slaves

Jeff to serve 2 years from Dec 1826, Humphrey to serve 6 years from Jan 1827, Lewis to serve 7 years from Oct 1827, Maria to serve 6 years from June 1827, Nancy to serve 13 years from July 1827, Emily to serve 16 years from June 1827, Henrey? to serve 17? years from July 1827, Milford to serve 21 years from July 1827, James to serve 22 years from Mar 1827

.... pg 222, 29 Dec 1826, appr for life

Fanny & 3 children, Lucy & 2 children, Eveline & 3 children, Jeff, Humphrey, Lewis, Susan, Maria

Susan MEADE ....pg 224, 21 Feb 1828, inv & appr

2 women named Lucy, girl Alice

Lucy F. MEADE ....pg 224, 21 Feb 1828, inv & appr

Barbara, Hannah, Caroline, Sam, Lucy, James, William, Sally, Peggy, Lucy; "...joint property between Miss Lucy F. MEADE dec'd and Miss Mary Meade...has never been divided..."

Vance BUSH...pg 225, 9 Feb 1826, inv & appr

woman Haney, men Jim, Tom, woman Alce?, men Bob, Aaron, woman Fanncy

boy Moses, girl Mariah, boy George, girls Harriet, Milly, boys Harrison, Joseph, girl Mary, boys David, Philip, girl Sarah to age 21

Hugh KENNEDY................................. pg 235, 7 Dec 1825, inv & appr

Reubin 22, Moses 16

Matthew PAGE.................pg 243, 9 Oct 1826 – 17 Feb 1828, estate acct

paid 89 negroes $5.00 each per will; "…paid Miss Judith PAGE on afc of a bond executed by Matthew PAGE dec'd being amt of her purchase of negroes"; slaves given to wife of Humphrey BROOK by Matthew PAGE; $5.00 paid to 2 slaves 16 years old per will; man sold to Alice McALISTER; negroes sold to John B. WILLIAMSON; negroes sold to Judith R. PAGE; negroe sold to Lewis LINDSEY; negroes sold to George SAYERS; negroes sold to Philip SMITH; negro sold to John of Alexandra; slaves sold to Walter FAUQUARY; slaves sold to John BUSHELL; slaves sold to Conrad HUNTSBERRY; slaves sold to Conrad KOWNSLAR; slaves sold to George WALLS; slaves sold to Stephen RUTTER; slave sold to George S. KERFOOT; slaves sold to Robert BUCKELEY and also for his mother; slaves sold to Jacob SENSENEY; slaves sold to George H. NORRIS; slaves sold to Joseph SHEPHERD; slaves sold to John BOWLES; slaves sold to David CATHER for? Washington GOLD; slaves sold to Jacob ISLER; slaves sold to David CATHER; slaves sold to Robert PAGE; slave sold to John BAKER; slave sold to Mandly TAYLOR; slave sold to William SOWERS; slaves sold to John CASTLEMAN; slaves sold to Sagamus PINE; slaves sold to Benjamin CRIGLER; slaves sold to Dr. Philip SMITH; slaves sold to Thomas BLAKEMORE; slaves sold to Lewis BERKELEY; slaves sold to John BUSHELL

Joseph GLASS .... pg 251, 18 Dec 1821, property delivered

men Cuffy, Frank, James, Joseph, old Abram, young Abram, woman Molly, girl Nancy, women Sarah, Rachel, boys Mingo, John, Robert, girls Louisa, Mary Ann, Betsey, Chloe, boy David, girls Sally, Chloe to widow, Mrs. Ann GLASS

.... pg 263, 29 Mar 1828, remarks

hired out the slaves

Joseph GLASS ....pg 263, 1 Jan 1824 – 1 Apr 1828, estate acct

boarding black man 10 days; Cuffy, Frank, Louisa, Rachel, Abram, Joseph, John, Joe, Mingo, Sarah, Abraham, Joe/Jos Molly

Henry FRANK ....pg 276, 9 Feb 1825 – 20 Mar 1828, estate acct

George,

Oliver FUNSTEN.............. pg 292, 26 Dec 1826, appr of slaves

Nicholas, Amelia & 2 children Susan & James, Charlotte & 2 children Louisa & Catharine, Washington, John, Nathaniel, Lucy & child Selina, Eliza, Clara, Mary, William, Henry, Charles, Alfred, Hannah & 2 children William & Arena?, Immanuel, Dennis, old Louisa & 3 grandchildren Lucinda, Mary, & Israel, Ellison

Isaac N. GANT.............. pg 295, 1 Dec 1827, inv & appr

Peter (pg 320); negro Jeminia, negro Jonas Baker, negro Richard Norris, negro Robin Lovet, negro Randle Ivens?; negro Fairfax, negro Ralph, negro Abraham ___, negro Sam at TAYLORS, negro Robert, negro Sharlotte, negro Abraham Hull

John W. BAYLIS .... pg 356, 15 Dec 1826, inv & appr

man Jack bought by H. VANMETER

John DRAKE..............pg 358, 30 May 1826, sales

girl was not sold

John DRAKE.............. pg 360, 1 May 1826 – 25 Apr 1828, estate acct

"...a negro girl...still in the possession of the widow (Mrs. Phebe DRAKE)..."

Oliver FUNSTEN.............. pg 364, Nov 1826 – 15 Apr 1828, estate acct

negroes taken to court; Polly died; Betty WILSON's bond for hire of boy

Robert MATTOX .... pg 378, 29 Mar 1826, will

all negroes to wife Nelly MATTOX except Emanuel age 5 or 6 given to wife's daughter Gizzle ANDERSON; Merial's oldest son Beverly to grandson James Harrson CARSON

Francis ASH .... pg 382, 13 Apr 1828, will

"...Kentucky lands...to my five eldest sons, namely Buckner, George B, William F, Francis F and Robert M. Ash to be equally divided among them...all the slaves in that country that Buckner took out with him namely Jack, Mary, Frank commonly called big Frank, Winny, little Frank, Isaac, Lyddy, Eliza, and Winny's increase in that country...by the name of Samuel..."; Frank, Winny, little Frank, Isaac, Lydia, Eliza, to George B., William T., & Francis T. ASH; Robert M. to have his share of slaves when he comes of age; Catherine, David now in his possession to son-in-law Robert ASHBY; Aaron, Charles, Henry, Baylis, Daniel, Jeffry, Seipio, Joanna, Beck, Rachel, old Jim to wife

Frances BUCKNER .... pg 389, 21 Apr 182_, will

Dick, his wife Diana, & all their children given to him by his father Horace BUCKNER to brother Otway G. BUCKNER; Kitty to brother William Strother JONES; boy Stepto to nephew Charles Marshall JONES

Alexander CLEVELAND .... pg 398, Dec 1823 - June 1828, estate acct

Moses, Washington, Augustin, Beverly; paid for slave appraisal

Hannah WHITING .... pg 400, 5 June 1828, inv & appr

man Jack, girl Mary Ann, old woman Molly?, men Godfrey, Jasper, Philip, Christopher, Charles, woman Harriett

Benjamin McDONALD .... pg 412, 17 Feb 1827, inv & appr

man Ned

Robert BAYARLY .... pg 416, 21 Apr 1828, will

all slaves to wife & at her death to be freed except my boy Tom to son Thomas until the age of 21; my boy James to daughter Mary Ann to the age of 20; my boy Albin? to daughter Elizabeth to the age of 21; my female child Lucy to granddaughter Elizabeth L.G. BAYARLY daughter of my son Daniel 21; "I order that the family shall not be broken up until two years after the death of my wife...each of my children as I have given my young negroes to if they will learn them to read in the new testament they shall serve them to the age of twenty three."

119

James MOORE.. pg 423, 19 Nov 1826, sales

  boy Robert (pg 444) to Frederick HOLTZMAN

David CASTLEMAN...................... pg 483, 29 May 1826, inv & appr

  man Peter

....pg 483, 29 May 1826, sales

  man Peter to John CASTLEMAN

William B. PAGE..............................pg 485, 23 Sept 1826, will

  slaves to wife Eliza

Charles CLIFTON... pg 488, 24 June 1828, will

  slaves to be freed except for John, Bob, & Henry subject to executors;
  Bob & Henry's mother is old Fanny

Joseph HEDGE ....pg 489, 6 Oct 1828 in court, will

  Peter to son Edward

John CATLETT.................................... pg 494, 2 Aug 1828, sales

  man Sam sold at private sale; Randle & Levi? sold by sheriff for
  STICKLEY; woman, sold to J. CATLETT Jr., died

Marquis Q. BLACKEMAN ....

..................................pg 500, 24 Nov 1823 - 23 Oct 1827, estate acct

  Rose died; George, Tom, Bill, Horace, Ben, Faithy, Larry?, Moses,
  Joe, Sidney, Jack, Kitty

Mary WORMLEY................................pg 505, 25 Aug 1823, inv & appr

  man Stepney

Oliver FUNSTON .... pg 509, 27 Sept 1826 - 28 Oct 1828, estate acct

  Amelia kept by Mrs. FUNSTON; negro Sam Wilson; Nicholas,
  Charles, William

Orphans of George ASH ....

.... pg 522, 14 Nov 1827 – 15 May 1828, gdn acct

  negroes

John HOPKINS .... pg 8, 10 Dec 1822, will

negroes; 4 youngest daughters to choose a maid each; Laura to daughter Lucy

Alice McALLISTER .... pg 14, 18 Sept 1828, inv & appr

Henry

Edward McGUIRE .... pg 19, 12 Nov 1828, will

boy Bill to son Edward D. McGUIRE

Lewis BURWELL .... pg 20, 20 May 1826 – 29 Nov 1828, estate acct

girl sold to B. BAN?; girl sold to Gabriel THI___ 2 boys to Matthew PAGE; boy to BRADSHAW; girl to Ezekiel DOUGHERTY; 6 negroes to ATWOOD; girl to Robert CRUPPER; Hanny, Fanny, Lucy; Andrew to W. PAGE; Wat to R. RHODES; man Lye? to W. BARTLETT?

Esaias EARLE .... pg 23, 25 Nov 1826, inv & appr

men Abraham, Jack Driver, Tom Sexton, Moses, boys Peter, John, Alfred, Tom Banister, Thornton, girls Millcy, Hannah, Evelina, Esther & her child George, Winney & her child Vina, Nancy & her 4 children Humphrey, Henry, Prestley, & Mary

exec note: "In the amended inventory there is a negro man named Tom Sexton a blacksmith included as the property of my testator, which is in fact my own property to which I do now and shall hereafter affect my right." signed James B. EARLE

Eliza DAVIS .... pg 38, 25 Oct 1828, inv & appr

Larry & his wife Winny, boy Joseph, girl Delpha

James STROTHER .... pg 47, 7 Mar 1823, will

Daniel, Jeffry, George, Alice, Letty, Vinny to wife Elizabeth; _e_ley & her child George to daughter Mary; Levi to son Enoch STROTHER; Ann to daughter Susan; Sarah & her 1st son to daughter Elizabeth; woman Clara in trust for daughter Delia wife of Nathaniel TEMPLEMAN; Armested to son John STROTHER; Frederick to son

George STROTHER; Nelly to son William STROTHER; girl Lucy to daughter Jane; girl Rachael to son James STROTHER

George BELL ....pg 49, 10 Sept 1828, will

woman Poll to son Harry BELL; fellow Edward to son Squire BELL

Esaias EARLE .... pg 50, 8 Nov 1826 – 1 Jan 1829, estate acct

negroes kept by Sally EARLE

James WILLIAMS ....pg 55, 17 Nov 1827, inv & appr

boy Bob, man Robin, Clary & her 2 children Armstead & Jack, old woman Jenny

Orphans of Oliver FURSTON...
....pg 58, 5 Nov 1827- 1 Jan 1829, estate acct

servant

Matthew PAGE .... pg 66, 6 Jan 1829 in court, appr of slaves

old Penny, Joe & Milly his wife & children; Katy, Peggy & 2 children; Charles, Nancy, Lucy, Anna, Randolph, Joe, Eleanor, Mary and children in the cabin (No 15

Molly, George, Daniel, Squire, William, Frederick, children in the cabin (No 6

Judy & 2 children, Jenny & 1 child; Hannah wife to a son of Nancy, no child (No 6

Hanover; Betty & her daughter Kiziah with 5 children; Custer & Bob sons of Betty; Sally a grown up daughter (No 10

Tom, Becky, Nancy & her husband Robin; Edmund, Parker (No 6

old Jenny, her son Johnny & Katy his wife, her son Robin who has a wife & children at W. TAYLOR's near Battletown (No 4

old Mat & his daughter China with 3 children (No 5

John & Milly with 4 children in the cabin; girl Sarah sister to Milly (No 7

Betty & Jim her husband with 4 children (No 6

Michael & Nelly & 4 children; Moses, Michael & his mother Franky (No 8

Sarah with 2 children her husband at W. BYRD's (No 3

Phil has a wife near W. BURWELL's island (No 1

Carey is husband to a young woman one of the legacy to W. BROOKE (No 1

old Gilbert who has a wife at Janeville (No 1

old woman Judy, Rachael her granddaughter; her mother dec'd (No 2

Bob, Franky & 2 grandchildren whose mother is dead; Thornton (No 5

Judy, Isaac & Ariana her children grown, her oldest daughter Alice is wife to Frederick, Judy has besides 5 children in the cabin her husband Matt at Janesville (No 9

Dicky (No 1

Harry & brother Tommy? his brothers, Judy, Sally; Aaron who lives at Pagebrook with great Sarah his grandmother & a smaller boy Ben named after his old grandfather, are brothers to the same family (No 7

old Sally & her daughter Esther, no children (No 2

Nancy wife to Bob at Pagebrook & her children Solomon, Joe, Jim, ___, Tom, & Nancy; Harry, Jack, Peggy, Betsy, Nancy has no child her husband is Lewis at Northend; old Moll mother to Nancy the wife of Bob (No 12

Suky wife of old Humphrey & her children Tommy who has a wife at the Meadow at Page Brook; Delphey with 2 children; Sukey, Tommy, Peggy & 2 children in the cabin (No 10

Lucy who has a husband at W. WHITING's & her 6 children (No 7

Peter & Sally & 2 children; Doll & her son Ralph at W. BROOKE's (No 6

Matt has a wife at the Meadows (No 1

Pat & her daughters Daisy? with 2 children, & grown daughter Lucy, Bill her son (No 6

Legacies:

to Mrs. PAGE of Janesville: Polly & 7 children, 6 grandchildren the children of her daughters Fanny & Betty (No 14

to Mrs. BROOKE: Fanny & her daughter Fanny, Hom?, George, Clara, Emily 4 years old (No 6 to Mrs. John W. PAGE: Israel & Lizzy his wife with 5 children; Milly & son; 2 children in the cabin; Penny & 2 children in the cabin (No 15

to William B. PAGE: 2 boys & a girl not yet chosen from the preceeding pages

to Mrs. Ann R. PAGE: Ruth & her 6 children, 2 are men, 2 are young women, a boy & girl; Gilbert & Mary & 4 children in the cabin, a boy son of Ann who died, & 2 little girls his sisters (No 16

Frederick

Matthew PAGE ....pg 75, 28 Dec 1826, sales

Thomas Strange? to John ALEXANDER; Dolly & her son Ralph to Judith R. PAGE; Carter, Rachael to Robert BERKELEY; Peggy to Morton BOWERS; Sarah to John BAKER; Judy, her youngest child & her 2nd daughter to John BOWLES; Billy to John CASTLEMAN; George to James CASTLEMAN; Sarah & her youngest child & her son Jacob to David CATHER; Franky to Benjamin CRIGLER; Delphy's daughter to Jacob ISLEE; Lucy's daughter Mary to William JENKINS; Jenny & her child, young man Tommy, Sawney, Isaac, Frederick & wife to Conrad KOWASLSKI; Nancy to George KERFOOT; Sally to Lewis LINDSAY; Harry to Alice McCALISTER; John, his wife & youngest child, their next youngest son & next child a female to George H. NORRIS; Peter, his wife & child & Peter's son Charles to Mann R. PAGE; Lucy & 4 children, Judy & her 3 youngest children, & her oldest child to Robert PAGE; Bob to Lax PINE; Lucy's son to Stephen RUTTER; Kizzy & her youngest child, her oldest male child, her oldest female, child her 2nd male child, & her youngest male child to George SAWYER?; John's son to J. SENSENEY; Sukey, Nancy to William TRAVERS; Clary/Casy, old Gilbert to James TRAVERS; Delphy & child to Joseph SHEPHERD; Charles to Marly TAYLOR; Katy to Walter TAUQUARY; Ariana to John B. WILLIAMSON; Mary to George WALLS

.... pg 76, 17 Aug 1827, sales con't

Michael, his wife & 2 youngest children, their 3rd child Betsey, their 4th child Leanna, their 5th child Lot, James, his wife Betsy, their children Francis & Anthony to Lewis BERKELEY; Sukey & her youngest child Maria to Thomas BLAKEMORE; Joe, William to John BURCHELL; Matt to Benjamin CRIGLER; Phill to Lemuel HUTCHINSON; Molly & her child Fred to Conrad HUNTSBERRY; Peggy & child, & her 2nd child to J.M. HITE; Drusy & 2 children to Thomas JACKSON; Robin to James M. MASON; Milly & her 2nd child Sukey to George McCORMISH Judy to George H. MORRIS; Aaron, Ben to William B. PAGE; Peter son of James, James son of James to Philip SMITH; Lucy to Bushrod TAYLOR

William B. PAGE...................................... pg 77, 31 Dec 1828, inv & appr

Clarissa, George, Elinor?, Preston, Lucy Ann, Mary & child, Lelia & child, Jane, Ben, Daniel, Anna, Squire, Henry, Betty, Evelyn, Jessy, Jacob, Solomon, Charles, Henry, John, Elinor, Richard, Charles, Anthony, Peter, Richard, Johnson, Aaron, Robert, Maria & child, Molly

William HAND............... pg 102, 19 Dec 1826 - 26 Jan 1829, estate acct

3 negroes sold; small boy, boy Frank, small girl Kit

William N. BURWELL.... pg 106, 25 Jan 1825 - 31 Dec 1828, estate acct

Frank, Sam sold to J. BAKER Nancy, Wat

Abraham HESS...................................... pg 111, 6 Dec 1828, inv & appr

man Joe, boys William, Isaac, girls Julia, Clarissa, old woman Molly, woman Ann, girls Eveline, Adaline, Joanah, boys John William, Harrison, girl Elizabeth

Sigismund E. STRIBLING..... pg 128, 1 Jan 1827 – 1 Nov 1827, gdn acct

paid Taliferro STRIBLING the difference in division of the negroes of Francis STRIBLING Sr, dec'd; Aaron sold

Edward McGUIRE................................ pg 129, 21 Dec 1828, inv & appr

old man Ned, Sarah 54, Collins 35, Matthew 42, Esther 27, Seipio 55, Aby & infant, Katilda 16, George 14, Bill 12, Sam 11, Dick 8, Charles 6, Jackson 4, Leonadas 6

John PAINTER .... pg 139, 9 Feb 1827 – 30 Jan 1829, estate acct

paid negro Franky her account

Matthew PAGE .... pg 143, 21 Feb 1828 - 16 Feb 1829, estate acct

slaves purchased by James M. HITE; slave purchased by James CASTLEMAN; slave purchased by James W. MASON; slave purchased by by Bushrod TAYLOR; slave purchased by Thornton? BOWEN; slaves purchased by William JENKINS; slaves purchased by William B. PAGE

Benedict RUST .... pg 145, 8 Mar 1827 – 4 Mar 1829, comm acct

Daniel, Dennis, Thornton

Richard L. REDMAN......... pg 147, 3 Dec 1825 – 4 Mar 1829, estate acct

Alice & 4 children in 1824, 5 children in 1825 & 1826, 6 in 1827 kept by Mrs. REDMAN; Ethalinda & children; Alfred Wells transported negroes to be sold in Winchester; George

John HADDOX .... pg 149, 26 Feb 1829, estate acct

Salley kept by Martha TRIPLETT; slaves; Ann, Kitty sold to Samuel GARDNER, Sally to Enoch R. ASHBY, Janney to James WHITE, Ailey, Mariah, Gabriel to James WAY, Mary to Daniel N. TRIPLETT

Jaby LARUE ....pg 173, 18 Dec 1823 - 19 Feb 1827, estate acct

negro hire

Richard L. REDMAN.........pg 181, 1 Jan 1824 – 30 Mar 1829, estate acct

negroes kept by Mrs. REDMAN; 2 negroes sold, other negroes sold

Eliza FURSTON .... pg 183, 1 Mar 1827 - 21 Mar 1829, gdn acct

Alfred

Hugh HOLMES..................................pg 190, 13 June 1825, sales

Jenny to Griffin FROST; girl to Townsend W. THOMAS

.... pg 192, 1 July 1825 - 1 Apr 1829, estate acct

boy hired by VANMETER

Reuben ROMINE .... pg 199, 1_ Dec 1828, inv & appr

Henry, Mary, Kitty, Margaret, Lucy, Jane

Augustine SMITH .... pg 200, 4 May 1829 in court, inv & appr

Lancaster 50, Dowdell 70, Robert 45, Taleferro 30, Judy 24, Lewis 41, Maria 24 & child 4 months, Mary 22 & child 6 months, George 9, Alexander 5, Eliza 5, Emily 3, Warner 3; Let & Israel to be freed at 21

Augustine SMITH..........................pg 201, 4 May 1829 in court, sales

hired: Letty to Thomas C. WYNSHAW; Bob to Lewis A. SMITH; Lewis to John GANT; Israel to Jacob STONE; Tolaver, Dowdell, Lang to Lewis A. SMITH;

.... pg 205, 6 Nov 1824 – 21 Apr 1829, estate acct

negroes; George, Lewis sold; "There are, as appears by the appraisment, eight slaves belonging to the estate, which have not been sold..."

Ann FUNSTON...................pg 210, 25 Oct 1828 – 2 May 1829, gdn acct

Nicholas

Richard L. REDMAN......................................pg 211, 3 Feb 1828, sales

at Winchester:

girl Mima to G. FROST; negro to Nancy REDMAN

4 May 1829: boy Bob, girls Jane, Catharine to T. SMITH; girl Betsey to D. CASTLEMAN

at Berryville: June 21

George, Ethalinda & child Henry to T. SMITH; Benjamin, Isaac, Jack to Griffin TAYLOR; Louisa to J.N. BLAKEMAN; Alice & child Moses to John JOHNSON; Jim to D. McCORMICK; Ame to Isaac McCORMICK

Lucy F. MEADE............. pg 211, 22 Dec 1823 – 21 Feb 1828, estate acct

paid for the education of an Indian child; servants; Barbara's family supported by Richard K. MEADE; Caroline hired by David MEADE

Susan MEADE.....................pg 213, 22 Dec 1823 – Jan 1826, estate acct

paid for the education of an Indian child; Alice; Lucy, Andrew & children boarded by Richard K. MEADE; little Lucy

Ann KERFOOT..................................... pg 215, 5 Apr 1829, will

John to be free at her death; Winney to be freed; the will was signed by Nancy KERFOOT

Robert MATTOX.................... pg 222, 26 May 1828, inv & appr

Mariel & child 10 months old, boy Madison, boy Joquilin, boys Beverly, Emanuel

John SELF .... pg 237, 1 Dec 1826, inv & appr

man Frederick, woman Rose, boy Samuel, girl Sophia, woman Jane, boys Alfred, James, girl Patsy, Milly & child Sidner, girl Caroline, woman Susanna, child Presley, boys William, ___, girl Maria, boy Deskin, girl Fanny, Fanny & child Lewis, girls Mary, Harriett

Isaac WILLIAMS.................... pg 242, 16 Oct 1828, sales

Daniel's time till Christmas to J. M. STILLMAN

Elizabeth GUNNELL late of Fairfax, Co.......... pg 249, 29 Mar 1827, will

all the interest of the negroes purchased by me or my agent (Henry GUNNELL) at the sale of William GUNNELL in trust of William H. HARRIS to daughter Nancy STANTHOPE wife of John STANTHOPE, also boy Harrison; woman Christeen to be free

Oliver FUNSTON .... pg 250, 15 Apr 1828 – 1 May 1829, estate acct

negro Daniel Wilkins

David FUNSTON.............. pg 254, 29 July 1827 – 29 Mar 1829, gdn acct

Israel, Elisa

Oliver FUNSTON ....pg 256, 29 July 1827 – 10 Apr 1829, gdn acct

paid negro Israel; Susan sold

Sally W. & Mary F. PAGE..
.... pg 257, 15 Apr 1828 – 1 May 1829, gdn acct

negroes

John CATLETT..............pg 259, 17 Jan 1828 - 26 May 1829, estate acct

Sam

Henry COE......................... pg 265, 2 Apr 1829, will

woman Margaret until she is 40, boy Isaac until he is 36, boy Warren? until he is 36 to wife Sarah COE; boy George until he is 36 to son Wesley COE; boy Isaac to son Henry COE and after wife's decease

128

then all to be free at stated age; Margaret's children should she have any to daughters Elizabeth SERVINER? wife of William SERVINER? & Mary BRUNER wife of John BRUNER & sons Wesley COE & Henry COE, be free at age 36

Francis ASH .... pg 267, 31 Oct 1828, inv & appr

old man Seipio, man Charles, Daniel 17, Henry 18, Aaron 22, Jeffrey 14, Bayles 12, Lucy 40, John 21, Bayles 21, Joanna 56, Lavinah 43, Beck 23, Kitty 11, Evelina 9, Lyddia 4, Benjamin 3, old woman Rachel

.... pg 270, 22 Apr 1829

young woman Beck died on 7 Feb 1829

James MITCHELL .... pg 271, 15 Oct 1821, inv & appr

Charity, Charlott, Harrison, Kesia, Venice, Violett, Judy, Benjamin, Salley, Betsey, Elias, Clary, Dafney, Arenia?, Hannah, Lucy, Federic, Bob, Ned, Harriott

Jane RAYNOLDS .... pg 273, 6 Jan 1814, will

girl Charlotte to Trustees for daughter Nancy & her children excluding her husband

Matthew PAGE .... pg 320, 3 Aug 1829 in court, inv & appr

these negroes are of no value, all old except & Milly & Randolph: Matt, Jenny, Persey, Judy, Sally, Molly, Patt, Franky, Great Sarah, Bob, Joe, Milly, Randolph, Nancy; Esther, Richard or Dicky, Michael, Ariana, Charles, China & her little boy, Sally has a child born since, Solomon, Thomas' wife Hannah; brothers Robin, Tom, Joe, Jim Cray, Sam, Harry, Jack; Nancy & 1 child, Peggy 15, little girl Betsy, Tom's wife Becky & 2 children, Nancy & 2 children, Thornton, Edmund, Parker, little girls Eleanor, Mary Ann, Johnny & Katy his wife; "16 negroes not enumerated here were devised specifically to Mrs. PAGE in addition to her dower..."

amount of George H. NORRIS' note for purchase of girl; amount of George H. NORRIS & Jacob ISLEE's note for slaves; amount for Mann R. PAGE & Joseph PAGE Jr.'s note for slaves

Henry CATLETT .... pg 344, 25 Oct 1827, inv & appr

Lemmon, Daniel, Jeny, Alexander, William, Lawson, Forten, George, Charles, Peter, David, John, Thomas, Harris, Alfred, Letty, Darcus, Fanny, Miles, James, Dinah, Lucy, Li__, Rose, Emily, Eliza, Sinah

John SENSENEY .... pg 346, 25 July 1829, estate acct

to hire 3 slaves; Eveline was sold contrary to law & was returned; Phill & Eveline kept by J. DANNER; Phill & Eveline died; Fann 26 & her 2 children kept by George BRINKER; Fanney & her 2 children all to be free at 30 years of age

William McLEOD .... pg 355, 4 Aug 1829 in court, inv & appr

Lewis, Mary & child, Maria, Reuben, Solomon, Milly & 3 children, Jane, James

Philip Fergurson, a free man of color .... pg 357, 24 Nov 1828, noncupative will

he had purchased his wife Franky who is to be left in trust by Humphrey & Sarah W. BROOKE to hire her out & act in the capacity of a master; Philip died the Wednesday following about day break

Charles GIBBS .... pg 364, 1 Oct 1824 - 31 Nov 1827, estate acct

Peter sold

Thomas T. & Mary A. BOYD .... pg 388, 8 Oct 1824 - 1 Oct 1829, estate acct

Robin, Tom, Ralph, Tom Cooper, George, Frank & Molly his wife, Kate, Richard, Hampton, Thomas Potter, Abby, midwife for Nancy, Matt; Letty purchased by Benjamin LEWIS __ E. DOUGHERTY; Robin purchased by Dr. HAY; boy Thomas Whiting sold

Jacob DEARY .... pg 398, 23 Sept 1824, codicil

man Harry to Mary HOFF/HOOF daughter of Elizabeth HOFF/HOOF

Benjamin KENDERICK .... pg 399, 25 Oct 1825, will

choice of 1 negro to wife Elizabeth; 1 slave to son-in-law John STEPHENSON

Oliver FUNSTON .... pg 401, 5 Nov 1828 – 1 Oct 1829, estate acct

free negroes removed as directed by the will & the legacies to said negroes

James WILLIAMS .... pg 414, Oct 1827 – 28 Oct 1829, estate acct

Gloria & 2 children; Armistead, Jack died, Clara died; Robin, boy Bob, old woman Jenny

Sarah I. DAVIS .... pg 416, Nov 1827 - 28 Oct 1829, estate acct

man

Mary TAYLOR .... pg 418, 31 Oct 1829, inv & appr

woman

Henry JANES .... pg 421, 2 Nov 1829 in court, will

lad David, boy Nelson to son Willy JANES; Chrisland or Crist, boy Spencer to daughter Elizabeth FISH; woman Mary to daughter Matildy TRESSALL; girl Ann to Matildy TRESSALL in trust for Miranda TRESSALL, Nimrod TRESSALL, & Thomas TRESSALL the children of dec'd daughter Arianna TRESSALL & to be sold when the youngest is of age; boy Sandy to son Willy JANES in trust for Henry Jackson FALKERSON & Thomas Willy FALKERSON the children of dec'd daughter Amealia FALKERSON & to be sold when the youngest is of age

James OLIVER .... pg 422, 6 Aug 1827 – 29 Aug 1829, estate acct

Henny? sold to James WAY

Abraham NEILL .... pg 423, 2 Nov 1826, will

woman Maria to wife & at her decease to son Joseph NEILL

Mary TAYLOR .... pg 428, 5 Nov 1829, sales

woman to Noah FRASHER

Sarah I. DAVIS .... pg 433, 14 Nov 1827, inv & appr

women Rose, Kitty, Ally & 2 children Lucy & Daniel, girl Eliza

Sarah I. DAVIS .... pg 436, 15 Nov 1827, sales

woman Rose to Henry BARTLETT; woman Kitty to William TOWERS; Ally & 2 children to David TIMBERLAKE; girl Eliza to John GILKESON for Julia DAVIS?

Charles BRENT .... pg 444, 30 Aug 1825, will

man Sam, woman Lydia to wife Rachel BRENT & not to be sold

Jane ASHBY .... pg 446, 4 Jan 1830 in court, inv & appr

boy Ben, woman Winney, boy Harry

.... pg 447, 4 Jan 1830 in court, sales

boy Ben to John ASHBY; woman Winney to Judith ASHBY; boy Harry to Lewis ASHBY

Lewis ASHBY .... pg 447, 10 Jan 1827, inv & appr

Maria, Mary

.... pg 448, 10 Jan 1827, sales

Maria & daughter sold to John ASHBY on 1 Jan 1828

Orphans of John REDMAN .... pg 450, 1827 - 1829, gdn acct

hire of negroes: Charles, Henry, Hannah, Adam, Winney, Maria, Felicia, Rachel, Eliza & Sarah with their children; to be divided among the 6 children

Charles, Maria to John LONTHAN; Adam, Else & 3 children to G.K. SOWERS; Rachel & child to Thomas GRUBBS; Felicia to James McDANIEL; Winney to John WALTER; Henry to Catharine NEWMAN; Hannah to Roger? RUST; Sarah & children to William MONROE; Adam, Else & children to Julia BERKLEY; Henry to William WRIGHT; Winney to Landon? BERKELEY; Hannah to A. RUST; Felicia to Thompson KIBBLE?; Sarah & children to D. SOWERS

Catherine B. REDMON orphan of John REDMAN ....
.... pg 450, 1827 - 1829, gdn acct

removing negroes to Frederick her part; hire of negroes

Frederick B. REDMON orphan of John REDMAN................................
.... pg 451, 1827 - 1829, gdn acct

removing negroes to Frederick his part; hire of negroes

Benjamin L. REDMON orphan of John REDMAN................................
.... pg 452, 1827 - 1829, gdn acct

removing negroes to Westmoreland your part; hire of negroes

John Milton REDMON orphan of John REDMAN................................
.... pg 453, 1827 - 1829, gdn acct

removing negroes to Westmoreland your part; hire of negroes

Thomas Jett REDMON orphan of John REDMAN................................
.... pg 453, 1827 - 1829, gdn acct

removing negroes to Westmoreland your part; hire of negroes

Eliza Ann SOWERS............. pg 454, 6 Jan 1828 – 15 Dec 1829, gdn acct

Joanna, James, Bill, Mary

Daniel SOWERS................. pg 456, 8 Sept 1828 - 15 Dec 1829, gdn acct

Orange, Jany, Ned, Flood

Julia A. DAVIS .... pg 457, 5 Nov 1827 – 31 Nov 1829, gdn acct

girl Eliza

James S. DAVIS.................. pg 458, 17 Nov 1827 – 1 Oct 1829, gdn acct

superannuated Nelly belonging to the estate of William DAVIS, dec'd

Abraham TAYLOR........... pg 467, 20 july 1811 –1 Apr 1826, estate acct

negroe

Marshall RUST .... pg 472, 27 Sept 1827 – 24 dec 1829, estate acct

David, Harrison, Winney, Adam, Sarah, Charles; negroes brought from Westmoreland County; Charles, Hannah, Henry, Adam, Maria, Felicia, Rachel; hire of negroes of J. REDMAN's estate

Benedict RUST .... pg 474, 5 Mar – 25 Dec 1829, comm acct

Thornton, Dennis

Jacob REED .... pg 478, 3 Oct 1829, inv & appr

    hire of girl of color till free

Maxwell DOWDALL .... pg 482, 7 Apr 1823 – 31 Dec 1829, comm acct

    Gilbert; Tom died

Reuben ROMINE .... pg 488, 1 Feb 1830 in court, sales

    Henry to Adison ROMINE; Mary & child, Lucy to Lydia ROMINE;
    Kitty to Mahaley ROMINE; girl Margaret to Elizabeth ROMINE

Robert MATTOX .... pg 493, 15 Aug 1829 - 7 Dec 1829, estate acct

    slaves purchased by J.W. COCKRELL

Vance BUSH .... pg 495, 4 Feb 1828 - 1 Jan 1830, estate acct

    Martha Ann

Mary McMURRAY .... pg 501, 25 Feb 1830, inv & appr

    boy Briston, girl Joannah

James WILLIAMS .... pg 3, 4 Nov 1827 - 31 Dec 1830, estate acct

Jane, Jane's child died; Jane & child

.... pg 5, 1 Mar 1830, notes

In 1792 Leroy PEACHY conveyed by deed to James WILLIAMS, Elizabeth his wife (who was Mr. PEACHY's daughter) and their son Leroy P. WILLIAMS...sundry slaves...In 1798 James WILLIAMS sold one of the slaves...and in 1802 another...Leroy P. WILLIAMS now claims one third of the price

Isaac N. GANT............... pg 10, 25 Dec 1827 - 24 Dec 1829, estate acct

Jonas Baker; Randell Evans, a free negro; Ralph; Abraham Swan

.... pg 17, 20 Feb 1830, uncollected debts

Robin Lovett, Randell Evans, Fairfax

Warner WASHINGTON .... pg 20, 7 July 1826, will

3 negroes of equal value with those I sold to daughter Elizabeth; girl to daughter Mary

Jane RAYNOLDS .... pg 22, 16 Nov 1829, sales

man David, Phebe & 3 children Mariah, Moses, & Henry, old woman Susan to Ebin TAYLOR; boy Charles to James McDONALD

William TYLER of Washington Co., TN............pg 25, 13 Aug 1820, will

"I will that Ira the boy of color that I have raised shall be under the care of my widow...to work for her until he arrives to the age of twenty one years...my negro woman Jenney for the support of the children..."

Thomas GRUBB .... pg 27, 16 Oct 1829, inv & appr

Davy & his wife Lindsy, man James, man Mage?, boy Jake, woman Ciller, Dinah & her son Ben, Fanny & her daughter M, women Lydia, Mariah, Betsey, Jane & her child Mariah, woman Edy, girl Lucy, boy Charles, girl Mary

Henry JANES .... pg 30, 14 Jan 1830, inv & appr

men Ned, Tom, John, woman Janny, boy Jarry, girls Nancy, Milly, Scig_?

Rev Joseph GLASS .... pg 40, 1 Apr 1828 – 1 Apr 1830, estate acct

Joseph GLASS .... pg 42, 1 Apr 1828 – 1 Apr 1830, second estate acct

Abram, Joe, Sarah, John, Louisa, Molly, Frank, Jim, Mingo, Cuffey; woman Louisa removed to Winchester for Capt. TIMBERLAKE; Louisa ran away

Michael MANCK .... pg 67, 31 Dec 1820, will

woman Phebe to choose her purchaser for herself & her youngest child Charlette & kept together, if not purchased or hired out to go to Solomon HARMAN till sold; young woman Mary to choose her purchaser; Sarah Catherine to Solomon HARMAN as part of his wife's division of the estate; remaining slaves to be sold

Nathaniel CARTMELL .... pg 75, 15 Mar 1830, inv & appr

men Jacob, Gilbert, boy James, woman Barbary, Matilda & child, girl Milly, boy Jackson, girl Nancy, boy William

James WATSON .... pg 78, 19 Mar 1830, will

Edward 13 to be sold for a term of 25 years & then be free

Rebecca HENRY .... pg 86, 11 July 1825, will

Mima, Stephen, Robert to son Bryant Hampson HENRY; Lucy, Wilford to son William Vannester HENRY; Washington, George to son Bryant Hampson HENRY in trust for Elizabeth ROBERSTON wife of William N. ROBERSTON

James HOLIDAY .... pg 87, 2 June 1830 in court, will

"I believe it has been the will of my deces'd wife that Evans one black servant should be given or left to Luisa now J. HOLLINGSWORTH and Hanna Marrion & Fanny to my Harriet…" it is my will that Evans to be free at age 45 & the 2 little girls at the age of 35

Francis ASH .... pg 88, 28 June 1829 - 1 June 1830, estate acct

boy, a part of Philip SWAN's wife Nancy's legacy; negroes; boy John delivered Philip SWAN

Benjamin KENDRICK.................pg 97, 16 Oct 1829, inv & appr

Gabriel, Charlotte & child, woman Amelia, girl Maria, man

....pg 107, 1 Jan 1830, sales

man Gabriel to John KENDRCK; woman Amelia to Samuel KENDRICK; Charlotte & child to Sam KENDRICK

Solomon VANMETRE.........pg 108, 16 June 1830, inv & appr

Celia, Eveline, Mary, Sarah, Anne Mariah, Louisa, Jerry, David, Henry, Robert, Jordon, Anthony, Jack, Ben, Jack, Manlia, Jacob on the farm

hires: Thomas, Nelson to John KENDRICK; Bill to Enoch HENRY; Isaac to Jacob CLINE; Sam to Isaac FUNKHOUSER; Jacob to Thomas PERRY; Isiah, Judah to Mrs. WILLIAMS; Phebe to SNAP?; Alice to Jacob HITT; Joseph in possession of William PAYNE; Barshaba to Mrs. CRYZER; Ann to David? STRIKLER; Patty, Eliza, child Alphias in possession of William LANE; Dan, Mahala, Mathilda in possession of B.H. HENRY; Marcus? in possession of Enos M. GRAY

Orphans of George ASH......pg 117, 1 June 1828 – 1 June 1830, gdn acct

boy Isaac supported by Hannah REED; young & infirm negroes; Maria

William BOWIN..............................pg 127, 7Aug 1824, will

Kisiah & her child to daughter Sarah HATHAWAY wife of Francis HATHAWAY; Armistead, Lidda to wife Milly BROWN & at her decease Armistead to son John & Lidda to son Andrew; boy Jacob, Ben (who is free at 21) to son William; girl Margate to daughter Lucy Ann; Lidda's daughter Asa to daughter Jane

Matthew PAGE.................pg 129, 5 Oct 1828 - 15 July 1830, estate acct

girl to George H. NORRIS; first sale of negroes; slaves purchased by Mann R. PAGE; slave purchased by Norton BROWN; slaves purchased by John ALEXANDER; slave purchased by William JENKINS; boy belonging to the estate of Nathan PAGE, dec'd, at widow's request to John E. PAGE

Sally W. & Mary F. PAGE... pg 155, 1 May 1829 – 1 Aug 1830, gdn acct

money to The Colonization Society; purchased negro cloth; hired hands

Mary GREEN...pg 162, 4 Sept 1823, will

negroes to niece Mary Ann GREEN

William HELM .... pg 164, 12 May 1829, will

slaves aged 28 & older to be emancipated after nine months, those younger hired out & then emancipated at age 28; those unable to work to be supported by the estate

Samuel MADDEN .... pg 169, 22 Aug 1829, sales

Louisa hired by George RISSLER

William B. PAGE..............pg 182, 10 Oct 1828 – 9 Sept 1830, estate acct

Solomon, Anthony, midwife for Lelia, Michael, midwife for Maria, Henry, midwife for Betty, Charles

James MOORE.....................................pg 186, 9 Sept 1826, inv & appr

Robert 19 to serve to age 35

James WILLIAMS .... pg 200, 29 Oct 1829 – 18 Oct 1830, estate acct

sales: Bob to James CASTLEMAN; Armistead to John PRICE; old woman Jenny to McCORMICK

James BAKER.. pg 201, 18 Mar 1829, will

Joe, Dasy, Sally & her son Henry to son Corban; Nelly, Betsy to daughter Sophia; Mary Ann, Catharine, Lucy to daughter Maria; Jerrard, Mary & chld George, Harry, Sally to son Alexander; girl Cla_sy to Mary I. MURRAY & her sister Betty

.... pg 202, 1 Nov 1830 in court, inv & appr

Jacob, Jerrard, Jim, Joe, Dave, Cesar, Dick, Ralph, Pat, Ampy, Nelly, Sally & her son Henry, Mary & child George, Harry, Mary Ann, Catharine, Lucy, Sally, Bill, Winney, Aaron, Dinah, Betsy, Jim, Dole; Claria, George? to Mary I. MURRAY & her sister Betty

.... pg 203, 1 Nov 1830 in court, division

Joe, Dasy, Sally & her son Henry to Corban BAKER; Nelly, Betsy to Sophia; Mary Ann, Catharine, Lucy (Mary's children) to Maria; Jerrard, Mary & child George, Harry, Sally to Alexander

138

Jacob DEARY ....pg 211, Feb 1830, inv & appr

Henry, girl Peggy; woman Fanny claimed by Mrs. Elizabeth HOFF

Bartholomew SMITH ....pg 215, 29 Dec 1826, sales

Jeff to serve 2 yrs to John LOCH; Humphrey to serve 6 yrs, Lewis to serve 7 years to Henry SMITH; Maria to serve 6 yrs to John CABLE; Nancy to serve 13 yrs to Michael SMITH; Emily to serve 16 yrs, James 22 yrs, Harry 19 yrs, Milford 21 yrs to Henry SMITH

Samuel MADDEN ....pg 221, 6 Aug 1829 – 2 Oct 1830, estate acct

Louisa hired by George RISLER; Sarah

Edward McGUIRE ....pg 242, 10 June 1829, sales

girl Matilda to Rebecca MACKY; woman Abby, ; man Seipio to John R. COOKE; boy George to John COPENHAVER; boys Tom, Jackson, Charles to E.D. McGUIRE woman Esther to Solomon DODDS; boy Leonidas to Reuben STRANGE; Collins to B.H. LEWIS; Matthew to E.D. McGUIRE

Maria FUNSTON ....pg 244, 2 Mar 1830 – 1 Jan 1831, gdn acct

hire of negro belonging to Elizabeth FUNSTON dec'd

Margaret FUNSTON .... pg 245, 23 Feb 1830 – 1 Jan 1831, gdn acct

hire of negro belonging to Elizabeth FUNSTON dec'd

Abraham HESS .... pg 246, 1 Dec 1828 – 26 Aug 1830, estate acct

Ann & her children kept by Nancy HESS; Joseph, Julia, Molly

Robert MATTOX............pg 254, 15 Aug 1828 - 23 Dec 1830, estate acct

slaves not devised purchased by J.W. COCHRELL

Vance BUSH .... pg 259, Feb 1826 – 27 Dec 1830, estate acct

slaves emacipated in court; woman sold; Joe Taper

Lewis BURWELL ....pg 267, Dec 1828 – 3 Dec 1830, estate acct

Hannah & child purchased by J.V. GLASS; purchase of Tenar & 2 children by ___ waggoner; Betsey, Arthur, Fanny, Lucy, Hannah, Mary Ann?, Fanny, Judy; child purchased by waggoner; boy purchased by HUMPHREYS; girl Lucy purchased by a stranger

Susan PEYTON................................pg 269, 30 Dec 1830, inv & appr

Daniel 60, boy William

Elizabeth SHUMER nee CRIGLER...
....pg 270, 9 Dec 1822 – 30 Dec 1830, gdn acct

amount paid for division of slaves to Christopher CRIGLER, Reuben CRIGLER, Robert CRIGLER from father's estate; boys Jno, George; man James; Reuben CRIGLER's amount due for his propotion of slaves from mother's estate

Benjamin GLASSCOCK.....pg 278, 9 June 1827 – 6 Jan 1831, estate acct

negroes sold

Ambrose BARNETT.............................pg 280, 25 Oct 1825, will

negroes to be purchased by children of dec'd only: daughters Nancy ALLEN nee BARNETT, Betsey BARNETT, Jane FOISTER nee BARNETT, Mildred BARNETT, sons Neile BARNETT, & George N. BARNETT

Edward McGINNIS........ pg 285, 16 Dec 1828 – 31 Nov 1830, estate acct

Tom hired by Rebecca MACKY; Dick; boy Leonidas raised by Reuben STRANGE; reward for Collins; Scipio, girl Matilda; Abbe, boy George; Scipio sold; boys Tom, Jackson, Charles, Esther; Collins, Matthew, Abbe sold

John LEFEVER............................pg 306, 3 Sept 182_, inv & appr

men John, Jerry, Barney, John, boys Hilyard, Albert, Richard, women Alcey, Frank

....pg 310, 20 Sept 1828 - 30 Jan 1831, estate acct

hire of negrees; 5 negroes vacinated

Elija Ann SOWERS ....pg 312, 29 Jan 1829 – 3 Jan 1831, gdn acct

negro hire; Mary

Children of William N. BURWELL ....
.... pg 315, 11 Oct 1824, - 17 Dec 1830, gdn acct

paid for passage of negroes from Jamestown to Norfolk, from Norfolk
to Alexandria; Emily, L___, Mo__, Senaca; lot of negroes in Low
Country; David, __na_

Isaac BAKER .... pg 328, 28 Feb 1831 in court, inv & appr

men Lewis, Thomas, boys Benjamin, John, James, Milly & infant
George Edward, girls Mary Ann, Sarah Jane, Susan Catharine, Susan
& infant Henriett Ann, girls Mary, Winny, woman Minny, girls Fanny,
Sarah

........................pg 335, 4 May 1829, sales

man Lewis to Lewis? WOLFE?; man Tom to Jacob KIGER; boy
Benjamin to Robert BRANNON?, girl Mary, Janny to Jacob
SENSENEY; girl Winny to Matthew RUST?; girl Susan to Jacob
NICHOLS; Sarah to John BAKER; Milly & her infant child George
Edward, Susan Catharine, Milly's children James, Mary Ann, & Sarah
Jane to George W. BAKER; boy John to William MILLER; Minny &
infant child to Nathan PARKINS

James BAKER......................pg 348, 16/17 Nov 1830, inv & appr

old couples: Aaron & wife Dinah, Billy & wife Winney, Jim & wife
Dolly; men Dick, Jim Dove, Jared, Ceasar, Ralph, Jacob, Joe, David,
Sally & child Henry, Nelly & child, Patty & child Tom, Mary & 4
children, girl Clara, boy Harry, girls Betty, Mary Ann

Rebecca BRINKER.....................pg 359, 23 Sept 1826?, will

Winny devised to wife from late husband George BRINKER; Jack, one
of her children, was sold a year ago; man Harry to be sold

James FOSTER .... pg 362, 5 Dec 1829, inv & appr

man

William BOURNE .... pg 364, 12 Nov 1830, inv & appr

men Armistead, Ben for 1 year service, boy Jaed?, Margaret, boy Ralph

Thomas McCONNICK............. pg 370, June 1827 – 1 Apr 1831, gdn acct

negroes kept by Isaac McCONNICK; division of negroes fee;
Solomon, Nancy

141

Charles McCONNICK .... pg 372, June 1827 – 1 Apr 1831, gdn acct

negroes kept by Isaac McCONNICK; division of negroes fee

Lucy McCONNICK ....pg 373, 16 May 1827 – 30 Mar 1831, gdn acct

Tom

Elizabeth GUNNELL .... pg 385, 11 June 1829, inv & appr

Harrison age 21/22

Edwin B. BURWELL............................ pg 392, 18 Mar 1831, inv & appr

Putnam 12, Aggy 17, Happy 50, Esther 25, Davy 2, Rachel 2, Henry 50, Jess 25, Spencer 20, Harriett 14, Jane 6, Elija 10

....pg 395, 2 May 1831 in court, sales

Jesse to John COLLINS; Henry to Jacob HUNSUCKER; Spencer to William WATSON; Putnam to Thomas CLARK; Elija to Ja__ D. MILLER, Hester to Lewis B. WYSONG; Aggy to William THOMAS

Isaac L. CAN........................pg 406, 5 Mar 1830 – 5 Apr 1831, gdn acct

share of sale of the slaves of Richard CAN deed

Cornelius B. CAN ....pg 407, 5 Mar 1830 – 5 Apr 1831, gdn acct

share of sale of the slaves of Richard CAN deed

Joseph S. CAN ....pg 408, 5 Mar 1830 – 5 Apr 1831, gdn acct

share of sale of the slaves of Richard CAN deed

Richard B. CAN ....pg 409, 5 Mar 1830 – 5 Apr 1831, gdn acct

share of sale of the slaves of Richard CAN deed

Mary E. CAN ....pg 410, 5 Mar 1830 – 5 Apr 1831, gdn acct

share of sale of the slaves of Richard CAN deed

Eliza DAVIS .... pg 412, 1826 – 1 Jan 1831, estate acct

Zachary, Winney, Jos?, Delphia

William HELM ....pg 416, 27 Sept 1830, inv & appr

Lucy, Dick, Fiday, Vilet 42, Horace 39, Becca 32, Sarah 42 & her child Fielding 13 months, Isaac 20, Nelson 18, Moses 14, Richmond 12,

Levi 8?, Emily 12, Leannah Jr. 11, Matilda Jr. 3, Louisa 6, Lucy 6, Caroline 3, Jim? 2, Reuben 3, Rose 40 & her child Evelina 7, Ralph 20, Henry 19, Henson 15, Louis Jr. 20, Jack 16, Sandy 9, Moses 35, Lewis Sr. 44, Eliza 22, Jemima 23, Pricilla 17, Mary 15, Leana Jr. 14, Matilda Jr. 9, Betsy Ann 10, Sally 23 & her 3 children Felicia 5, Jane 3, & William 1, Harriet 9

Sarah HENDREN .... pg 424, 14 May 1831, appr slaves

Providence, Thornton, Mike, Catherine

Thomas LITTLETON .... pg 426, 26 Oct 1830, inv & appr

girl Mary, man Elijah, Jack, boys Willis, Charles, man Timathey?, William, woman Venis, boy Edward, girls Fanender?, Hanah?, girl Christian, Elizabeth, boys Fielding, Dorsey, old Jinncy?

Stephen PRITCHARD ...... pg 434, 26 May 1819 – 1 Jan 1826, estate acct

a slave died

Henry COE .... pg 438, 18 June 1829, inv & appr

Margaret, Isaac, George, Warner

William HOLMES .... pg 458, 17/18 Mar 1831, sales

Beck? to Edward B. JACOBS

John BOWLES .... pg 469, 4 July 1831 in court, inv & appr

men Joshua, Reuben, Isaac, boy Jerry, Judy & her child Emily, woman Molley

James JACKSON .... pg 472, Aug 1822? – 1827?, estate acct

negroes

Orphans of George ASH .... pg 489, 3 Sept 1830 – 1 July 1831, gdn acct

maintained young & usless slaves; negroes; slaves

Isaac BAKER .... pg 490, 1 Apr 1829 - 2 Aug 1831, estate acct

midwife for Minney; Negro Roberts; Nat, Payton; received from Matthew RUST for girl Winney; from Jacob KEGER for Tom; from Jacob NICHOLS for Susan; from Lewis WOLFE for Lewis; from George W. BAKER for Milly & children; from William MILLER for John

Benjamin KENDRICK ....
..................................pg 507, 22 Sept 1829 – 20 July 1831, estate acct

negroes

Benedict RUST ....pg 518, 29 Apr 1829 – May 1831, estate acct

old Betty kept by Jane M. RUST; woman Sidney's purchase by
Madison HITE for Mrs. BALDWIN is in dispute

Jacob REED .... pg 7, 20 Oct 1829, sales

girl's service till free to Lewis SMITH

Philip D. WILLIAMSON .... pg 21, 18 July 1831, will

girl Charlotte Temple? & any issue to be free at age 30 & sent to Liberia, if refuses to go to remain in service of wife Mary; old man Valentine to wife Mary M. WILLIAMSON

Thomas COOPER .... pg 24, 15 July 1831, will

Jack, Tom to be freed

Elizabeth BRUCE .... pg 36, 16 Nov 1831, will

maid Sophia

Rebecca BRINKER .... pg 38, 15 Mar 1831, inv & appr

Fielden, Robert Brown, Harry, Nelly, Benjamin

.... pg 40, 15 Mar 1831, sales

Harry, Nelly the hire of George BRINKER; Benjamin the hire of George LANICK & Lewis STEPHENS; Fielding, Harry purchased by George BRINKER; Robert purchased by Isaac SCAGGS; Benjamin, Nelly purchased by Joseph BRINKER

Maxwell DOWDALL .... pg 49, 5 Oct 1831, estate acct

Gilbert sold 1 June 1830

Margaret SEEMER .... pg 50, 1 Dec 1829 - 21 Nov 1831, estate acct

paid Rebecca Johnston black woman for services rendered

Rebecca BRINKER .... pg 51, 1830 - 21 July 1831, estate acct

negroes sold; Ben

Joseph LUPTON .... pg 52, 9 Jan 1829 – 3_ Oct 1831, estate acct

Ricky & wife

Benedict RUST .... pg 74, 25 Dec 1829, inv & appr

old woman, man Thornton, boy Dennis, woman Sidney

Benedict RUST .... pg 75, Dec 1829, sales

Thornton to William A. CARTER; Dennis to Matthew RUST; Sidney to James M. HITE

Daniel W. SOWERS .... pg 80, 28 Dec 1829 – 22 Nov 1831, gdn acct

negroes sold/hired; Ned, Flood, Orange, Jenny

Ann FUNSTON .... pg 82, 29 Apr 1829 – 16 Jan 1832, gdn acct

cash due Sally Y. BRYCE in the division of negroes due from Ann & Eliza FUNSTON; Nicholas, Alfred

Jared WILLIAMS .... pg 83, 17 Aug 1831, inv & appr

Tom, Sarah, Maria & her child, Winney & her child Thornton, Moses, Matilda & her child Henry, Juliana, Peyton, Charles, Harriet, Lucy, George

Sarah STRIBLING of Butler Co. KY .... pg 86, 15 Oct 1823, will

all slaves to Isham L. WATKINS & Martin HOGAN in trust for daughter Dulcibella BECSON wife of Edward BECSON

Henrietta CATLETT .... pg 90, 3 June 1830, will

Fortin to be hired out until the mony is enough to convey him to Liberia & to emancipate him

Maria FUNSTON .... pg 96, 5 Apr 1831 - 1 Jan 1832, gdn acct

sale of man belonging to the estate of Eliza FUNSTON, dec'd

Margaret FUNSTON .... pg 96, 5 Apr 1831 - 1 Jan 1832, gdn acct

sale of man belonging to the estate of Eliza FUNSTON, dec'd

Emily FUNSTON .... pg 97, 5 Apr 1831 - 1 Jan 1832, gdn acct

sale of man belonging to the estate of Eliza FUNSTON, dec'd

Matthew PAGE's children: L.W. & M.F. PAGE ....
.... pg 98, 1 Aug 1830 – 14 Nov 1831, gdn acct

Harry

James MITCHELL .... pg 101, 16 Oct 1821 – 1 Jan 1830, estate acct

Lucy, Venice, Harriet, Ned, Bob, Violett, Clary, Charity, Federick, Maria, Dafney; Sally & 2 children kept by Samuel J. SHACKELFORD; midwife for Maria & Harriet; Juda? & 3 children kept by Charles G. MITCHELL

Ebin TAYLOR, Fayette Co., KY .... pg 107, 28 Nov 1831, inv & appr

men Bob, Samuel, boys Alfred, Charles, girl Nancy

.... pg 108, 28 Nov 1831, sales

Bob to George BOSWELL; Samuel to David BRYANT; Alfred, Charles to John PARKER; Nancy to Dr. RITCHIE

Adam BROWN .... pg 110, 12 May 1831, sales

negro Ben bought items

Ambrose BARNETT .... pg 116, 22 Feb 1831, inv & appr

Ginny 47 yrs, Sam 40, Jim 19, Ben 17, Ann 15, Presley 12, Sidney 8

.... pg 118, 23 Feb 1831, sales

Ben to William ALLEN; Jim to Joseph W. CARTER; Ginny, Ann, to Jane H. FORSTER; boy Presley to Neil BARNETT; man Sam to George _. BARNETT; girl Sidney to Mildred _. BARNETT

Bartholomew SMITH ...... pg 132, 21 June 1824 - 20 Feb 1832, estate acct

2 children kept by E. SMITH, 2 kept by Fanny BAKER; Jeff, Humphry, Lewis, Louisa, Mary; 9 negroes sold for a term

Mary McMURRAY .... pg 135, 1828 - 13 Feb 1832, estate acct

cost for dividing slaves

Nathan C. BAKER .... pg 151, 3 Apr 1832, inv & appr

woman Anne

.... pg 155, 15 Mar 1831 - 22 Mar 1832, estate acct

girl sold

147

Joseph GLASS .... pg 160, 1 Apr 1830 - 31 Mar 1832, estate acct

man Mingo, Molly, Louisa, Cuffy, Sarah, Frank, Abraham, John, Jim, Sally, Joe

John B. HARRIS .... pg 169, 31 Mar 1832, inv & appr

woman & child, man Quiller

Mary STEPHENS .... pg 183, 21 June 182_, will

Nace, Sarah his wife, Frank, Isaac, Robert, Emily & her children, Milly & her children to nephew William HENING of Winchester; boy Nelson to John NEWCOMER husband of niece Polly

.... pg 186, 21 Feb 1828, codicil

man Nelson sold; Isaac to John & Polly NEWCOMER in Nelson's place

James STROTHER .... pg 191, 5 Jan 1829 - 15 Oct 1830, estate acct

boy Marshall sold

Thomas JACOBS .... pg 223, 15 Nov 1834, appr

woman Betty, girl Maria, boy George, man Daniel

James WATSON .... pg 234, 7 June 1830, inv & appr

boy aged 13

.... pg 237, 19 Aug 11830, sales

boy Edward to Joseph RITENOUR

Dudley BURWELL .... pg 241, 8 Feb 1832 in court, inv & appr

Billy 65 & his wife Winny 60

John MORGAN .... pg 257, 26 Dec 1831, will

Dick & Nelley and all of their children Edman? & Virginia and and all of her children to son John at the deaths of wife Elizabeth MORGAN & son Benjamin MORGAN

Henry BERKHAMER .... pg 262, 1816 – 14 Dec 1831, estate acct

Isaac, Ann, Jacob

James WATSON .... pg 262, 16 Aug 1830 – 1 June 1832, estate acct

hire of 2 negroes belonging to the heirs of George ASH

William BOURN .... pg 265, 17 Aug 1830 – 11 May 1832, estate acct

negroes

Michale MANCK .... pg 267, 3 May 1830 – 26 May 1832, estate acct

Solomon HARMON trustee for Phebe; Mary

Susan MEADE ....pg 270, 1828 – 10 Feb 1832, estate acct

Alice died; Lucy, Andrew

Lucy MEADE ....pg 271, 29 Jan 1829 – 5 Mar 1832, estate acct

Caroline's hire from D. MEADE; Barbara, husband Jack & children went out West; transfer to the Colony Society; "Balance in the hands of the Exceutor retained in order to meet any expenses which may be incurred by Barbara & her family & Caroline's child Tr__ who is the only one not liberated."

Adam BOSTEYON.............................. pg 274, 27 June 1832, inv & appr

George, Polly, Harriet, Lydia, Charles, Chancy, Charity, Sam

Ebin TAYLOR ....pg 276, 24 Oct 1831, inv & appr

Milly & her child Thornton, boy Nelson, girls Fanny, Loulsa, boy Charles, Hannah, Silvy, Mary, Harriet & child, Evelina & child, girl Hannah, Violet & child, girl Nelly, woman Ann, Caroline, Bob & Polley his wife, boys Buckner, Reuben, Frank, John William, Jackson, Joseph; Palace & child, Martha Ann, Jasper, Bill, Spencer, Bob, Armistead, Sam, James, Tony, Joseph, Sharlotte, Lousia, Ginny & child, Lucy, Jane, Lucy & 2 children, Ellen, Ammanda, Catharine, Lucy, Fanny Ann, Dinah, Warner, Rachel, Lucinda, Peggy, Elizabeth, Ruth, William, Henry, Simon, Masse, Mahala, Nan, Ambrose, Sarah, Nancy, Nelson, Jack, George, Emily & child, Bushrod, Benjamin, Charles, Harry, Amy & her 4 children, girls Evalina, Rachel, man Carter

.... pg 285, 26 Oct 1831, sales

boy Charles to Paul SMITH; boy Joseph to Samuel ENGLE; boy Spencer to Benjamin LEWIS; boy Simon to Leonard Y. DAVIS; boy Harry to Charles M. CONNICK, boy Jack to Bushrod TAYLOR; boy

Ben to William STEPHENSON; man Bob to Joseph SMITH; man Armistead to William CASTLEMAN Jr.; man Samuel to Abraham ISLER; boy Buckner to Joseph SMITH; boy John William to Nat SEEVER; boy Charles to James TAYLOR; boy Jackson to Peter GARDNER; boy Reuben to John H. LEWIS; boy Joseph to Joseph LANE; boy Warner to John SMITH; woman Jane, Jane, Caroline to Jeremiah RICHARDS; boy Nelson to Griffin TAYLOR; woman Syliva to Dr. QUIGLY; woman Mary to James TAYLOR; woman Ruth to Conrad KOWNSLAR; woman Rachael to Joseph ANDERSON; boy Frank to Ebin CRAIG; girl Hannah to William TAYLOR; girl Martha Ann to Edward HART; Harriet & child Marshal to Joseph MEYERS; girl Louisa to Dr. John HAYDEN; woman Anna to John HAY; woman Sharlotte to Thomas G. HUMPHREY; girl Hannah to Parkinson SHEPHERD, Evelina & child Alfred to Paul SMITH; girl Dinah to Bushrod TAYLOR __; woman Nancy to Theophilus F. CORNADT?; girl Lucy to Paul SMITH; girl Nelly to Joseph SMITH; Milly & child Thornton to Nat SEEVERS; Palace & child Presly to Oliver CROMWELL; girl Elon to Joseph LANE; girl Lucinda to Joseph MYERS; Lucy & 2 children Catharine & Ely, girl Amanda to John McKNIGHT; girl Judy to Samuel MARTIN; girl Violet, Elizabeth, Amanda to David CATHER; girl Caroline to Daniel MUMPHRY; girls Massie, Mahala to Samuel STARET?; man James, old man Fini?, Amy & her 4 children, girls Fanny, Louisa to Mrs. TAYLOR; girl Janney Ann to Samuel MARTEN; Peggy, boy William to William CASTLEMAN Jr.; woman Nan to Alfred CASTLEMAN; man Toney to Daniel CABLE; man Ambrose to Nathan SEEVER; woman Mary? to William CASTLEMAN Jr; girl Evelina to R.E. PARKER; girl Rachel to Bus. TAYLOR; man Carter to William CARTER; woman Hany to William CARTER Jr.

Nelly C. BALDWIN .... pg 300, 3,4 Nov 1831, sales

man Bob to E.J. DAVISON; woman Sidney to Samuel BERKELEY

Miss Frances McCORMICK ....
.... pg 309, 11 Nov 1829 -1 Apr 1832, gdn acct

amount from division of negroes from the dower estate; Rachel, boy Moses

Lucy Catharine WARE .... pg 314, 10 Nov 1822 - 1 Jan 1832, gdn acct

negroes; midwife for Milly

Thomas Marshall WARE ....pg 320, 11 Dec 1829 - 18 June 1832, gdn acct

kept 3 children too small to hire out; Eliza; negroes

Orphans of James WARE .... pg 324, 7 Jan 1823 – 1 Jan 1830, gdn acct

negroes; Billy Lightfoot , Milly & children, midwife for Mary, Susan & children, Jacob, man Nelson, Dick died, man Jerry, James, Mary Lightfoot died; Mary Ann, midwife for Milly, Spencer died; James Lightfoot, J_ed, Beatty, Lewis, Harry, Peter, Presley, Betty, Amy & child, Rachel, Fanny, Jacob, Sawney; Harry, Tom?, Mortimer; Amy sold due to murdering her child

James WARE .... pg 331, 1 Oct 1821 – 1 Mar 1831, estate acct

Sam & Betty's jail fee; Amy

Harriet Mary T. WARE ....
.... pg 335, 17 July 1828 – 1 Oct 1831, estate acct

negroes

James William WARE .... pg 336, 3 June 1828 - 1 Oct 1831, estate acct

boy Peter

Michael MANCK .... pg 341, 1 Apr 1832, inv & appr

Phebe 40, Charlotte 3, child about 6 weeks, Sarah Catharine 5, Mary 17, Daniel Ransel 12, Joseph Reuben? 8, Thomas Harrison 10, Richard 70

Mary STEPHENS .... pg 345, 19/28 May 1832, inv & appr

boys Isaac, Robert, girls Milly, Emily, boy Charles, girl Fanny, women Fanny, Sarah, man Nace

Orphans of John HOPKINS ....
.............................pg 366, 12 July 1830 - 30 Aug 1832, gdn acct

midwife for Nancy; men

Alfred H. POWELL ....pg 376, 20 Sept 1831, inv & appr

men William, Jonathan, Patrick, boy Jack

151

Alfred H. POWELL .... pg 378, 7 Nov 1831, sales

man William to Margaret MERCER; man Jonathan, boy Jack to Leven M. POWELL; man Patrick to Thomas GLASS

Thomas CATHER .... pg 389, 28 Aug 1828, will

boy Frank to wife Elizabeth until he is 25 years old

Davis STUTLY .... pg 392, 16 June 1832, inv & appr

John 36, Hannah 30 & child 2 months, Harry? 13, Sarah 9, Levi? 7, Jo? 5, Pete 3, Jim newborn?

Davis HOLMES .... pg 395, about 1825, will

Lewis & Nancy his wife to sister Rebecca CONRAD provided she will remove them to Virginia from Mississippi, also Sylvia & her child or children; Jack to nephew David Holmes CONRAD; Emanuel to be liberated & remain in Mississippi

.... pg 396, 19 May 1828, codicil

man Manuel, man Jack, Lewis & his wife Lucy to be emancipated & permitted to remain in Mississippi or Louisianna; Sylvia has 2 children

.... pg 397, 23 Nov 1831, 2nd codicil

man Jerry

Joseph W. CARTER .... pg 406, 10 Jan – 10 Aug 1832, estate acct

Mary Coat's account, a woman of color

Orphans of George ASH ....

.... pg 407, 11 July 1831 – 1 Sept 1832, gdn acct

negroes, young usless slaves, Sarah

William CASTLEMAN .... pg 410, 1 June 1832, inv & appr

Alfred, Bob, Jos, James, Fanny, Hannah, Matty, Sipio, Tom, David, Emalina, Pompoy

Philip D. WILLIAMSON .... pg 412, 5 Oct 1831, inv & inv & appr

Valentine 65, Charlotte 15 to be free at age 30 if she chooses to go to Liberia

Archibald MAGILL .... pg 415, 31 Mar 1831, will

Polly Ann & her family & other negroes may be sold if necessary after consultation with wife Mary Jane

William B. PAGE .... pg 420, 4 Oct 1830 – 15 Oct 1832, estate acct

midwife for Clarissa; Evelyn, Mary, midwife Sarah for Anna, Peter, midwife Sarah for Maria, Solomon

Elizabeth BAZZEL .... pg 425, 21 July1830, will

William hired in Fairfax County

William HELM .... pg 428, 13 Sept 1830 - 2 Nov 1832, estate acct

old Dick, Lucy, Fidy?, Violett & her 3 children, Sarah & her 2 children, midwife for girl Mary; Evelyn, Ralph, Henry, Jacob, Isaac, Elija, Mima, Sellar, Betsy Ann, Emily, Leannah, Nelson, boy Lewis, Beck

Matthew PAGE .... pg 436, 4 Oct 1830 – 1 Jan 1831, estate acct

Note: "delivered to D. MEADE...all the slaves not sold for the payment of debt...in full discharge of his administration on the estate..."

Moses GREEN .... pg 445, 8 Feb 1830 - 1 Dec 1832, estate acct

Thompson ADAMS, Elizabeth GREEN, Ann GREEN, Lane GREEN, Elijah KERCHEVAL, Richard GREEN & James GREEN equalized their or their children's share of negroes; Cate, William, Joseph, Orang, Gilbert, Edward, Mary Jane

Rebecca CONRAD .... pg 450, 9 Nov 1832, will

Sylvia & her children to choose her master from Rebecca's sons Daniel Holmes & Robert Young CONRAD

Margaret FUNSTON .... pg 452, 6 Aug 1832 – 1 Jan 1833, gdn acct

servant

Edwin B. BURWELL ...... pg 454, 24 Jan 1831 – 21 Aug 1833, estate acct

Esther, Putman, Jesse, Harry, Spencer

.... pg 456, 20 Jan 1831 – 18 Jan 1833, estate acct

Ben; old negroes sold; negroes; Spencer, Jesse

153

James BEAN ....pg 457, 4 Mar 1833 in court, inv & appr

women Lucy, Peggy, boys Jesse, Philip, man Jack, boy Charles, man Ned

Edward McGUIRE ....pg 465, 1 Jan 1831 – 19 Jan 1833, estate acct

boy Dick died; Abbe

Daniel M. CAULEY .... pg 468, 24 Aug 1829 – 13 Jan 1833, estate acct

William & wife died

Stewart REDMAN .... pg 469, 1 Jan 1830 - 1 Mar 1832, gdn acct

negroes, Betty sold

WILL BOOK 18
1833 - 1835

Thomas CATHER .... pg 41, 2 Apr 1833 in court, inv & appr

boy Frank to serve 8-9 years

Jacob ANDERSON .... pg 52, 25 Apr 1833, will

housekeeper Margaret Camar; Emily Susan Camer

Daniel LEE .... pg 53, 6? Apr 1833, will

Charles & his daughter to be sold

John HAMILTON .... pg 56, 30 Apr 1828 - 17 Apr 1833, estate acct

old Toby died

.... pg 58, 1 Nov 1827 – 19 Apr 1833, estate acct

Abraham sold to DOWELL

George W. NELSON .... pg 66, 20 Dec 1832, inv & appr

man John

Adam BROWN .... pg 68, 12 May 1831 – 28 May 1833, estate acct

paid Ben, paid Joe?, Sally, girl

William HOLMES .... pg 70, Mar 1832 – 1 June 1833, estate acct

Moses

David HOLMES .... pg 72, 2 Oct 1832 - 17 May 1833, estate acct

Jerry

Lewis HOFF .... pg 79, 20 June 1831 - 3 June 1833, estate acct

Jesse

Joseph W. CARTER .... pg 85, 7 Feb 1832, inv & appr

man Jim, boy Presley, women Nancy, Amy; girl the lifetime of Miss
Jabez LANIE?

.... pg 87, 8 Feb 1832, sales

Presley, Nancy hired to Elizabeth N. CARTER; Sopha to Joseph R.
CARTER, Amy to Sol S. SPENGLER, Jim to Elizabeth JACKSON

Anthony SPENGLER Jr..............pg 91, 3 Nov 1832, inv & appr

woman & child

Anthony SPENGLER Jr...................... pg 92, 9 Nov 1832, sales

woman & child to Ann SPENGLER

Province McCORMICK...............pg 98, Dec 1830 – 1 July 1833, gdn acct

child kept by Bushrod McCORMICK; Richmond, Bob, Anthony

Robert WHITE.............................. pg 101, 4 May 1831, inv & appr

old Davy, old Becky & child, boy John

....pg 102, 3 May 11831, sales

Becky & child to John MAYHEW; old Davy to Baker WHITE

Joseph GAMBLE............................... pg 108, 30 July 1833, inv & appr

Lucy & child

Joseph BAKER .... pg 110, 14 July 1831, will

all negroes except Jim to wife Sarah BAKER; Jim age 10 to son Franklyn BAKER

Charles BRENT.................................pg 113, 12 Mar 1830, inv & appr

men Samuel, Henry, Solomon, Lydia & 2 children, Janey

Penelope J. BLAKEMORE................... pg 116, 20 June 1833, inv & appr

Nancy 27, Phil 9

.... pg 118, 7 Aug 1833 in court, sales

Nancy hired to Thomas SEEVERS; Phil hired to Jacob ENDERS

Francis ASH..................... pg 120, 3 May 11831 - 5 July 1833, estate acct

Bayless, Eveline

Francis BROWN ....pg 127, 1 Aug 1825, will

slaves to be hired out; Howard to daughters Ann BROWN & Elizabeth BROWN as long as they are unmarried & then sold; Betty & her increase in possession of daughter Susannah DAVIS wife of John C. DAVIS to be returned to the estate subject to division

Philip D. WILLIAMSON...
....pg 138, 1 Oct 1831 - 17 Aug 1833, estate acct

servants, woman

Joseph W. CARTER ....pg 142, 15 Feb 1832 - 20 July 1833, estate acct

Dennis

John Von RIESEN ....pg 147, 3 Oct 1831 – 2 Sept 1833, estate acct

negro Robert Mason

George Henry & Mary Sophia ASH ....
....pg 150, 15 Sept 1832 – 1 Oct 1833, gdn acct

slaves

Lewis LEFEVRE............................pg 151, 1833 – 18 Sept 1833, gdn acct

slaves of John LEFEVRE sold, his share of proceeds

Robert H. CHAPMAN of Tipton Co., TN .... pg 162, 18 June 1833, will

man purchased by me since the making of my will, his wife, & children
to wife

Henry JACKSON...pg 173, 2 Oct 1833, will

Mynna & her youngest child Anna Sa___ & their future increase to be
liberated; also boy John; boys Hyram & Lee to be free at the age of 21
to friend Simon CARSON; Larina? & her child Enoch, Jane & her
child to niece Mrs. Eveline WATSON late Eveline LONGACRE; Bill
age 16, boys Lewis, Antony to nephew Andrew Shannon?
LONGACRE; Hannah & her unnamed infant daughter, girl Henrietta
to niece Sarah LONGACRE

Alfred H. POWELL ....pg 176, 26 Aug 1831 – Oct 1833, estate acct

Milly died; negroes

Mary CATLETT .... pg 185, 24/25 Oct 1827, sales

Lynn?, Sina, Peter, Thomas to Marian CATLETT; Lawson, Alfred,
John to Jas. V. GLASS; Alexander, Lucy to William STEPHENSON;
Daniel, Dina, Lemmon, Jerry to Henry CATLETT; Eliza, Fentin to
Henrietta CATLETT; William, Emily to Elizabeth CATLETT; Rose,

George, Horace? to Sarah CATLETT; Charles, David to Susan CATLETT

Joseph K. CARTER ....pg 196, 19 Aug 1833, inv & appr

man Bob?, girl ___, woman L__

Joseph K. CARTER .... pg 198, 21 Aug 1833, sales

Elias hired by Daniel S. BONHAM

David STULTZ .... pg 208, Aug 1832, sales

man John to David _. DAMIER?; Hannah & child to Jacob SENSENEY; boy Henry to Anderston BROWN; boy Levi to George WRIGHT until he is age 15; boys Jo, Pete to Mrs. STULTZ until they are age 15; boy Jim kept by Thomas SPERRY; girl Sarah to Mrs. STULTZ

Mary STEPHENS .... pg 229, 1832 – 1 Jan 1834, estate acct

Robert & Emily are special legacies received by Mrs. __NGHT

Dudley BURWELL.............pg 236, 8 July 1832 – 1 Feb 1834, estate acct

negro, man

Margaret FUNSTON..............pg 248, 22 Apr 1833 - 1 Jan 1834, gdn acct

boy Washington

Francis ASH .... pg 253, 31 July 1828 - 1 Sept 1830, estate acct

negroes, Eveline

Henry JACKSON .... pg 263, 31 Mar 1834, inv & appr

woman Winney, Vine & child, Henrietta, Jane & child, Hannah & child, men John, William, boys Hiram, Lewis, Anthony, Legrand, child Anna Semerica?

Joseph GLASS ....pg 269, 31 Mar 1832 – 1 Apr 1834, estate acct

Abraham

Joseph GLASS ....pg 270, 1 Apr 1832 – 25 Mar 1834, estate acct

woman Rachel, Cuffee, Mingo, girl Sally, Louisa, Frank, John, Jim, Eliza

William ABBOTT .... pg 274, 7 Apr 1834, inv & appr

Janney 40, Emily 20, Dolly 19, Morgan 17, Fanny 15, Armisted 13, Reuben 11, Francis 9, _a_c_y 7, Mary 4, Betty 2, Matilda 4, Malinda 1

Orphans of William N. BURWELL ....
.... pg 278, 1 Jan 1831 – 17 Apr 1836, gdn acct

Ann?

Elisha J. HALL, Baltimore Co., MD .... pg 282, 14 Mar 1833, will

Mary, Harriet to wife Catharine HALL; man Albert, Presley, girl Ellen to son Edward E. HALL; slaves to wife Catherine HALL & children Susan J. HALL, Caroline L. HALL, Elizabeth L. HALL, Edward E. HALL, George W. HALL, & James W. HALL; the Eastern part of a tract of land & slaves to be sold

William ALEXANDER .... pg 299, 2 Jan 1833, will

Yamah/Tamah?, infant Milly, Lucinda, Diannah, Thomas, Becky, Phill to wife Mary ALEXANDER & at her death divided between daughters Ann, Jamima, & Eliza

Thomas CASTLEMAN .... pg 302, 20 Mar 1833, sales

man Vincent to John KERFOOT; man Bob, woman, Jackson to Joseph TULY; girl Kitty to William SOWERS; girl Jane to James CROSS

negroes hired: Ambrose, John, Charles, Gabriel, Polly, Mary & 2 children, Aggy, Hilbind?, Mary, Hary

Ann VANNOSDELNS .... pg 317, 1 Apr 1834, inv & appr

man Thomas

George PAYNE .... pg 319, 21 Dec 1833, inv & appr

John William Norman age 9 as of 1 Aug last, to serve until age 21

.... pg 320, 21 Dec 1833, sales

boy John William Norman to Anderton BROWN

Adam BOSTEYON .... pg 323, 29 June 1832, sales/ inv & appr

George, Patty, Harrt, Lydia, Charles, Clary, Charity, Sam

Adam BOSTEYON........pg 327, 18 June 1832 - 30 May 1834, estate acct

George, boy Charles, Harriet, Lydia

James LITTLE.................................... pg 363, 31 May 1834, will

boy Jack to stay in the family until he is 30 & then freed provided he is sent to Africa

Orphans of John HOPKINS ......pg 367, 1 Sept 1832 - Mar 1834, gdn acct

negroes, midwife for Nancy

Michael MANCK.............pg 371, 5 June 1832 - 21 June 1834, estate acct

Dick

Joseph BAKER ....pg 380, 17 Oct 1833, inv & appr

Jack, Alice & family Daniel, Isaac, John, George, Emily; Aaron, Sally & family Kitty, Mary, Harriet; Reuben, Charles

Daniel LEE................................ pg 383, 1 Sept 1834 in court, inv & appr

Charles. Sarah & child, Sally, Louisa

Nathan ANDERSON.......................................pg 388, 30 July 1831, will

man James to wife

....pg 390, 20 Apr 1832, codicil

James shall not be sold

Daniel LEE...pg 391, 1 Sept 1834 in court, sales

Sally to T.H. CROW, Joseph? SHEPHERD; Charles to D. Anderton BROWN?

James WILLIAMS .... pg 392, 1 Mar 1830 – 6 Nov 1832, estate acct

James; paid Dr. THOMAS bill for negro Fairfax?; John, Jane

Remarks: "...Leroy WILLIAMS claimed One Third certain negroes...On examining the deed it appears that Leroy is entitled to one half..."

John E. DANGERFIELD ....
.... pg 396, 4 Aug 1831 - 1 Sept 1834, estate acct

negro died, Abraham, Virgil?, negroes

161

David BROWN ....pg 401, 10 Aug 1834, will

Nancy to daughter Eliza; Suky & child to daughter Sarah Maria; Sarah, Caroline to wife; Jefferson, Elias to sons Newton & Hiram

Eliza G. WILLIAMS .... pg 404, 28 Mar 1831, will

man Jack to son Leroy P. WILLIAMS; boy Addam to grandson Peachy WILLIAMS; woman Maria, man Obanion to son Allen WILLIAMS; boy Bob, boy Tate, Jim, boy Lee to son James I. WILLIAMS

Charles C. BYRD .... pg 406, 6 Aug - Nov 1831, estate acct

girl Fillis sold; Ralph, Lewis

Lyles R. ROBINSON ....pg 407, 15 Sept 1834, will

Benah, Jenny, Henry to be sold

....pg 407, 17 Sept 1834, codicil

girl Mary Ann to daughter Angelina; girl Mary, now in his possession, to Rev. J.E. JACKSON

David BROWN ....pg 412, 7 Oct 1834 in court, inv & appr

man Jefferson, Elias, Sucky & child, Sarah, Nancy, Caroline

William ALEXANDER ....pg 413, 22 Aug 1834, inv & appr

Tamer, Becky, Philip. Lucinda, Thomas?, Dianah, Milly

Archibald MAGILL .... pg 414, 28 Nov 1832 – 6 Oct 1834, estate acct

girl Mary to D.H. CONRAD; boy Harry/Henry to David? DINGES; girl Harriet to Maj. MASON; Polly & 2 children to T.? CROW; woman Jenny to A.J. TRIBULL?

William HELM ....pg 424, 20 Dec 1832 - 6 Sept 1834, estate acct

negroes kept by Jacob GIBBONS

William HELM .... pg 426, 2 Nov 1832 – 1 Oct 1834, estate acct

Sarah & 3 children kept by John RICHARDSON; Sally & 4 children kept by M. HELM; Sarah & 3 children kept by William EDDY; Violet's 2 children kept by P.N. HELM; Lucy, Fridy; old Dick kept by Ann B. HELM; Sally & 3 children kept by John RICHARDS; Silla, Eliza, Henry, Betsey Ann, Emily, Ralph; Len?, Harriet, Isaac, Leannah, Mary, Matilda, Nelson

William B. PAGE.............pg 432, 15 Oct 1832 – 1 Nov 1834, estate acct

Buck, Charles, Solomon, Daniel; Lucy Ann, a midwife, Jane

George Henry & Mary Sophia ASH ....
....pg 436, 1 Oct 1833 - 1 Nov 1834, gdn acct

woman & children, Isaac, young negroes

Josiah CRAIG .... pg 441, 31 Oct 1834, sales

Rebecca to L_sinderf CRAIG; boy Dick to John CRAIG

Elizabeth W. BERKELEY ....
....pg 447, 5 June 1826 - 12 June 1834, gdn acct

Sam, money from sale of negroes belonging to the estate of Robert
BERKELEY; money from sale of negroes belonging to the estate of
Edmond BERKELEY

Julia BERKELEY ....pg 453, 5 June 1826 - 12 June 1834, gdn acct

Sam, money from sale of negroes belonging to the estate of Robert
BERKELEY; money from sale of negroes belonging to the estate of
Edmond BERKELEY

Frances A.T.. BERKELEY ....
....pg 459, 5 June 1826 - 12 June 1834, gdn acct

money from sale of negroes belonging to the estate of Robert
BERKELEY; money from sale of negroes belonging to the estate of
Edmond BERKELEY

Sophia C. BERKELEY ....pg 464, 5 June 1826 - 12 June 1834, gdn acct

money from sale of negroes belonging to the estate of Robert
BERKELEY; money from sale of negroes belonging to the estate of
Edmond BERKELEY

Lucy H. BERKELEY ....pg 466, 5 June 1826 - 12 June 1834, gdn acct

money from sale of negroes belonging to the estate of Robert
BERKELEY; money from sale of negroes belonging to the estate of
Edmond BERKELEY

John RUSSELL .... pg 476, 3 Dec 1834, will

Peter to wife Elizabeth

Jane E. WILLIAMS .... pg 479, 13 Dec 1834, will

woman Crese to daughter H. LONG

Thomas T. & Mary A. BYRD...
.... pg 480, 1 Oct 1829, - 27 Dec 1834, gdn acct

Frank, old woman & children; coffins for dec'd negroes; division of
negroes; paid Phillip BURWELL midwife fee of his negro woman;
Tom Potter, Watt, Tom Cooper, William Laws?, Richard Potter

died: Hampton, Ralph, George White, Abby, William White

Elizabeth G. WILLIAMS .... pg 485, 28 Aug 1834, inv & appr

legacies: Jack to Lucy P. WILLIAMS; Dinah & children to Hannah
WILLIAMS; Caroline & children to Eliza P. WILLIAMS; Obanon,
Maria to Allen WILLIAMS; Hampton, Robert, Tate, Lee, Jim to James
G. WILLIAMS; Adam to Erasmis Peachy WILLIAMS

Washington, Earnest?, Mary, Rachel, Ruthy, Simon, Eliza & child,
Harriet, Daniel, Lucy, Emily & child, Ann, Abner, Juliet, Henry,
Charles

Elias EARLE .... pg 486, 2 Aug 1834, inv & appr

boys Washington, Tom Bannister

Richard K. MEADE .... pg 488, 16 Apr 1833, inv & appr

man Jacob, Betsy & children Betsy, Jacob, Mary, boy Phil, boy, man
Harry, Edward, old Hannah, Vina, Quigly, Ireland, Sally & children,
Eliza & 3 children

Lyles R. ROBINSON .... pg 490, 13 Oct 1834, inv & appr

Henry 45, Biny & youngest child 2 years old, Mary Ann 3, Sam 16,
Charles 11, Henry 9, Robert 7, Jenny 40, Emily 13, William 10,
Hannah 30, Matilda 11, Isaac 9, Mary 10, Ann 5

Richard K. MEADE .... pg 497, 1 Apr 1833 – 31 Jan 1835, estate acct

woman Tab

Isaac BAKER .... pg 503, Mar 1833 – 26 Jan 1835, estate acct

Peter __stone jailed; negroes

Isaac BAKER ....pg 505, 22 Mar 1833 – 26 Jan 1835, estate acct

    Milly & child

Thomas MITCHELL .... pg 507, 4 Jan 1835, will

    Moses to be hired out for 3 years and then freed; woman Beck to be hired out unless she will leave the state and then she may be freed; old Hetty & old Sarah to be cared for from proceeds of rented land; slaves to be sold and equally divided between all the children of my son William

Harrison CLEVELAND .... pg 508, 31 Dec 1834, inv & appr

    Phillip, Henry, Celina

Benjamin S. REDMAN .... pg 508, Feb 1833 - 28 Feb 1835, gdn acct

    money paid in dividing of negroes; hire of negroes

Mary Catherine REDMAN ......pg 509, Mar 1833 - 28 Feb 1835, gdn acct

    money paid in dividing of negroes; hire of negroes

Frederick B. REDMAN .... pg 510, Feb 1833 - 28 Feb 1835, gdn acct

    George sold; hire of negroes

Robert CRIGLER .... pg 511, 1834, gdn acct

    negroes

Orphan children of French F. GLASSCOCK...
.... pg 511, 21 Oct 1830 - 14 Apr 1834, gdn acct

    boy Jackson

David STULTZ ....pg 514, 20 June 1832 – Jan 1835, estate acct

    man James?, woman Hannah; boy Pete to be kept until age 15

Jane E. WILLIAMS .... pg 1, 7 Jan 1835, inv & appr

old woman

John RUSSELL .... pg 20, 26 Jan 1835, inv & appr

man Peter

Edwin B. BURWELL.........pg 24, 7 Feb 1833 – 11 Mar 1835, estate acct

negroes kept by William STONE; Spencer, Elias?, Putnum

....pg 25, 5 July 1833 – 7 Apr 1835, estate acct

Esther, Aggy, Eliza, Jesse, Harry, Jim

James LITTLE.. pg 28, 14 July 1834, inv & appr

boy Jack

Christopher CRIGLER .... pg 37, 1 Nov 1825 – 2 June 1835, gdn acct

Lydia, man, woman

Maza McCORMICK .... pg 43, 21 Apr 1831 - 18 Mar 1834, estate acct

2 negroes sold

Lucy McCORMICK.................pg 45, Sept 1831 – 1 July 1835, gdn acct

young negroes kept by Isaac McCORMICK; Tom, Juliet, Maria; Juliet
sold

Province McCORMICK........ pg 48, 10 May 1832 - 1 July 1835, gdn acct

equality in division of negroes

Joseph SNAPP..................pg 51, 9 Nov 1832 - 26 Dec 1833, estate acct

John

Harriet HOPKINS .... pg 53, 23 June 1834 – June 1835

Frank?

Lyles R. ROBINSON .... pg 56, 28 Oct 1834, sales

Henry to Jonathan SMITH; Biny & child age 2, Emily, Robert to A.S. TIDBALL; Jenny, William to Jacob BAKER; Sam to Mathius RITTER; Charles to Joseph SHEPHERD; Henry, Hannah & her children Matilda & Isaac to Branch JORDAN; Ann to J.E. JACKSON

Alexander MILLER .... pg 63, 30 June 1834, will

all slaves to wife Elizabeth MILLER & daughter Maria B. EARLE

Joseph K. CARTER .... pg 64, 27 May 1833 – 3 Aug 1835, estate acct

servant, negroes

Alexander CHURCHILL ....pg 67, 11 Aug 1835, inv & appr

boy, girl

George BLAKEMORE ....pg 68, 25 Sept 1833, inv & appr

Jerome, Big Peter, Little Peter

Catharine R. MILLER ....pg 71, 25 July 1835, inv & appr

man Henry Morgan, woman Sinah; "...appraise..with the exception of a negro man who has run off..."

Francis BROWN ....pg 74, 25 Sept 1833, inv & appr

L__, Tr_y__, Larkin, Hansford, Furlong, George, Howard, Thomas, William, Russell, Marcus, Paracutis?, Agnes, Charlotte & child Eli, May, Brient?

Levi HICKS ....pg 76, 5 Nov 1834, inv & appr

men George, Charles, boy Richard, Amy & her child, Maria 9 or 10, Maria 2

Orphans of William N. BURWELL ....
.... pg 93, 30 Apr 1825 - 31 Sept 1835, gdn acct

negroes moved from James Town to Norfolk to Andriana?; negroes in lower county; paid Old Lydia for a midwife for a woman of the estate; Emily, Jim, Mos?, Seneca; lot of negreos to Phillip BURWELL; Daniel

Henry JACKSON............. pg 101, 9 Nov 1833 - 23 Sept 1834, estate acct

slaves delivered to: Eveline WATSON, Sarah G. LONGACRE, & Ebenezer LONGACRE

James H. CARSON Jr. .... pg 106, 16 Jan 1834 – 30 Sept 1835, gdn acct

Beverly

James WILLIAMS .... pg 109, 1831 – 18 Sept 1835, estate acct

NOTE: man Robin absconded in Nov 1829 & has not been heard of since; Robin's wife Clary died 21 Mar 1829; their son, boy Jack, died in the fall of 1829

John DUCKWALL ....pg 111, 12 Mar 1834 - Oct 1835, gdn acct

John

Orphans of George ASH ...... pg 112, 24 Dec 1834 - 1 Nov 1835, gdn acct

women & children were boarded out; young Tom & John died; Neill, defended in court by D.W. BARTON was sold under court order – he attempted to kill Marcus D. BAKER

David CATHER .... pg 126, 5 Dec 1835, inv & appr

Benjamin 45, Sarah 40, Michael 5, Elizabeth 6, Isaac 1, Grace 11 months

.... pg 131, 7 Mar 1835, sales

Ben to James CATHER from 1 Apr to 25 Dec

Samuel J. SHACKELFORD .... pg 136, 15 May 1835, inv & appr

man Lewis?, Jerry, David, Thornton, Hampton, Sanford, Alice, Catharine, Sidney & 2 children John & William, Emily & child Elizabeth

Joseph BERRY Jr........................ pg 140, 4 Jan 1836 in court, inv & appr

Alia_, Emily & child, William, Rubin, Harriet

Thomas MITCHELL ....pg 145, 12 Aug 1835, inv & appr

Moses emancipated at the expiration of 3 years as stated in the Testator's will; woman Rebecca

Ann FUNSTEN.................pg 151, 24 May 1834 – 1 Jan 1836, gdn acct

Nick

Joseph GLASS ....pg 154, 31 Mar 1834 – 1 Jan 1836, estate acct

cash received for Louisa & her child Charles; Teller, Molly & 2 children, Frank, Abram, John, man Mingo, Cuffee, Rachel, Jim, girl Sally, Eliza, Isaac

"Negro man Mingo who was devised by Jos. GLASS dec'd to his daughter Emeline was sold...stealing...publicly whipped...believed he was making his arrangements to elope during the Christmas holidays. Given under my hand this 1 day Feby 1836." signed Samuel BENT?

Thomas GRUBBS............pg 162, 26 Aug 1830 - 28 Jan 1836, estate acct

negroes kept by R. WAY 3 years; negroes sold; negroes hired

Francis BROWN ....pg 163, 25 Dec 1834 – 15 Feb 1836, estate acct

William/Wm, George, Larkin, Agnes, Lewis?, Brent, Pat, Furlong

William Byrd PAGE ....pg 168, 6 Oct 1834 – 20 Mar 1836, estate acct

30 blankets for negroes; Charles, Solomon, Daniel

Joseph W. CARTER ....pg 170, 31 July 1833 - 8 Mar 1830, estate acct

Sophia, girl, Jim

Elias EARLE..................pg 174, 21 Aug 1834 - 17 Mar 1836, estate acct

2 negroes sold; cash received for Washington, Tom

David HOLMES.............. pg 219, 24 Oct 1833 – 9 May 1834, estate acct

paid Robert Y. CONRAD for Jerry

Susan BALDWIN ....pg 220, 8 Mar 1836, will

man Amos to be emancipated after sister Judith's decease

George RAYNOLDS .... pg 223, 23 Apr 1834, will

all slaves, except man Jesse, to be hired & then set free after debts have been payed; Jesse to daughter-in-law Frances C. RAYNOLDS the widow of dec'd son George H. RAYNOLDS

George RAYNOLDS ....pg 224, 17 Apr 1835, codicil

Jesse was disposed

Adam BOSTEYAN........ pg 225, 11 Dec 1834 - 10 June 1836, estate acct

George, Harriet, Lydia; boy Charles sold

Robert VANCE ....pg 228, 8 Sept 1836, inv & appr

man 45?, girl 16

....pg 230, 10 Sept 1836, sales

girl Eliza to Bryan M. STEPHENS; man Adam to James H. SOWERS; boy West? to serve until 21 years of age to Isaac B. VANCE

Francis STRIBLING ....pg 238, 18 Nov 1823 – 1 July 1836, estate acct

valuation of slaves; Hannah; paid Robert MONTGOMERY for Giffy; girl conveyed to Magmus & Nancy STRIBLING by F. STRIBLING dec'd

Christian HALL............................ pg 245, 1836 - 1 Feb 1836, estate acct

slave acct settled

Levi HICKS ....pg 247, 20 Oct 1834 - 27 July 1836, estate acct

negro, girl

Robert CUGLER ....pg 253, Oct 1835 – July 1836, gdn acct

negro

Edwin B. BURWELL........pg 261, 7 Apr 1835 – 25 July 1836, estate acct

Esther, old Henry

William BRENT...pg 269, 1 Aug 1836, gdn acct

court decree for a difference in negroes

Rebecca DUCHWALL.............pg 269, 3 Jan 1835 - 1 Jan 1836, gdn acct

Bob

Charles HULET....................................pg 270, 24 Aug 1836, inv & appr

woman Sally

171

Charles HULET .... pg 271, 25 Aug 1836, sales

Sally to Mrs. ENDERS

Dawson McCORMICK .... pg 274, 12 Aug 1834, inv & appr

women Lucinda, Fanny, Maria; Sarah, Rose, Tom, John, James Jones, Bob, Samuel Thompson, Jim Lee/See, Nat Mossie, Lorenzo, Caty, Molly, Jnda, William

Mary A. POLK .... pg 297, 25 June 1835 - 7 July 1836, gdn acct

negroes

Duvall POLK .... pg 298, 15 Jan 1835 - 7 July 1836, gdn acct

negroes

Susan N. POLK .... pg 298, 6 Jan 1834 - 1 July 1836, gdn acct

negroes

Robert W. POLK .... pg 298, 20 Dec 1833 – 7 July 1836, gdn acct

negroes

Elizabeth ROADS .... pg 301, 22 Sept 1836, will

negroes to Jane WATERS

Archibald MAGILL .... pg 303, 10 Mar 1832, inv & appr

George 60, John, Enoch, Phil, boy Harry/Henry, Harriet, Kitty, Mary, John, William, Polly & 2 children, Jenny

.... pg 309, 29 Nov 1832, sales

Harriet to Maj. John D. EARLE; Mary to T.H. CONRAD; Polly & 2 children to Thomas CROW; Harry/Henry to Daniel DINGES; John to Richard TIMBERLAKE; William to P__ McCORMICK; Enoch to John __ANDE; John to Joseph LONG; Phil to John L. MAGILL; Jenny to __ _. MAGILL; old George to __ CRISER?

Josiah CRAIG .... pg 323, 31 Oct 1834, sales

Maria to Miss Emily CRAIG; Ned? to Parkinson CRAIG?; boy Duke to John CRAIG

172

John HICKS ....pg 329, 1 Apr – 1 Oct 1836, gdn acct

cash for proportion of negroes

Mary HICKS ....pg 330, 1 Apr – 1 Oct 1836, gdn acct

cash for proportion of negroes

Levi HICKS ....pg 330, 1 Apr – 1 Oct 1836, gdn acct

cash for proportion of negroes

Amelia HICKS ....pg 331, 1 Apr – 1 Oct 1836, gdn acct

cash for proportion of negroes

James MITCHELL .... pg 332, 29 June 1830 - 25 Dec 1836, estate acct

Ned, Charity, Violett, Venus, Lucy & 2 children, Clarey, Frederick, Charlott, Sally & child, Harriett, Betty, James, Harrison, Bob, Maria & child, Judy & 2 children, Hannah & 2 children, Daphney & child, Elias, Ben, Eliza, Kissey, Jared, Louisa, Jack Thruston, Amnias?, Arena, Carstine?, George, Ned; negroes sold 2_ Dec 1833; boarded out: Anna & 2 children by David ___, Hannah & 2 children by T. HUMSTED, Lucy & 2 children by John SOUTHAN

John MORGAN ....pg 338, 6? Nov 1837, inv & appr

Solomon, Isaac, Jeny, Philip, Dangerfield, Sawny, big Dick, Edmund, Abram, Frederick, young Tom, Hezakiah, Willis, big Tom, Pete, James, George, Harry, Andrew, Daniel, John, Sarah, Rachel, Minny & 3 children Daniel, Frederick, & Lewis, Lavina & 4 children Lucy, Margaret, Robert, & Jeny, Betty & child Joseph, Milly & 2 children _dson & Susan, Emily, Sucky, Virgin & 2 children James & Charly, Hannah & 4 children Harriet, Barnet, Nelly, & Gracy, Molly, Lucy, Nelly & 2 children Eliza & Della; Matilda & 3 children not considered worth anything in consequence of a suit depending __ her freedom

Philip C. SPENGLER ....pg 340, 11 Aug 1836, will

Richard, Nathan, Judy & her child Thornton, Caroline to wife Margaret E.

Orphans of George ASH .... pg 342, 2 Nov 1835 - 7 Oct 1836, gdn acct

woman & children put out to lowest bidder; negroes supported at HOLYDAY for 8 years; by hire of negroes for 1835 deducting __ __ __ reason of his prosecution for crime & sale; old Gabriel a runaway?

Elizabeth BRUCE .... pg 343, 6 May 1835 – Oct 1836, estate acct

paid R. MONTGOMERY legacy to Sophia | negro girl

Dawson McCORMICK ...... pg 345, 5 Apr 1834 – 5 Sept 1835, estate acct

Florinda, woman; midwife for Molly; woman Katy kept by Samuel McCORMICK; Kate died; cash of Herbert WASHINGTON for sale of _att

Isaac HITE .... pg 354, 31 Oct 1827, will

slaves from the Guildford Tract to son Madison; slaves from the Bellgrove Tract to wife Ann; wife is to give 2 young men & 2 young women to her sons when they reach legal age; daughters to receive negroes when they are of legal age or marry

.... pg 358, 18 Feb 1837, 3ʳᵈ codicil

after the death of my wife her slaves are to be divided between the children living at the time of my death

Elizabeth G. WILLIAMS ....

.... pg 366, 19 Jan 1833 – 2_ Aug 1834, estate acct

difference in distribution of negroes

Isaac BAKER .... pg 367, 8 Apr 1835 - 10 Oct 1836, estate acct

Lewis, Milly & her children

George RAYNOLDS .... pg 369, 29 Dec 1836, inv & appr

Joseph Davis, Thomas Pollard, William Pollard, James Pollard, Charlotte Pollard, Mary Pollard, Francis Pollard, Simon Ball

Westley COE .... pg 376, 16 Feb 1835, inv & appr

George, Isaac, Warner, Susan

Westley COE .... pg 377, 16 Feb 1835, sales

George to to widow; Isaac to John C. MILLER; Warner, Susan to Thomas HOOK

Josiah CRAIG .... pg 379, 30 Oct 1834, inv & appr

women Rebecca, Maria

Philip C. SPENGLER .... pg 384, 29 Dec 1836, inv & appr

man Richard, Juda, Mary Carstun?, Nathan

Anna FUNSTON .... pg 388, 27 Feb 136 – 25 Dec 1836, gdn acct

Dick

children of Richard K. MEADE ...... pg 406, 20 Sept 1833- 1837, gdn acct

"...from Langly in part payment for his daughter Hannah who was sold for $150 at the request of all the family being 38 years old and having had six? children..."; Jared, Phil, Simon, Ireland, old Lewis, Israel, Vina, Viny, Cymon

Gabriel H. DAVIS ....pg 418, Feb 1837, will

Bet, Ket, John to wife Mary to serve until they are intitled to their freedom; boy Bill to son David DAVIS to serve until he is intitled to his freedom

Rebecca DUCKWALL .... pg 426, 20 Jan – 24 Dec 1836, gdn acct

Bob, Molly

Isaac HITE .... pg 433, 17 Jan 1837, inv & appr

Nat?, Flank? Thornton age 61-69, Frederick 60, Reuben 65, Job? 61, Walter? 55, Sam 49, Anthony 47, Jerry 36, Jim 35, Carter Lane? 30, Frank Jennings? 50, Ben 50, Bill 44, Manuel 21, Marcus 18, Robert 17, Franklin 14, Westley 9, Jim or James 7, Elias 6, Elijah 4, Frank 7, Washington 2, Charles 50, Abby 67, Priscilla 58, Nelly 62, Hannah 63, Nancy 59, Fanny 40?, Truelove 53, Betty 41?, Sally 28 dec'd, Milly 17, Mary 15 dec'd, Betsey 12, Margaret or Peggy 12, Frances 10, Lucy 11, Elizabeth 8, Maria 11, Emily 2, Louisa 2, Hannah 1

Orphans of Margaret LARUE ....
....pg 446, 13 Feb 1834 - 25 Mar 1837, gdn acct

Orphans: James W., Alfred L.P., John D., Francis C., & Robert A.I?. LARUE

use of woman for 2 years; cash at division of negroes

Henry JAMES .... pg 448, 18 Sept 1832, estate acct

negroes

Conrad CREBS ....pg 449, 31 Mar 1831 – 12 Apr 1837, estate acct

cash paid David W. BARTON fee against Dick

William C. WILLIAMS ....pg 452, 29 Aug 1836, inv & appr

Moses, George, Lucy

John WHISSENT ....pg 454, 21 Mar 1837, inv & appr

James, Caroline, Sarah, Dorcus

Lucy McCORMICK................... pg 460, July 1835 - 1 Jan 1837, gdn acct

Tom, man

Thomas MITCHELL........... pg 464, 3 Mar 1835- 5 June 1837, estate acct

2 invalid slaves; man Moses

Robert CRIGLER............................ pg 465, Oct – 31 Dec 1836, gdn acct

negroes

Benjamin S. REDMAN .... pg 465, Feb 1835 - 1837, gdn acct

negroes, girl Esther; Winny sold

Mary Catharine REDMAN .... pg 466, Feb 1835 - 1837, gdn acct

George, Adam; George sold; old man sold to Benjamin BERKLEY

Martha BARTON .... pg 47, 7 Apr 1829, 2nd codicil

men Charles & Willis purchased by Dr. Robert B. BARTON, part of mother's legacy to me, to granddaughter Martha Virginia BARTON daughter of son Thomas W. BARTON

WILL BOOK 20
1837 - 1841

Henry J. JACKSON............ pg 5, 9 Dec 1833 - 31 July 1837, estate acct

Negro Winny, negro

Samuel J. SHACKELFORD..
..................pg 9, 25 May 1835 – 11 July 1837, estate acct

David sold; Tony, David in jail; George, woman; negros sold;
Hampson

Solomon VANMETRE...... pg 12, 26 Feb 1833 – 1 June 1835, estate acct

negroes; 32 negroes boarded by H. VANMETRE

Daniel MYTINGER.............................pg 15, 17 Oct 1836, inv & appr

Ambrose 17/18, Calvin 16, Lucy 50, Frances 10

David CATHER.................pg 25, 25 Jan 1835 - 1 Sept 1837, estate acct

child kept by Joseph FISHER; Sarah sold; Ben

John M. BROME.............. pg 26, 19 Mar 1835 – 28 Aug 1837, estate acct

___? Moses; Waverly sold

Robert McCANDLASS............................ pg 32, 2 May 1837, inv & appr

Walnut Grove Farm

negroes

.... pg 35, June 1837, inv & appr

Spont? Run Farm, Clarke Co

Matt 36 & 2 infants, Eliza 5, Jim 11, Aaron 50, Daniel 60

....pg 35, 25 Oct 1837, inv & appr

Walnut Grove

Nacy 80, Dale? 75, Jacob 65, Ann 13, Amanda 14, Caroline 19 &
female child 17 months, Sam 10, Josiah 11, Jacob 20, Mary 15,
Ralph 40, Bailly? 40, Sam 36, Edward 10, Frederick 13, Henry 19,
Zack 19, Nat 16, Tom 7, Priscilla 16, Jane 6, Sarah 35 & female

child 18 months, Joe Sutton 8, Francis 7, Drucilla 3, Mazy 32 & female child 9 months, Lucy 10, Nelson 6, Milly 26, Sophy 8, Archy 5

Mary STUBBLEFIELD ...... pg 36, 5 Dec 1834 - 23 May 1837, estate acct

Chloe & children sold to John RICHARDSON

Benjamin KENDRICK ...... pg 42, 31 Oct 1835 – 23 Dec 1836, estate acct

negroes sold, girl Clara sold

Orphans of George ASH .... gp 45, 14 Dec 1836, - 1 Nov 1837, gdn acct

negroes, woman & children

Daniel TAGGART .... pg 47, 3 Feb 1836, sales

residue of time for William, a free boy, to B. TAYLOR; man William to Joseph McGOVERN; girl Amie? to John W. PITMAN; Evans wife & child to Taylor L.? DANIELS

Sarah Ann BAKER .... pg 52, 29 Dec 1835 – 1 Jan 1838, gdn acct

negroes; Caroline

Robert W.BAKER .... pg 53, 29 Dec 1835 – 1 Jan 1838, gdn acct

negroes; Hannah, Charles

Solomon VANMETRE .... pg 53, 1 June 1830 - 12 July 1833, curator acct

girl; child kept by D. EYSLERS; 2 negroes to Samuel M. SPINGLER until Christmas

Joseph GLASS .... pg 57, 1 Jan 1836 – 1 Jan 1838, estate acct

man Cuffee, Frank, Rommey, woman Teller, Molly, Sally, Mingo, Jim, Rachel, Eliza

Mary SHIP .... pg 71, 12 Nov 1825 – 5 Oct 1837, estate acct

difference in negro interest

James BAKER Jr. .... pg 72, 4 Oct 1823 - 1 Jan 1838, estate acct

Caroline

Nicholas HOOPER .... pg 76, 22 Mar 1836 – 29 Dec 1837, estate acct

Rachel

Daniel TAGGART .... pg 78, 3 Feb 1836 - 31 Jan 1838, estate acct

girl Amy; Billy sold to Joseph McGOVERN; Evan's wife & child, girl Ann also sold? to Joseph McGOVERN

Rebecca DUCKWALL .... pg 81, 12 Jan 1837 - 1 Jan 1838, gdn acct

boy Bob, girl Molly

Robert CRIGLER .... pg 82, 1 Jan 1837- 1 Jan 1838, gdn acct

negroes

Joseph DUCKWALL .... pg 99, 1833 – 15 Mar 1838, gdn acct

Harry, John

John BELL .... pg 106, Dec 1837, will

boy George to son John _. BELL; woman Lotty to be free if she wishes, otherwise to go to William? GILKESON or son John

Conrad HUNTSBERRY .... pg 115, 30 Mar 1838, inv & appr

men Elijah, Michael, Edwan, Joe, woman Grace, woman, 4 children named Susan

William CAMPBELL .... pg 120, 9 Apr 1838, will

women Ailcia, Hannah to wife & at her death Ailcia & her daughter Charlotte to son James Harrison CAMPBELL; child Mary Elizabeth to daughter Eliza CARTMELL; boy Willoughby, girl Barbara to son Franklin CAMPBELL

William LYNN .... pg 123, 27 Feb 1837, inv & appr

five? negro slaves (not sold)

Charles J. LOVE .... pg 137, 20 May 1837, will

Betsy & child, Stephen, & John sons of Betsy to daughter Frances M. FALLS; Betty & children little Jim, Easter, Mary, Gustavus, & Bill, Barbara & children Edwin & Moses; Fisher, Thomas, & Wilson sons of Sucky to Samuel T. LOVE in trust for Charles J. LOVE; Edmond, Barny, Randall, to son Richard M.S. LOVE; Betty daughter of Edy, Lucy & children under the age of Thomas? to daughter Mary Sijeniora? LOVE; Euordo?, Jane & her children & Eliza her nurse, to Harriet Campbell LOVE; Eliza's son Thornton to John DYSORE? & at his death to Harriett Campbell LOVE

James LITTLE................. pg 139, 12 July 1836- 20 June 1838, estate acct

woman

Catharine R. MILLER.... pg 143, 21 Apr 1835 – 25 June 1838, estate acct

Henry, a runaway; Sinah

Dawson McCORMICK........ pg 145, 5 Oct 1836 – 1 Jan 1838, estate acct

negroes

Evelyn & Mary A. PAGE............. pg 147, July 1832 - Dec 1837, gdn acct

servants; Squire, property of Mary PAGE; George, property of Evelyn PAGE; Ben property of Mary A. PAGE; Molly sold to Mrs. Ann R. PAGE she belonging to Evelyn PAGE; George, Carston, Charles, Solomon

Henry C. & George S. BAKER............. pg 148, 31 July 1838, inv & appr

share of proceeds of slave

Catharine BAKER................................ pg 155, 19 June 1838, 1st codicil

girl Sarah to daughter Julia Ann BAKER

Hetty Z. ARTHUR .... pg 157, no date, will

woman Rody & her brother Henry, woman Lucy to brother Robert; Silla & her only child Charles, left to me by my grandmother, to brother David

.... pg 157, 4 Aug 1838, 1st codical

Jacob sold

Henry W. BAKER.................... pg 160, 3 Sept 1838 in court, inv & appr

woman Sally, man Jefferson, girls Charlotte, Sarah

.... pg 162, 31 May 1838, sales

Sally, Jefferson, Charlotte, Sarah to Catharine BAKER

Edmund SHACKELFORD .... pg 165, 28 June 1838, will

negroes to be hired out; boy Thornton, who is about the same age of my nephew, to nephew Edmund Shackleford DARLINGTON –

Thornton is to learn the trade of blacksmith until he is 21 & then serve nephew Edmund; Edmund to care for old James & his sister Berella

George RAYNOLDS ....pg 167, 4 July 1836 – 1 Sept 1838, estate acct

boy, girl, man, boys James, William, woman

Ann T. SHIP.....................pg 169, 15 Jan 1837 - 5 Jan 1838, gdn acct

Jerry

Rebecca Morgan, a free woman of color.......... pg 173, 22 May 1832, will

granddaughters are Rebecca Fountain & Charlotte Spencer; brother is Frank Robinson; son is Nicholas; daughters are Charlotte & Judy

Eleanor MAGRUDER.................................pg 174, 11 Sept 1838, will

Monimia?, Moses, Robert to son William who he has carried to Kentucky; David, Lucy to son Thomas who he has with him in Kentucky; Mary, Agnes, Thomas to son Daniel; Frank, Juliet, Jerry to son Robert; Albert, Fanny, Dolly to son Adrian; Peyton, Matilda, Godfrey to daughter Frances; William, Sarah to daughter Maza; Hampton, Augusta to daughter Susan; Joseph, John Thomas, slaves for life, to daughter Ellen; "further support for my said husband,...to my daughter Maza my negro woman Nancy during his life and at his death...shall be emancipated..."

John PAGE...........................pg 179, 9 Nov 1835 - 17 Oct 1838, gdn acct

John, Solomon, midwife Sarah

Orphans of George ASH ..... pg 181, 14 Dec 1837 – 1 Nov 1838, gdn acct

Henry, old & useless slaes supported, midwife Milly

Catharine BAKER................................. pg 189, 17 Dec 1838, inv & appr

man Jefferson, woman Sally, Charlotte, Sarah

Isaac BAKER .... pg 192, 6 June 1837 – 24 Nov 1838, estate acct

Milly & her children to George W. BAKER administrator of Johnathan ROBINSON dec'd

Ann FUNSTON................... pg 201, 17 June 1837 - 4 Feb 1839, gdn acct

servant, Nick

Robert CRIGLER..............pg 202, 1 Jan 1838 - 1 Jan 1839, gdn acct

negros

Thomas MITCHELL......... pg 206, 5 June 1837 - 1 Dec 1838, estate acct

Moses

Susan C. APPOLD late Susan C. Von REESEN.......................................
.... pg 214, 20 Feb 1838 - 28 Feb 1839, gdn acct

woman died

Cornelia F. TOWERS..........pg 215, 20 Feb 1838 – 11 Feb 1839, gdn acct

woman died

Gabriel H. DAVIS..............................pg 223, Mar 1837, inv & appr

boy William servitude for 6 years, girl Kitt servitude for 4 years, boy
John servitude for 10 years

N.C. BAKER's Orphans .... pg 225, 10 Dec 1838, supplement inv

"Memo...from the Estate eof Mrs. C. Baker, was due from her for the
purchase of certain slaves belonging to the Estate of H.M. Baker dec'd
which has been sold by special commissioners..."

Jacob FRYE .... pg 225, 4 May 1838, will

Patty & her daughter Truelove to daughter Judith FRYE; girl Cilia? to
son Mordecai B. FRYE; girl Rachael to Mordecai B. FRYE in trust for
daughter-in-law Martha FRYE wife of son James FRYE

John RUSSELL ....pg 227, 1 Jan 1835 – 1 Jan 1839, estate acct

runaway estate negros

Robert McCANDLESS .... pg 252, 2 Jan 1838, slave sale

Mall & 4 youngest children, Ann, Amanda, Caroline & infant, boys
Sam, Isaac, Mary, Sam, Zach?, Nat, boy Tom, Priscilla, Mazy & infant,
Lucy, Nelson, to Branch JORDAN; Jacob, Bartly, Ralph, Aaron,
Frederick, Milly & 2 children Sophy & Archy to Robert P.
McCANDLESS; boys Edward, Joe Sutton to Conrad HUNTSBERRY;
Henry to Mrs. STEPHERSON; old man Daniel to Otway
McCORMISH; old man Wall to R. HAWKINS

20 Sept 1838: Francis to John PRICE

8 Jan 1839: Sarah & children Druscilla 4, Winnifred 3, & infant to R.P. McCANDLESS & G.W. SEEVERS; Amanda 6 to R.P. McCANDLESS

William JACKSON............pg 266, 12 July 1826 – 1 Jan 1839, estate acct

Daniel, Robin

William LYNN................pg 269, 15 Feb 1837 - 1 Apr 1839, estate acct

negroes sold

George L. BAKER...................pg 275, 1838 - 1 Mar 1839, gdn acct

slaves sold from the estate of Henry W. BAKER

Henry C. BAKER................pg 277, 1838 - 1 Mar 1839, gdn acct

slaves sold from the estate of Henry W. BAKER

Robert McCANDLESS...... pg 286, 2 Apr 1837 – 8 May 1839, estate acct

negroes, woman, cash of Robert P. McCANDLESS of his purchase of negroes; cash of Conrad HUNTSBERRY for boys Edwin, Joe Sutton; cash of Branch JORDAN for purchase of negroes; for Mall; cash of Mrs. STEPHERSON for Henry; girl Frances purchased by John PRICE; cash from Otway McCORMICK for man Daniel; cash of R.P. McCANDLESS & George W. SEEVERS for Sarah & her 3 young children; cash of R.P. McCANDLESS for girl Amanda

Thomas ROBERTS........................ pg 303, 4? Aug 1837, sales

man Osburn to John ROBERTS; man Harry to B. JORDAN

.... pg 308, 2 June 1837- 25 July 1839, estate acct

superannuated Lina cared for by Marshee? WEAVER & supported by Philip HOOVER; Lucy; hired servant belonging to Dr. McGUIRE

George RAYNOLDS .... pg 324, 6 Sept 1838 – 6 Sept 1839, estate acct

girl, William, Charlotte, James, Thoms, Mary, Amelia, Simon

Joseph DUCKWALL .... pg 327, Nov 1837 - 1 Jan 1839, gdn acct

Harry. John

Orphans of R.K. MEADE .... pg 329, 19 Feb 1837 – 1 Mar 1839, gdn acct

Langley, Harry, girl, Cymon (Simon?), Betsey, Jacob, Ireland, Vena, little Jacob, Cymon purchased by Mrs.? STRINGFELLOW, big Jacob, Eliza's child, old Lewis, Eliza, Brutus' children

William MEADE................ pg 334, 19 Feb 1837 – 1 Mar 1839, gdn acct

old Lewis

Nathaniel BURWELL .... pg 349, 15 Sept 1835- 13 Feb 1839, gdn acct

Jim, Miles, Randolph, Maria, Charlotte, Martin?, Jerry, Jenny, Nancy

Orphans of George ASH ....

....pg 352, 31 Dec 1838 – 31 Dec 1839, gdn acct

negroes, Maria & 3 children kept by Robert WIDDOWS; child

George H. ASH .... pg 353, 22 Dec 1838 – 1 Dec 1839, gdn acct

Milly, Strother, & 2 children

Benjamin L. REDMAN......pg 359, June 1837 – 4 Oct 1839, gdn acct 188

Esther hired to John SHUMATE

Sarah A. BAKER .... pg 359, 1 Jan 1838 – 1 Jan 1840, gdn acct

Catherine, woman Caroline, George, girl Mary

Robert W. BAKER.................. pg 361, 1 Jan 1838 – 1 Jan 1840, gdn acct

woman Hannah, negroes, Charles

William CAMPBELL........................... pg 362, 24 May 1838, inv & appr

boys John, Jim, woman Nancy

....pg 364, 25 May 1838, sales

man John, boy Jim to George M. WALL; woman Nancy to M.B. CARTMELL

William CAMPBELL...................... pg 366, 25 May 1838 – 16 Jan 1840

Ceaser sold

Robert HETERICK .... pg 377, 4 July 1839, will

slaves to wife Mary Ried HETERICK & at her death to her children; little Rachel to daughter Elizabeth

Peter LAUCK .... pg 378, 12 Mar 1838, will

all slaves to wife

Rev. Joseph GLASS .... pg 380, 1 Jan 1835 - 21 Dec 1839, estate acct

old negro kept by R.M. CAMPBELL; Cuffee supported by Stephen JENKINS, Jim, Henry, Molly, Rachel, girl Eliza, Frank, boy Harry, man Mingo

Francis ASH .... pg 386, 18 Nov 1836 – 9 Jan 1840, estate acct

Bayly apprehended & sold

"Note, Negro Bayly belonging to the Estate of Francis Ash dec'd (one of the slaves bequeathed to Mrs. Ash for life)...apprehended in New Orleans, and lodged in jail at Natchez, was sold in jail on the 16th of September 1836 to Francis J. Ash..."

Hetty Z. ARTHUR .... pg 388, Sept 1838, inv & appr

Frederick County:

woman Silla & her son Charles bequeathed to D.W. BARTON; Jesse in jail & then sold

.... pg 391, 22 Sept 1838, inv & appr

Rockbridge County:

old woman Lucy, Rhody, Harry, boy Charles belonging to D.W. BARTON

George N. BLAKEMORE ....
.... pg 393, 5 Aug 1833 - 8 Dec 1834, estate acct

old women Jenny, Maria kept by _____

Conrad HUNTSBERRY ....
.... pg 395, 7 Mar 1838 - 19 Dec 1839, estate acct

Edward, Elijah

Philip HOOVER .... pg 400, 28 Jan 1840, will

girl Julianna to daughter Elizabeth AFFLICK until age 28 years at which time she may choose to go to Liberia & if she declines to remain a slave & the property of Elizabeth; woman Harriett to daughter Rebecca at which time she may choose to go to Liberia & if she declines to remain with Rebecca

Joseph DUCKWALL ....pg 404, 1 Jan 1839 - 1 Jan 1840, gdn acct

Harry

William GEORGE .... pg 408, 14 Dec 1839, inv & appr

Jack 35, Harry 2 1/2

Warner & Mary WHITE .... pg 409, 3 Jan 1838, inv & appr

woman Harr? 26, Ellen 7, child Ann, girl Sydney

Mary WHITE .... pg 414, 21 Dec 1837 – 11 Mar 1840, estate acct

paid B. BISON for his interest in 2 slaves sold by Mrs. WHITE; paid Warner WHITE for his interest in 2 slaves sold by Mrs. WHITE; Jesse T.? WHITE's share of 2 slaves sold by Mrs. WHITE as Exec of Warner WHITE; Westly GRUBBS' (being ¼ part) of the slaves of Warner WHITE sold since her death

Warner WHITE ....pg 416, 1838 – 11 Mar 1840, estate acct

cost incurred in sale of negroes

Robert HETERICK .... pg 416, 6 Apr 1840, inv & appr

Jarad 40, Patty 60, James 15, Rachel 13, girl Sidney 10, Fanny 9, Ann 4

Henry BEATTY ....pg 430, 23 Oct 1838, will

man Phil to son-in-law John WILSON; old woman Judy, young woman Evelina to daughter Sarah Matilda CHENOWETH wife of John W. CHENOWETH; amount of William ABBOTT's Deed of Trust on negroes

"William HENNING administrator of William ABBOTT's estate some years ago sold some negroes to William LINN...a suit has been threatened by Louisa HILL...to set aside the said sale..."

Abraham & Mary Ann HESS...
......................................pg 512, 1 Jan 1836 - 24 Sept 1840, gdn acct

negroes sold

Jacob FRYE ....pg 515, 20 Nov 1839, inv & appr

Rachel 8

Henry BEATTY ....pg 517, 1840, inv & appr

man Phil, old woman Judy, Evelina

James LITTLE.................pg 531, 14 June 1838 - 23 Jan 1841, estate acct

Robert, woman Hannah, Jim, boy

John LYNN ....pg 536, 28 Feb 1839 - 1 Mar 1841, estate acct

cash of Francis SILVER for man George & woman Chloe

Edward WALKER ....pg 539, 21 May 1833 - 26 Feb 1841, estate acct

man

Orphans of George ASH ....pg 544, 26 Dec 1839 – 19 Dec 1840, gdn acct

negroes

George ASH ....pg 545, 2 Dec 1839 –15 Dec 1840, gdn acct

negroes

Ann FUNSTEN ....pg 546, 4 Feb 1837 – 2 Feb 1941, gdn acct

Nick

Joseph DUCKWALL ....pg 547, 3 Jan 1840 - 1 Jan 1841, gdn acct

Harry, John

John PRICE ....pg 553, 3 May 1841 in court, inv & appr

women Maria, Frances

Lucy BALMAIN .... pg 559, 11 May 1839, will

Phillis, William, John, Kitty, George, Poindexter, Robert, Judy,
Alexander, Frank, Sally, John, Robert, Louisa, Elizabeth, David,
William & any future children to be free as authorized by will of
husband the Rev. Alexander BALMAIN

WILL BOOK 21
1841 - 1845

George L. BAKER.................pg 11, 1 Mar 1833 - 1 Sept 1841, gdn acct

slaves belonging to the estate of H.W. BAKER to be sold

Henry C. BAKER.................pg 14, 1 Mar 1833 - 1 Sept 1841, gdn acct

slaves belonging to the estate of H.W. BAKER to be sold

Thomas ROBERTS..............pg 19, 6 Aug 1839 – 5 Aug 1841, estate acct

superannuated woman Lina supported by Susan HAYMAKER

Margaret GALLOWAY .... pg 29, 25 May 1822, will

Polly & her child Henry to granddaughter Margaret GALLOWAY daughter of son Richard S. GALLOWAY; William age 14 to grandson James B. GALLOWAY son of Richard S. GALLOWAY; one half of the remaining slaves to daughter Helen C. GALLOWAY & the other half to the children of son Richard S. GALLOWAY

.... pg 31, 31 Aug 1841, codicil

Jeny & Winny age 45, Lindsey 40 to remain in the service of daughter Helen C. GALLOWAY for 2 years & then be emancipated

Rev. Joseph GLASS...........pg 48, 16 Jan 1840 – 31 Dec 1841, estate acct

Jim, Cuffee, Rachel, Frank, woman Molly, boy Henry, girl Eliza, man Mingo

Sarah BAKER ....pg 49, 8 Aug 1837, will

girl Mary to granddaughter Sarah Virginia McINTOSH on condition daughter Caroline has possession and full benefits of her services until her decease; remaining slaves to be divided between daughters Rebecca Ann & Sarah Alcinda

William MEADE...pg 50, 1 Mar 1839, gdn acct

division of servants; boy Ireland, Eliza, James

Lucy MEADE ....pg 52, 1 Mar 1839, gdn acct

division of servants; Betsy, Eliza, Mary Tabs

Drayton G. MEADE .... pg 53, 1 Mar 1839, gdn acct

division of servants; Eliza, Harry

Harriet MEADE .... pg 54, 12 Mar 1839, gdn acct

division of servants; Vina, Eliza, Jacob

Orphans of George H. ASH ....

.... pg 56, 21 Dec 1840 - 11 Oct 1841, gdn acct

Henry a runaway; Maria & children kept by Alexander NEWMAN

Sarah A. BAKER .... pg 58, 1 Jan 1840 – 1 Jan 1842, gdn acct

division of slaves recorded; Caroline, woman

Robert W. BAKER .... pg 59, 4 Mar 1840 – 1 Jan 1842, gdn acct

division of slaves recorded; negroes

Noah FRASHER .... pg 63, 15 Jan 1842, will

"...that John H. FRASHER and my wife Mary FRASHER have all my colored people which are not to be sold out of Frederick & Clarke Countys."

.... pg 63, 15 Jan 1842, codicil

"...with regard to my slaves disposed of in said will, I will & desire that all the slaves born after this date belonging to me be freed at twenty five years of age."

.... pg 67, 19 Mar 1842, inv & appr

man Armstead, old Harry, Charles 13, Tom 5, Bob 12, James 2, Winny 35, Eliza 25, Mary 17, Frances 3, Ann 7, Susan 6, Phebe & child; man Stephen to serve 3 years and then be free

Fielding LUTTRELL .... pg 73, 19 Jan 1842, will

man Harry owned? by sister Frankey LUTTRELL

Orphans of Marshall RUST .... pg 81, 17 Sept 1830 - 3 Apr 1841, gdn acct

paid John M. REDMAN on division of negroes; young Daniel, old Daniel, little Daniel

Ann FUNSTEN .... pg 83, Feb 1841 – Mar 1842, gdn acct

Dick

William ABBOTT .... pg 84, Mar 1834 - 9 Apr 1842, estate acct

child died; women; Morgan, Fanny, Armstead, Dolly

Joseph DUCKWALL .... pg 91, 1 Jan 1841 - 3 May 1843, gdn acct

Harry, John

George RAYNOLDS .... pg 92, 3 Nov 1840 – 8 Apr 1842, estate acct

man to Front Royal, old woman Frances, Wagoner, James, William, Charlotte, Amelia, Joseph, Thomas, Meary?

Orphans of David STULTZ ....pg 351, 13 Mar 139 – 1 Jan 1842, gdn acct

boys Leg, Joe

Margaret GALLOWAY .... pg 95, 12 Feb 1842, inv & appr

Jerry 47, Lindsey 40, Winney 45, Thomason 35, little Sam 27; Jerry, Lindsey, Winney emancipated by will after 2 years of her death

Isaac COLE .... pg 97, 7 June 1842, inv & appr

women Henny, Maria

John JOLLIFFE .... pg 99, 7 Sept 1838?, inv & appr

Willoughby, Alfred, Dennis, Ned, Ambrose, Jeney?, Jack, Charles, John, Bob, Ned, Joe, Nancy, Matilda, Lucy Ann, Mary, Evalina (Peggy) or Margaret, Selina, little Matilda, Lavinia, May

Lewis ASHBY .... pg 104, 1 Jan 1826 – 1 June 1842, estate acct

man sold

Robert HETERICK .... pg 106, 22 Feb 1840 - 30 July 1842, estate acct

negro

Sarah BAKER .... pg 124, 15 Mar 1842, inv & appr

Jack, Davis, Isaac, John, George, Emily, Francis, Charles, Kitty, Mary

Isaac HOLLINGSWORTH .... pg 129, 6 May 1842, will

man Cook to son Joseph P. HOLLINGSWORTH; woman Patty & her 4 children to son John HOLLINGSWORTH; man David to son Cyrus; man Jacob to son Isaac Milton HOLLINGSWORTH; man Shadrack to daughter Eliza the wife of Alfred PARKINS; man Phil to daughter Eleanor HOLLINGSWORTH wife of David HOLLINGSWORTH

Joshua GORE .... pg 135, 24 Nov 1841, will

slaves to be hired out then freed except for girls Mary & Harriet; Mary to serve sister Betty COE & at her death to be free & any children she may have; Harriet to serve Catharine COE the wife of Samuel COE & at her death to be free & any children she may have; man Bill to be set free

Abraham MILLER .... pg 147, 11 Nov 1842, will

John, William to wife Rebecca & at her death to be emancipated

John JOLLIFFE .... pg 151, 1 Feb 1841 - 31 Dec 1842, estate acct

negroes apprehended; slaves

Zachariah SANKS .... pg 154, 28 Mar 1842, will

man Isaac to William B. SLACK for 3 years and then be set free; man Andrew, at the death of SANKS' wife, Nancy SANKS, to serve William B. SLACK for 4 years and then be set free; woman Harriet, at the death of SANKS' wife, to serve William B. SLACK for 3 years and then be set free, any children to serve William B. SLACK until age 21 but if Harriet moves to a free state she may take her children with her; girl Winney, at the death of SANKS' wife, to live with James SANKS for 4 years and then be set free, any children to serve James SANKS until age 21 and then be set free

Edmond PAGETT .... pg 157, 8 Oct 1835, will

slaves (all one family), obtained by right of wife Jane, to wife Jane & at her death to be emancipated

Sophia BAYLESS .... pg 158, 17 Dec 1842, inv & appr

old woman Sarah, Charlot 32, Adam 3, Eve 3, Jacob 18 months old

Andrew PITMAN .... pg 165, 22 Sept 1838 - 9 Jan 1843, estate acct

Lucinda, Shadrack, Linsey, Nancy

Robert GLASS ....pg 168, 14 Feb 1843, inv & appr

man Harrison

Armistead T.M. McCORMICK ....
.....................................pg 175, 17 May 1830 – 7 July 1838, gdn acct

Nancy & family, Nancy & child; 3 children kept by B. McCORMICK; Nanny, Charlotte & children

Thomas W. McCORMICK ....
.... pg 177, 5 Jan 1830 – 27 Nov 1842, gdn acct

Kissy kept by Brockenbrough McCORMICK; Beckey kept by B. McCORMICK; Hannah, Eve

Eleanor MAGRUDER ....pg 187, 5 June 1843 in court, inv & appr

Frank, Joseph, Hampton, William, Peyton, Mary, Juliet & 2 children, Nancy & child William, Albert, Fanny, Tom, Sally, Agnes, Augustan, Matilda, Louisa, John, Ann

Mary Sophia ASH .... pg 195, 26 Mar 1841 - 26 May 1843, gdn acct

Sarah & child; Henry apprehended

Henry STIPE .... pg 197, 4 Apr 1843, will

girl Polly to wife Tabitha STIPE

Ephraim PIFER .... pg 199, 1 Jan 1842, inv & appr

girl hired until Christmas

.... pg 200, 27 Feb 1843, sales

girl hired until Christmas

Edmond PAGETT ....pg 205, 14 Feb 1843, inv & appr

Malah 32, Alah 19, Mary 17, Winney 65

Mary WILSON................................. pg 206, 10 Dec 1838, will

"...Mary & her 5 children also one black girl named Jane the same I purchased of my son David WILSON & their increase..." to daughters Mary WILSON, Eliza LONG, Isabella THOMPSON, Jane M. WILSON, & Ann S. WILSON

Sarah HASKILL .... pg 212, 15 July 1842, will

woman Juda to daughter Anne Elizabeth HASKILL; woman Anne to daughter Emilia Susan HASKILL but if Anne has children the first child goes to son John White HASKILL, her second child goes to daughter Anne Elizabeth HASKILL, & her third child to daughter Emilia Susan HASKILL, if she has more children they are to go to my children in rotation as above.

C.B. HITE .... pg 213, 6 Jan 1842, inv & appr

Jim 40, Marcus 24?, Elijah 9, Peggy 17

John WHITE .... pg 217, 20 Apr 1836, will

woman Jenny to wife Elizabeth WHITE; "...to my son James A. WHITE my negro woman Judy conveyed to him by John HASKILL by a bill of sale and my negro woman Anna? who was bound mine to be held by him in trust for...my daughter Sarah HASKILL wife of John HASKILL..." ; girl Eliza, boy Henry to daughter Susan Gilkerson WHITE; man Tom & his wife Hannah to be sold

George RAYNOLDS .... pg 220, 7 Sept 1842 – 5 June 1843, estate acct

man Joseph punished, Franky, Mary, Charlotte, William, James, Thomas, Amelia, Simon

Joshua GORE .... pg 224, May 1843, inv & appr

men Ned, James, David, Bill, women Jane, Hannah, Sarah, Fanny & child Elizabeth, Margaret, Milly, girls Lucy, Eliza, Julian, boys Isaac, Thomas, Aaron, men Henry, Adam, girls Mary, Harriet, men Umphrey, George, Peter, woman Elizabeth

Mankin & Thomas K. CARTMILL .... pg 267, 31 Mar 1843, sales

boy Robert to John M. MILLER; Abraham to Caspar RINKEN; Asy? to John N. BELL; Peggy & 3 children to Stephen PRITCHARD; Sarah, Bill, Jem, Mary, Tom to Laban F. CAMPBELL; Ben to Mordicai B. CARTMILL

.... pg 269, 3 July 1843, sales

Susan & 2 children to James JOLLIFFE; Maria & 3 children to John S. MAGILL

194

Cornelius B. HITE..........pg 270, 18 July 1842 - 19 Aug 1843, estate acct

negroes

David EVANS..............pg 281, 7 May 1841 – 4 Sept 1842, estate acct

negro Harrison

Zachariah SANKS.....................pg 285, 15 Feb 1823, inv & appr

Isaac, Andy, girl Winney, Harriet & her 4 children, Harriet's oldest child Moses

Nicholas KERN.................................. pg 293, 13 Jan 1842, will

girl Charlotte to wife Mary; balance of slaves to be sold

Philip MARTIN...............................pg 301, 29 Sept 1817, will

Leeds Castle in the County of Kent Esquire a General in His Majesty's Army

servant Peter Ferris of Leeds Castle

John CARTER........................ pg 314, 7 Dec 1842, inv & appr

men Buoy?, Jesse Beksmith?, Lee, John Poss, Dick, Ned, George, Andy, women Matilda, Lucy, Adelphia, Emily & child Billy

David WILSON............................ pg 325, 28 Dec 1843, inv & appr

Fanny 75, Milly 35 & her son Lewis 18 months, Samuel 40, Lewis 25, Sophia 16, Sidney 13, Sarah 11, John 8, George 6, Harriot 4, Charles 5

Mary WILSON........................ pg 326, 28 Dec 1843, inv & appr

Mary 38 & her daughter Sidney 18 months, Selena 14, Rubin 11, Evelina 9, Seatta? 8, Emily 6, John W. 4, Jane 17

Isaac HOLLINGSWORTH ....pg 326, 30 Dec 1843, estate acct

Patty & 4 children legacy to John HOLLINGSWORTH; man Jacob legacy to Isaac M. HOLLINGSWORTH; man Phil legacy to David HOLLINGSWORTH; man Shadrack legacy to Alfred PARKINS

Christiana RUSSELL .... pg 328, 22 Dec 1843, inv & appr

woman Lucy

Lucy SCHULL .... pg 340, 26 Jan 1844, inv & appr

  Elizabeth & her 3 children Ambrose, Moses, & Elizabeth

Daniel McDONALD ....pg 355, 28 Oct 1841 – 14 Feb 1844, estate acct

  hands boarded by Mrs. HETERICK

George PAYNE .... pg 356, 16 Jan 1844, will

  girl Sarah to wife

John BAKER ....pg 365, 25 Nov 184_, will

  girl Sarah to wife & at her death to be sold

Sarah HENKELL .... pg 371, 3 June 1844 in court, inv & appr

  women Ann, Judy

John WHITE .... pg 372, 3 June 1844 in court, inv & appr

  woman

Sarah BAKER ....pg 378, 14 Jan 1822 - 1 Jan 1844, estate acct

  settlement with R.A. & S.A. BAKER legatees, 25 Mar 1842

  Jack, John, Francis, David, George, Charles, Isaac, Emily, Kitty

Rev. Alexander BALDMAN ......pg 380, Jan 1822 - June 1844, estate acct

  slaves registered; John

Westly COE .... pg 387, Feb 1835 – 1 Jan 1844, estate acct

  George sold at the sale of the personal estate to the widow

Noah FRASHER .... pg 388, 15 Jan 1842 – 19 June 1844, estate acct

  cash paid James C. BAKER for hire of negroes

Elizabeth BUSH .... pg 400, 12 Dec 1842, will

  2 small negroes, Martin Van Buren & Annear? Nancy, to daughters
  M.C. & S.E. BUSH to be held until the period when they are to be free

John BAKER .... pg 407, 6 Aug 1844 in court, inv & appr

  girl age 18

196

Shapleigh FRENCH .... pg 413, 8 Jan 1841 - 17 July 1844, estate acct

amount of William MILLER over charging ___ slaves; Nelson, George, Harrison, Timothy, Robert, Henry, Bill, Horace, Eliza, Winney, Mary, Jared "...any balance that may remain my Exectors hands to be equally divided among my four negro women viz Winney, Lucy, Esther, and Maria...Winney is since dead leaving 5 children to wit Lucy Parker and Esther Webb two of the above named negroes who are entitled to one fourth part of Testators Estate and Timothy Nelson and Jared who are entitled to one fifth each of Winney's share..."

William BYWATERS ....pg 419, 5 Nov 1844 in court, will

choice of the black men and women and a girl called Judia to wife; girl Lucy to Mary Ann BAKER the wife of Henry BAKER; girl Hannah to daughter Asenath BYWATERS

Adam BOSTYON? ....pg 424, 1 Sept 1836 – 5 Nov 1844, estate acct

George, Hannah & her child sold

Henry STIPE ....pg 427, 16 Aug 1843, inv & appr

James 28, Jane 14, Alley 10; girl Patty in possession of the widow as long as she remains a widow; Joseph 5, Benjamin 3, Aggy 2

Joshua GORE .... pg 436, 6 Mar 1843 - 1 Dec 1844, estate acct

slaves

.... pg 437, 26 Jan 1843 – 28 Nov 1844, estate acct

Adam, Sarah, Ned

Robert D. GLASS .... pg 440, 9 May 1842, will

Bill & any slave who may be superannuated to son Robert

.... pg 442, 3 Mar 1843, codicil

Jinny, 4th daughter of Rozetta, to granddaughter Mary Elizabeth MAGILL

.... pg 442, 16 Jan 1845, inv & appr

Daniel, Fielding, George, Charles, Willonphy?, Jacob, Jim, Joe, Alfred, Dick, Mary, Rozetta & child, Martha, Caroline & her child Kitty, Lucy, Rose, Mimia

Peter COONTZ .... pg 450, 9 Jan 1845, inv & appr

boys Manuel, John, George, girl Becky, woman Betsy

....pg 452, note

"To the sheriff of Frederick and as such committee allow with the Will amended of Peter Coontz dec'd...a list of personal property which was conveyed to me in March by the late Peter Coontz on the 4th day of March 1843 for the benefit of Mary COONTZ, Lewis P. COONTZ, William H. COONTZ, George M. COONTZ & John P. COONTZ...and the following slaves viz Dennis, Manuel, John, George, Becky, & Rebecca...about to sell the said property..." 27 Jan 1845, signed by W.G. SINGLETON for the benefit of Mary COONTZ

William C. WILLIAMS .... pg 453, Aug 18_7, sales

Moses to Branch JORDAN, George to Jefferson WILLIAMS, Lucy to Martha WILLIAMS

John JOLLIFFE ....pg 456, 1 Jan 1843 – 29 Dec 1844, estate acct

Bob; young & old negroes kept by Mrs. JOLLIFFE; Jack apprehended; Charles sold

James LITTLE...................pg 468, 24 Feb 181 – 24 Feb 1845, estate acct

Cyrus, Hannah

Peter SPERRY..pg 474, 14 Feb 1845, will

Peter to wife Barbara & at her death to choose his master

Obed WAITE ....pg 479, 21 Oct 1842, will

Leroy, Evelina, Henry the latter have been disposed of; "Martha and her child James, I never had any right or claim whatever to, my wife obtained the said woman Martha when a small girl from her brother Charles C. STEWART, Esq, the girl Molly is my said wife's slave to which I have no claim."

John CARTER...................pg 481, 5 Dec 1842 – 12 mar 1845, estate acct

paid slave taxes

Alexander MARK .... pg 493, 10 Apr 1845, inv & appr

Joseph 7, Pheh? & child age 4 -7

Alexander MARK ....pg 494, 14 Apr 1845, sales

girl & child time to M__ MARK; Joseph's time to Samuel MARK

Jacob BRANCH ....pg 499, 15 Mar 1845, inv & appr

woman Dinnah, girl Ann

.... pg 500, 17 Mar 1845, sales

woman Dinnah & girl Ann to Joseph BYNON__

Peter SPERRY ....pg 504, 18 Mar 1845, inv & appr

Peter

Thomas DENT ....pg 509, 5 Oct 1837, will

negroes except man Stephen to be sold; daughter Cassandra McCOOL
to take remaining property, land or negroes

Edmond PAGETT .... pg 512, 15 Feb 184_ - 14 Feb 18 45, estate acct

men Alexander, Malack

Zachariah SANKS ....pg 515. 15 Mar 1943 – 21 Dec 1844

Jane, servant, negro

Thomas DENT ....pg 534, 22 Aug 1845, inv & appr

Stephen 46, Pamela 32, Jackson 16, Amanda 12, Lucetta 10, Patsy 8,
Emma 2

William S. JONES ....pg 536, 13 Nov 1841, will

Rebuen, Mary, Kitty, Thomas to wife Ann & at her death "Reuben and
Kitty over and above his share of my negroes also an equal portion or
shre of my slaves with my other children, but as one of his negroes he
is to have William that he may be convient to his wife..." to son
William S. JONES; __ of negroes to son James; "...at the death of my
wife to sell Mary and Thomas and the increase of Mary if any. My
other slaves not specificially bequeath to be equally divided amongst
all my children... Fanny, Marshall, James, Frances, & Beverly..."

....pg 538, 23 Apr 1844, codicil

Mary & all her family to Ann should she wish them during her life

199

Sarah A. BAKER ....pg 539, 1 Jan 1842 – 1 Oct 1845, gdn acct

girl Mary

Nicholas KERN.......................... pg 542, 4 Nov 1845 in court, inv & appr

man Jim, girl Charlotte, boy Lewis, boy Phebe

.... pg 545, 30 Nov 1843, sales

man Jim to William C. McNEILL; boy Lewis to George GETTES; woman Phebe to Fortunatus SYDNOR

WILL BOOK 22
1845 - 1850

that amount in negroes from the estate of my brother Edward MUSE dec'd..."

Moses SHEPHERD .... pg 63, 4 Sept 1845, inv & appr

boy Henry ___; woman Martha to serve until 15 Nov 1856 & her child 13 months old slave for life

.... pg 67, 8 Sept 1845, sales

boy Henry to Mary R. SHEPHERD; woman & child to T.H. CROW?

Joseph W. CARTER .... pg 69, 9 Mar 1826 – 23 Oct 1843, estate acct

Jim

Daniel CATHER .... pg 73, 1840 – 9 Nov 1845, estate acct

Ben, boy Mike, Betty

Job S. HENDRICK .... pg 77, 18 Feb 1846, will

man Robert Mason is to be emancipated

Seth MASON .... pg 80, 12 Dec 1838, will

old man James to choose his master; his wife Cate & youngest child Sandy; Rebecca R. PARKHAM, a relation of my dec'd wife, to receive money any part of which she may allot in negroes or personal property; girl Marinda to daughter Lucretia; girl Mary to daughter Jane; girl Judith to daughter Ann; Nick, Ned, Cate Jr. & her children & now in my possession as well as several I have sold willed to me only for my life & then to my children

.... pg 82, 12 July 1845, codicil

Dec 38: Advances made

to David TIMBERLAKE who married daughter Elizabeth - Leanna, Lewis, Winney, Abram, Frank, Isabel & 2 children

to Rebecca I. KEN – Thornton sold; Fanny

to James W. MASON – negroes

to James W. TIMBERLAKE who married daughter Jane – Israel, Eliza, Robert, Frederick?, Charles, Polly, Anna, Eliza

Job S. HENDRICK .... pg 85, 9 Apr 1846, inv & appr

man Bob liberated by will

Lucinda SHULL ....pg 87, 27 Jan 1844, sales

25 Dec: Ambrose to William A. CARTER; Jeff to James AFFLICK; Elizabeth & 2 children to W.O. HEADLEY

....pg 90, 1844 - 10 Jan 1846, estate acct

negroes sold; Lizzy & 3 children kept by administrator Thomas A. JACKSON

Robert MUSE .... pg 94, 4 Mar 1846, inv & appr

Bob, Bill, Isaac, Miranda, Eliza, Celia, Jane, Maria, George, Frank, Amos, Daniel, Charly, Caroline, Henry; note on John CANGH__ for hire of man allotted to Martha MUSE

Henry HITE .... pg 102, 10 May 1846, inv & appr

boy

....pg 104, 4 May 1846, at auction

boy to Mrs. Susan C. HITE

James G. FICKLIN .... pg 112, 1 July 1845, will

slaves to be sold

Elizabeth GLASS .... pg 113, 20 June 1837, will

Hannah, Mahala to be freed; executor to purchase boy Horace now in the possession of brothers Thomas & Robert GLASS & set him free

James G. FICKLIN ....pg 116, 18 Aug 1846, inv & appr

Henrietta & child, women Fanny, Judy, Emily, men Frederick, Aaron, boys Warren, Charles, women Jane, Betsy

Stephen GRUBBS ....pg 122, 18 Oct 1844 - 31 Aug 1846, estate acct

negroes kept by Caterania GRUBBS; Davy sold; Henry, Mahala, Sarah, Elizabeth, Mary Eliza, Manley, John

Hannah M. RUST ....pg 128, 6 Oct 1846, will

Caroline to son Robert RUST

Seth MASON .... pg 131, _ May 1846, inv & appr

David, Willis, Cate, Marinda & 3 children Frank, Charles?, & Milley?, Philip, Bailley?, John

25 Dec 1846: Chance, Betsy, Harry?, Nelson, Frederick, Bennet, Cyrus, Cate, Jordan, Alfred, Horace, Isam, Thornton, Sandy, Judy, Mary, Dorcas, Edmond

the following are claimed by Seth MASON Jr?: Lucy, James, Wyate? George, ____

.... pg 133, 7 Aug 1846, sales

26 Dec 1846: boy Thornton to Warren McKE__; Henry to KEMP; Horace to George W. WARD; Isam to David TIMBERLAKE; Edward to David TIMBERLAKE; Willis to William? HO__D; Dorcas to Gabriel NEVILLE

Joseph LANICK .... pg 137, May 1845, inv & appr

woman

Joshua GORE .... pg 145, 1 Dec 1844 – 1 Feb 1847, estate acct

women & 3 children kept by Samuel COE & boarding other negroes; Henry?, Ned

.... pg 147, 1 Dec 1844 - Jan 1847, estate acct

Edmond; negroes transferred to J.C. BOYER; Adam, David

Robert D. GLASS .... pg 162, 6 Jan 1845 – 19 Feb 1847, estate acct

negroes

Elizabeth GLASS ....pg 166, 2 Sept 1846, inv & appr

Hannah 55, Horace 27, Mahala 23? were directed by the will to be emancipated

Joseph LANICK ....pg 177, 1 May 1845 - 9 Feb 1847, estate acct

negroes; transfer of boy ___; woman

Henry RICHARDS .... pg 183, 29 Mar 1833, will

all slaves to son Joseph RICHARDS

Richard WILLS..................pg 194, 6 Feb 1847, inv & appr

men Charles, Peyton, boy John, women Francis, Molly, girl Asy?

.... pg 196, 25 Mar 1847, sales

man Charles, boys John, Peyton, girls Francis, Molly, Asy? to Jane R. WILLS

Brian M. STEPHENS.........................pg 217, 15 ___ 1845, will

first choice of negro men to sister Caroline & one of the younger set of negroes ___ Lucy; Charles to daughter Harriet McKAY; a negro child to son Brian; a child to son George; remaining negroes, including Dick now with daughter Maria BRAKEN?, to be sold; one woman to wife Emma until her death

Mabra MADDEN Jr............pg 220, ,25 Sept 1830 – Oct 1846, estate acct

negro sold; woman & children, belonging to the estate of Mabra MADDEN Sr., sold

Martha Rebecca CARSON........................ pg 236, 26 Apr 1847, gdn acct

girl Frances

George PELTER ....pg 238, 3 Aug 1847, will

Bill to be free at wife's death; Le_ to be free at age 35

Francis B. JONES .... pg 241, 17 Sept 1845 – 4 Sept 1847, gdn acct

servants; Harriet kept by William L. JONES; negroes

William S. JONES.............. pg 246, 2 Oct 1847, supplemental estate acct

value of slaves; share of negroes amount

Robert MUSE........................pg 268, 15 Apr 1846, div of slaves

Bill, Eliza, Celia, George, Caroline to Mrs. E.B. MUSE, widow; Maria, Daniel, Henry to Julia A. DAVIS; Jane, Charles to Rob B. MUSE; Isaac, Miranda to John N. MUSE; Bob to Martha E. MUSE; Frank, Arnod? to Joseph R. MUSE

Bushrod TAYLOR .... pg 271, 7 Dec 1947, inv & appr

Dandridge 42, Henry 56, Samuel Bell 22, Ned 48, Tom 45, Robert Shirly 22, Sawney Bell 26, Charles 32, Robert Smith 16, Mary

16, Lucinda 24, Elizabeth 30, Kitty 60, Jack Blacksmith 27, George 6, Aley? 45 & child 1, Jim? 14, Highland 22, Jane? 26, Betsy 20, Henrietta 22 & child Hannah 3, Judy 21

Beverly R. JONES......................pg 300, 4 Oct 1845 – 1 Jan 1848, gdn acct

boy, girl Cattrerine

Christiana TOUCHSTONE.............. pg 308, 18 June 1836, will

George, Barbara to daughter Polly TOUCHSTONE; man Charles emancipated; Betty & her infant daughter Betsy to be emancipated at her death; old Benjamin & old Lucy to be cared for by daughter Polly; Joe, Chinman?, John, Sarah to be emancipated at age 25

William SMITH................................. pg 310, 12 Apr 1848, will

girl gift to son Crizer SMITH; man John to son Alfred; slaves to be divided between son Crizer W. & Stephen F. SMITH after the death of their mother

....pg 311, 12 Apr 1848, codicil

Martha, Virginia, Scott? to son Stephen

James D. FICKLIN........pg 318, 28 Aug 1846 – 13 may 1848, estate acct

Emily, Henrietta & child. Judy, Jane, Betsy, Fanny, Warner, Frederick sold

Benjamin M. MASSIE......pg 322, 1 May 1846 – 1 May 1848, estate acct

negroes sold

Sarah McLINN.................................pg 325, 13 Mar 1844, will

Reuben to son Samuel McLINN; Lexington to daughter Mary now Mary WINSTON

Henry BAKER ....pg 326, 13 Aug 1846, inv & appr

woman Jane

.... pg 328, 26 Sept 1846, sales

girl to Harrison BOWERS

Grizzella G. ANDERSON..................... pg 333, Jan 1846, will

boy Emanuel to be free

206

William SMITH .... pg 334, 22 July 1848, inv & appr

man James, Sarah & her 4 children Michael, George, Martha, & Sea_; Lucy & her children Milly, Sylvania, & infant Sama?

Thomas LITTETON .... pg 346, 1830 – 27 Oct 1847, estate acct

Dorcey, Edward, Henry, old Jenny died

George REYNOLDS .... pg 360, 10 June 1843- 21 Sept 1848, estate acct

Simon to pay for his freedom; William; coffin for child of the estate; old Franky Pollard, old Hannah, Charlotte Pollard, Amelia Pollard, Mary Pollard, William Pollard, Thomas, James Pollard, Tom, Joe

Maria HELM .... pg 362, Aug 1827 – Jan 1847, estate acct

man Ned, amount purchase girl

William McCORMICK .... pg 366, Oct 1835 – 1 Jan 1848, gdn acct

Fanny, midwife for Milly & Rose; Lorenzo, Nat, Lucinda & child

Ann McCORMICK .... pg 371, Oct 1835 – 1 July 1848, gdn acct

Fanny, midwife for Sukey, Lorenzo, Nat

Edward McCORMICK .... pg 376, Oct 1835 – 1 July 1848, gdn acct

Fanny, midwife for Suckey & Rose, Jim, Maria, Lorenzo, Nat, Tom

Seth MASON .... pg 382, 10 Apr 1846 – 1 May1848, estate acct

negroes sold; old Hannah kept by James W. MASON; John/Jno, girl Margaret?, boy Harry, Thornton, Willis, Horace, Edmond, Isaac, boy Jim, Cyrus, Adam, Cynthia, George, John, Charles, Betsy, Bennett?, Nelson, Philip, Bailley, Judy, Mary, Dora?, Frederick, Maranda & 3 children, boy Isaac

Stephen GRUBB .... pg 394, 1 Sept 1846 – 1 Sept 1848, estate acct

negroes kept by Caterania GRUBB

Ann KINNEY .... pg 397, 30 Dec 1848, inv & appr

Joseph, Milo, Paul, George, Lucinda, Charity

Henry St. George TUCKER............... pg 410, 5 Apr 18_9, inv & appr

Judy 70, Emily 37, Mary 12, James 10, William 8, James Flanegan 15, George 45, Hetty 3, Ca_ty 10, Sandy 6

.... pg 414, 2 Apr 1849 in court, inv & appr

boy, Edward, George, Wesley, Isaac, Ned Lowry, Jim Lowry, Carter, Ben, Eliza

.... pg 414, 25 Feb 1849, appr slaves

in Albemarle Co: Becky 56, Dolly 22

Judith ASHLY............... pg 425, 6 Mar 1849, will

John to niece Julia Ann; Isaac, Maria, Edward, "B__t & white..." to nephew John B. MASSIEHenry?, Fanny to niece Mildred MASSIE, all children of sister Sidney MASSIE

William M. ATKINSON............... pg 426, 30 May 1846, codicil

"...servants to be sold...avoid the breaking up of families, except Cloe whom I leave to my daughter Mary Francis..."

.... pg 432, 3 Apr 1849, inv & appr

Robin, Rachel, James, John, Peter, Maria & her child Tody?, Jacob, William; added property: Chloe, Peter to BROAD___

Henry St. George TUCKER............... pg 435, 29 Feb 1849, slave appr

Eliza & child, Henry, Ned Lowry, James Lowry, Ben Smith little Betsy, George, Carter, Bill Doctor, old Betsy, Reuben, William, Reuben

William S. JONES............... pg 474, 5 Sept 1845, inv & appr

slaves in families where they have families:

Patsey 51 & her child Margaret 17, Margaret's child Jane 1 1/2, Thomas Hunter 8, Lavinia 55, Lavenia Jr 19, Charles 45, Maria his wife 41, Ben 23, William 15, Vincent Sr 45, Hannah his wife 49, Vincent Jr? 21, Harriet 17, Catharine 10, Eliza 8, Peter 50, Catharine 42, George 15, Austen 9, Nelson 7, Lucy 3, Lucinda 43, Anthony 17, Thornten 15, Moses Turner 8, Tayler 5, Harriett 35, Sarah Ann 16, Robert 13, Lucinda 12, Washington 7, Patsy 5, Frances 3, Gabriel 40, Maria 30, Spencer 11, Otway 10, Columbia 8, Fanny 6,

Hattey Tayler 3, Steptoe 1 ½, Markam 36, Nancy Cook 33, Moses Holter 45, Sauney B. Smith 40, Daniel 38, James 77, Harry 63

slaves specially bequeathed:

William 44. Mary 38 to STROTHER; Thomas 19 to Mrs. JONES for life; Mahale 14 to __; Flora 12, Mary Ann 7, Sally Ann 3; Reuben 60, Kitty 52 to Mary JONES for life remander to STROTHER

Frances B. JONES .... pg 480, 9 Sept 1847 – 3 July 1849, gdn acct

Anthony, Harriet & children kept by William S. JONES; negroes advertised; Armestead, Anthony sold, midwife for Levina

John GROVE, Sr. .... pg 502, 42 Dec 1849 in court, will

slaves to wife Susan GROVE; woman Hannah & her 3 children Mary, Martha, & Caty to receive firewood annually from grandson John William RITEN__, a tract of land with house for life, her children to be hired out until the age of 30 & then be free; man Jesse "...shall be free at the decease of myself and wife..."

Joshua GORE .... pg 512, 1 Feb 1847 – 27 Aug 1849, estate acct

Isaac, George, Humphry, Adam, Ned; Fanny & children died; man, negroes to be registered, Sally, Daniel

.... pg 515, 12 May – 1 Feb 1850, estate acct

Dave, George

WILL BOOK 23
1850 - 1854

Bushrod TAYLOR .... pg 1, 4 Aug 1847 - 19 Feb 1850, estate acct

old Bennet Taylor, old man John Marshall; Samey? purchased by H.H.. McGUIRE; Elizabeth purchased by Samuel BELL & David FAUNTLEROY; old Henry purchased by Harrigen BOWERS

Mary B. MAGILL .... pg 30, 21 June 1849, will

servants of son Charles L. MAGILL were purchased from his mother Mary

George PELTER ....pg 33, 10 Sept 1847, inv & appr

man Bill, boy Lewis

Joseph PARKINS ....pg 41, 16 Aug 1848, inv & appr

Maria & child claimed by the widow

.... pg 44, 16 Aug 1848, sales

Maria & child Mary to H. PARKINS, widow

.... pg 46, 1 July 1848 – 1 July 1850, estate acct

John; girl Hannah a runaway; Jane; cash paid for absconded girl Hannah; Hannah sold

Seth MASEN ....pg 51, 1 May 1848 – 8 May 1850, estate acct

Hannah kept by J.W. MASEN; cash paid James R. BROOKING for Lucy & 2 children; old Hannah died; Amanda & 4 children kept by J.W. MASEN; boy Dave; boy George sold; Chance, Cyrus, Kate, Cynthia, Judy, Bailly, John, Philip, Nelson, Betsy & 2 children, Jordan; Cyrus, Kate, Judy, Cynthia sold

Benjamin KECKLEY ....pg 53, 1 July 1850 in court, will

woman Jane to daughter Margaret RUSSELL after she serves wife Mary for 8 years; boy Billy to daughter Mary Jane, man Charles to son Benjamin Franklin; boy Harvey to son Josiah

Christina TOUCHSTONE .... pg 65, 16 May 1848, inv & appr

George 23, Barbary 25

211

John GIFFEN ....pg 68, 31 Aug 1850, inv & appr

    girl to serve for 11 years

....pg 69, 17 Sept 1850, sales

    girl to Sarah GIFFEN

Brian M. STEPHENS..............................pg 74, 11 Dec 1847, inv & appr

    John 50, Dave? 35, man William, girl Sydney, Eliza & 2 children Ned
    & Joe, girl Harriett, boys Ben, Bush, woman Sharlott, Mary 3, Lucy 6,
    Daniel 42

....pg 80, 14 Sept 1847, sales

    man John to Joseph LEVY; man David, boy Benjamin to B.M.
    STEPHENS; man William, girl Mary to Caroline STEPHENS; Eliza
    & 2 children to Nancy WHITE; girl Sidney to Emma STEPHENS; boy
    Dick to Maria BRABSON; girl Sidney to widow

William M. ATKINSON...
................................pg 95, 20 Mar 1849 - 29 July 1850, estate acct

    9 slaves transported from Winchester to Petersburg; Robin & family
    sold to I.G. RUSSELL; Peter, James sold; Chloe; Robin, Rachel &
    their children, Maria & her 3 children sold

Ann T. HITE ....pg 100, 5 Jan 1851, will

    man John to choose his master

Benjamin KECKLEY.................pg 112, 3 Mar 1851 in court, inv & appr

    woman, boys Charles, Harvey, Bill

Beverly JONES ....pg 138, 1 Jan 1849 - 31 Dec 1850, gdn acct

    Margaret & child, Harriet & children, young Vincent, Eliza, Catharine

    "The guardian supported certain slaves of his ward viz old Patsy a
    small boy Jim & an infant girl Eliza and...boy Tom about 12 years
    old."

Ely BEALL ....pg 148, 13 May 1851, will

    Landen, Cornelius, Alexander, William Henry to daughter Harriet A.
    BURGESS wife of James H. BURGESS; slaves not to be sold unless
    needed to pay debt

Isaac COLE .... pg 158, 12 June 1851, inv & appr

woman Henny 76-80, Mariah 51

Edmond PAGETT .... pg 163, 25 Dec 1845 - 18 May 1851, estate acct

midwife for Mary, Alexander, Matlock

Ann T. HITE ....pg 184, 24/25 Feb 1851, inv & appr

Jim, Elijah, Sally & child Martha, Bill

.... pg 206, 27 Feb 1851, legatees

woman Sally, girl Martha to Isaac F. HITE; boy Elijah to Alexander
N. DAVISON; man Jim chose Dr. HITE as his master

John WRIGHT ....pg 211, 7 Aug 1851, inv & appr

girl Sally to be free about March 1854; Charles to serve until he is 25;
Emily to serve until age 25

Drayton G. MEADE................pg 229, 7 June 1842 - 1 Jan 1851, gdn acct

Harry sold; Catherine

Harriet G. MEADE .... pg 233, 7 Jun 1842 – 29 July 1850, gdn acct

Jacob, Vina

Lucy F. MEADE .... pg 238, 18 Jan 1843 - 1 Jan 1846, gdn acct

Betsy & Mary Tab died

Jared William CARSON ....pg 241, 7 Aug 1851, will

Jonas, John, Stephen, Milly to be hired out until age 21 & then freed;
"...in regard to the other two negro children...as their mother may
desire if the contract is fulfilled - they are to be hired out as the others
– and receive the same..."

Henry St. George TUCKER ....
...................................pg 242, 19 Sept 1848 – 1 Oct 1850, estate acct

boy, Ben, Jim Lowry, Carter, Eliza, Ned; H.T. TUCKER's bond for
purchase of negroes; James; Jim purchased, Meg?

William SMITH .... pg 245, 2 May 1848 – 1 Jan 1851, estate acct

Sam

William KERR ....pg 250, 11 Feb 1845, will

girl Harriet to daughter Virginia; man Harrison's remaining time to be sold

.... pg 250, 25 Aug 1849, codicil

"All the slaves that I may own at my decease, except the one given by the foregoing will to Virginia shall be divided among my children..."

George LYNN .... pg 252, 9 Dec 1844, will

all slaves to wife Mrs. Ann W. LYNN & at her death to the children & grandchildren of late brother Daniel LYNN

Jared W. CARSON .... pg 255, 2 Dec 1851, inv & appr

Jonas to serve to Feb 1853, John to 4 years & 5 months

Stephen GRUBB .... pg 265, 1 Sept 1848 – 1 Sept 1851, estate acct

negroes sold, hired

Rebecca LARRICK ....pg 269, 26 Nov 1850, will

woman Nancy Ann to son Jacob B. LARRICK; girl Annetta to daughter Rebecca & at Rebecca's death "...the said girl & her descendants to go to my son Jacob and his heirs Providing however that neither Jacob nor his heirs shall sell either the woman or the girl her daughter..."; "...Executor shall retain half of Catharine's share in trust for the use and benefit of my faithful servant Dick..." Dick may chose to go to a free state

Fielding LUTTRELL .... pg 271, 2 Feb 1850 – 1 Jan 1852, estate acct

Mary died

William M. ATKINSON ....

.... pg 276, 20 July 1850 – 30 July 1851, estate acct

Peter

Benjamin KICKLEY ...... pg 282, 12 Apr 1845 – 20 Apr 1850, inv & appr

man Charles to Benjamin F. KICKLEY; boy Harvey, to Josiah KICKLEY; boy William or Bill to Mary Jane KICKLEY; woman to Margaret RUSSEL after serving Mary KICKLEY, widow, for 8 years

Daniel GOLD .... pg 285, 24 Mar 1852, will

man Amistead, girl Susan

Peter KEEDING .... pg 286, 10 Apr 1852, inv & appr

George 50, Umphry 28; John 23 to WEAVER; Mariah 30, Doss or Lee 11, Selene 9, Mary about 10 months old

....pg 291, 2 Sept 1851, will

girl Let to son-in-law David WEAVER now in his possession; girl Maria, boy Lee, child Ann to daughter-in-law Eliza KEEDING; George, Humphrey, John, the infant child of Maria not yet named to grandson William WEAVER

Henry St. George TUCKER ....
....................................pg 299, 1 Oct 1850 - 1 Oct 1851, estate acct

negreos advertised; Ben sold to BYERS; Bill

Mary SPERRY .... pg 301, 1 May 1852, will

Peter given land

William KERR ....pg 307, 25 Apr 1852, inv

Frederick & his wife Peggy & their children Mary, Benjamin, Margaret, & Robert

....pg 311, 4 Aug 1852 in court, appr

Frederick & his wife Margaret Ann, Mary, Benjamin, child Margaret, sucking child Robert

Daniel GOLD .... pg 324, 10 May 1852, inv & appr

Armestead, Susan, Elija

Thomas BROWNING .... pg 327, 10 July 1852, will

29 slaves to wife Elizabeth BROWNING to be free at her death; "...Executors do lay out in purchasing land in some of the free western states on which to settle my slaves..."

Philip PITMAN .... pg 328, 10 June 1852, inv & appr

men Cyrus, Jeff

215

Philip PITMAN .... pg 329, 4 Oct 1852 in court, sales

man Cyrus to C.A. PITMAN; man Jeff to Casper RANKER

Francis SILVER .... pg 350, 1 Sept 1845, will

woman Pirnitta? to daughter Lucy Ellen S. JEFFERSON wife of Benjamin W. JEFFERSON now in their posession & at her death to her heirs; woman Milly & all her present & furture increase, woman Harriet commonly called Pampy? to daughter Ann Amelia McKOWN wife of Warner McKOWN & at her death to her heirs; man David, woman Mariah to son Zephaniah SILVER "...I gave him a Bill of Sale for them some years since."; boy Bill grandson of Ned & Rebecca to grandson Francis Samuel Silver McKOWN son of Warner & Ann Amelia MCKOWN; woman Elizabeth now living at Tatis to granddaughter Ann Elizabeth JEFFERSON daughter of Lucy Ellen JEFFERSON; girl Hannah Susan commonly called Suky to granddaughter Lucy Ann McKOWN daughter of my daughter Ann Amelia McKOWN; Ned & his wife Rebecca to son Zephaniah SILVER; the "...remaining slaves... and the three children now in Hampshire County in care of George SHARP and his wife Nancy SHARP be all appraised and divided into three separate lots...to son Zephaniah SILVER...daughter Ann Amelia McKOWN... and daughter Lucy Ellen S. JEFFERSON..."

.... pg 354, 26 Apr 1849, codicil

old Jack to choose his master; "...Ned and his wife Rebecca...the Law which prohibits slaves from trading as free persons..."

Robert BRANNON .... pg 359, 19 Feb 1852, inv & appr

boys Henry, George, John Hayden, girl Sarah Jane, boy Charles, girl Mary, boys Ben, John Tucker

James V. GLASS .... pg 369, 1 Mar 1851, inv & appr

men Charles, George, Rosetta & 2 children

Ann T. HITE .... pg 375, 20 Jan 1851 - 1 July 1852, estate acct

servant Bery? Jennings; negro

Jared W. CARSON .... pg 380, 8 Sept 1851 – 1_ Nov 1852, estate acct

Jonas, L. Stern

216

Rees HILL .... pg 388, 20 Jan 1853, inv & appr

Margaret, Mary, Amy?

"...the slaves therein named we state that they are held under the will of William ABBOTT decd (the first husband of Louisa HILL...in her marriage settlement..."

Frances SILVER .... pg 391, 1 Dec 1852, inv & appr

Ned, Rebecca, Jack, Bill, Terry, Francis, David, Mary, Zephaniah, Rebecca Jr., Milly, More?, infant Julia Ann, Charity, Lucy, John, Fanny, Virginia, Jacob, Amos, Black or Frank, Ann & infant child, Arianna

Daniel METZGER now in Baltimore, MD ....
.... pg 404, 13 Mar 1846, codicil

Henrietta 22 to be free at the age of 40, her son William age 2 to be free at age 45, any furture children to be free at age 45 for males & age 40 for females

Rebecca LARRICK .... pg 405, 28 Feb 1853 in court, inv & appr

Special Legacies: Antinett age 5 to Rebecca LARRICK & at Rebecca's death to J.B. LARRICK; Nancy 46, a slave for life, to J.B. LARRICK, not to be sold

Joseph MILLER .... pg 432, 5 May 1847, will

slaves to wife Mary MILLER

John COE .... pg 435, 4 Mar 1853, will

negroes to be sold at public auction

Virginia LITTLE .... pg 444, 17 Sept 1850 – 1 Jan 1853, estate acct

paid Betty for attendance

Jacob DANVER .... pg 454, 19 July 1850, inv & appr

Jared

.... pg 455, 20 July 1850, salaes

Jared to widow

Irene P. GREEN .... pg 460, 19 Apr 1853, will

woman Phoebe to son John in trust for his wife Sarah N. who was Sarah N. TAYLOR; Rachel to my children

John COE ....pg 466, 1 Aug 1853, inv & appr

Alcy & 3 children, woman Winey, man Frank, boy Jesse; boy John to serve 8 years

Josiah LOCKHART .... pg 470, 11 June 1849, will

man Dave to grandson Jonah PHILLIPS; Hannah, Kitty, Sally to daughters Margery D. GORE, Rebecca CAMPBELL, & Mary J. McDANALD

Joseph MILLER .... pg 474, 12 Apr 1853, inv & appr

Bill, Abron, Robison, Jim, Moses, Jack, Obed, Mance? & 2 children, Harriet & child, Nelly & 2 children

Henry St. George TUCKER ....
.... pg 501, 1 Oct 1851 – 1 Oct 1852, estate acct

Ned to William H. CRAYBILL

Emily S. HEISKELL .... pg 502, 18 Oct 1853, inv & appr

"The said Emily S. owns a negro woman who is now in the employ of W. CATHER but without hire..."

Thomas BROWNING ....pg 506, 11 Sept 1852, inv & appr

Joseph, Hiram, Jesse, Lewis, Burwell, Robert, Mariah, Caroline, Kitty Ann, Delila, Hannah, Mary, Lucinda, Susan, Martha, Malinda, William, John, James, John, Emily, Frances, Alis, Joseph, Roy, Mariah F., Jane, Joseph W. Augustus

Henry RICHARDS ....pg 508, 30 Step 1853, will

old Fanny, Thomas, Thornton & his wife Charlotte & their youngest child Fanny, Hannah, Rachel, B_ttlen? to wife Lydia; Hetty & her child to daughter Harriet LONG; Phlake & her 4 children Henry, Betty, Ellen, & Hannah to daughter Eliza BLAKEMORE; boy Jim to daughter Margaret E. SMITH; men John, Allen to son James R. RICHARDS; remaining slaves to be hired out; girl Hannah to grandchild Alice McKirn? Quinney BLAKEMORE at death of my wife; negroes at the death of my wife, except Hannah & her increase, to be divided among daughter Margaret SMITH, son James R. RICHARDS, son Moses R. RICHARDS, Henry LACY, James R. LACY, Harriet LONG, Eliza BLAKEMORE wife of T.L. BLAKEMORE, daughter Jane KIGER & her son Thomas W. KIGER

Magdaline BEAN .... pg 511, 9 Aug 1853, will

man Jesse to son Mordicai BEAN; "Jesse having been sold by the administrator of my deceased husband and I having purchased him..."

Samuel ALEXANDER .... pg 512, 7 Mar 1853, inv & appr

boy Thompson?

.... pg 513, 8 Mar 1853, sales

negro hired by Mary LANICK

Daniel POWERS .... pg 515, 5 June 1852, will

girl Bell, boy Alexander, girl Eancy to grandchild William Frances son of Charles William should he live to be age 21

James B. HALL .... pg 516, 10 Nov 1853, inv & appr

Hannah & youngest child, Flora, Frederic, Lucinda & youngest child, Eliza, Barbara Ellen, Sarah Frances, Aaron, Judith

WILL BOOK 24
1854 - 1856

Martha Rebecca CARSON Jr. ....
..................................pg 6, 23 Aug 1851 - 26 Mar 1853, gdn acct

Fanny

..............................pg 8, 8 Nov 1851 - 23 Sept 1853, gdn acct

Fanny

William DENNY ....pg 20, 8 Oct 1853, will

Haney? born 21 Mar 1824 to be free at age 40; Martha born 27 Feb
1827 to be free at age 37; John born 14 Jan 1848 to be free at age 27;
Elias born 15 Oct 1849 to be free at age 25; Anna born 8 Mar 1853 to
be free at age 25 to wife Sinna

Robert C. BERKLEY ....pg 40, 6 Feb 1854, inv & appr

man John Carter

Mary POWERS .... pg 40, 24 Jan 1854, will

Nancy, George to be sold; Isabell, Alice to grandson William
POWERS as they become of sufficient age; Edney, James to grandson
Joseph _. POWERS; remaining servants to be divided between sons
Charles William & John W. POWERS

John WRIGHT .... pg 46, 6 May 1851 – 1 Sept 1853, estate acct

negro child supported by Sarah WRIGHT, widow

Daniel POWERS ....pg 52, 6 Mar 1854 in court, inv & appr

Betty 13, Jesse 23, Mary 13, girl Bell 10, Sarah 9, Nancy 58, Easter 58
& child, Marian? 28, Joseph 10, Edna 4, Alex 3, George 17, Phebe 80

Josiah LOCKHART .... pg 53, 9 Sept 1853, inv & appr

Mike, Page, Dave, N__, Emily & her child, boy Isaac

.... pg 57, 6 Mar 1854 in court, sales

Page, N__

221

Joshua GORE .... pg 62, 12 Oct 185_ - 15 Jan 1851, estate acct

negroes kept by W.J. FLEECE; Dave

Jane B. EMMETT .... pg 63, 8 Mar 1854, will

girl Julia to daughter Mrs. Julia BELL; remainder of slaves to be hired out to pay debts then go to Mrs. Jane THOMPKINS & Miss Maria Catherine EMMETT

P.S. boy Jason age 6 to go to a good master near his relations until age 12 or 15

Isaac RICHARDS .... pg 66, 1 May 1854 in court, inv & appr

Peter

Jane EMMETT .... pg 69, 14 Apr 1854, inv & appr

man Ming?, girl Jude at Strother BELL's; boy Jesse, old woman Lucy

Ann W. LYNN of Cumberland, MD .... pg 72, 7 Nov 1851, will

Patty's son Joe to be free; Patty's daughter Sarah to Ann B. TILGHMAN widow of George TILGHMAN; remainder of slaves to be divided among brother James VENABLE of Kentucky, sister Martha D. MOSELY? of Kentucky, & niece Ann SCOTT daughter of sister Mrs. France ROBINSON dec'd of Kentucky

.... pg 73, 15 Feb 1854, codicil

girl Susan called Ann to Ann B. TILGHMAN; girl Lucy to J. Galloway LYNN of Cumberland; girl Martha to Virginia LYNN wife of George LYNN of Alleganey County, MD to hold for daughter Ann LYNN until she reaches age 18

Daniel & Mary POWERS .... pg 75, 31 Mar 1854, inv & appr

boy George, woman Nancy, boys Jesse, Harry, Joe, Ellick, Jim, Easter, girls Mary, Sarah, Letty, Bell, Mariah, Edny, woman Phoebe

.... pg 77, 1 May 1854, sales

George to D. STEPHENSON; woman Nancy to M.R. KAUFMAN; Jesse hired, Easter & child, child Mary, child Sarah, Mariah & child to C.W. POWERS; Harry hired, Letta, Bell to J.W. POWERS; Joseph hired to A.W. KLINE

Joshua GORE ....pg 82, 1 Feb 1850 – 1 Feb 1851, estate acct

Fanny Bartlett, Hannah, Peter

Frances SILVER ....pg 92, 2 Nov 1852 – 1 Feb 1854, estate acct

Mary, Jacob, Ann; Jack sold per will

Ann BYWATERS ....pg 108, 13 Feb 1847, will

girl Caroline to daughter Asaneth; girl Matilda to daughter Elizabeth wife of Thomas DUNCAN & the heirs of daughter Lucy dec'd wife of William SMITH; remaining negroes to daughters Mary Ann wife of Henry H. BAKER, Asaneth BYWATERS, & Rebecca wife of Zebulon PERRILL

Beverly JONES ....pg 112, 1 Jan 1852 – 1 May 1853, gdn acct

Vincent, Catherine, Eliza, Margaret & child, old Patty & 2 children, Jim, Patsy, Tom, Vincent's wife; Vincent, woman & children sold

Martha Rebecca CARSON ....pg 114, 9 Dec 1851 – 31 Dc 1853, gdn acct

Fanny

Thomas BRYARLY ....pg 129, 30 Sept 1853, will

man Nat to be free but if he cannot give security he is to go to brother James BRYARLY

James V. GLASS ....pg 137, 23 Nov 1850 – 1 June 1853, comm acct?

woman & children kept by M.B. CARTMILL

Ann BYWATERS ....pg 145, 2 Oct 1854 in court, inv & appr

Richard, Matilda, Judy, Cartine?, Taylor

John MARKER ....pg 159, 5 Sept 1854, will

use of land slaves to sons Alpheus & Cornelius B. MARKER; after the death of present wife Sarah MARKER when the above will expire, all slaves to be divided among children of present wife Jacob A. MARKER, John H. MARKER, Mary A. RAMEY wife of John RAMEY, Reuben MARKER, Alpheus MARKER, & Cornelius B. MARKER

Mary FIZER .... pg 164, 9 Sept 1854, will

    Henry to be sold

Isaac COLE .... pg 171, May 1842 – 14 Mar 1852, estate acct

    negroes, servants

Isaac HITE .... pg 173, 1 Jan 1839 – 1 Jan 1854, estate acct

    old negroes kept by W. ALLISON; slave died; old Frank & Freelove kept by Jacob F. LARICK

.... pg 176, 1 Jan 1854, estate acct

    "Statement showing the balance due to the Legatees....equalizing negroes...paid by the 4 sons to the 6 daughters." Isaac, Priss, ___; boy taken by W.M. HITE

.... pg 179, Oct 1838 – 1 Jan 1857, estate acct

    Frank; old negroes kept by ALLISON

Dorcas COMPTON .... pg 181, 14 Mar 185 – 1 Jan 1854, estate acct

    Ambrose, Judy, Caroline, Reuben

Orphans of John WRIGHT .... pg 182, 1 Nov 1851 – 1 July 1854, gdn acct

    woman, child

Dr. George LYNN .... pg 188, 31 Dec 1847 – 1 June 1854, attorney acct

    Joe, Harrison, Jane, Patty

Miss Ann LYNN .... pg 191, 18 Nov 1851 – Mar 1854, settlement

    amount of negro sales; Joe emancipated

Jesse COMEGYS .... pg 198, 15 May 1854, will

    George Copper, age 18, to be freed on 1 Jan 1860

Ann Evelina TUCKER .... pg 200, 11 Feb 1854, will

    Emily's daughter Mary to granddaughter Evelina Tucker MAGILL; man James Brooks to granddaughter Evelina Hunter TUCKER child of St. George TUCKER & A.E. GILMER; Hetty's daughter Betty to granddaughter Evelina Hunter TUCKER daughter of Randolph & Laura TUCKER; Emily's son Jim to son Tudor; Hetty & her daughter

Catherine & Emily's child William to son Alfred; Emily & George to choose their masters; old woman Judy died

Mary FIZER .... pg 203, 13 Nov 1854, inv & appr

boy Henry

Mrs. Ann Amelia McKOWN .... pg 204, 24 Apr 1854, inv & appr

Julia Ann 31, Harriet called Pony 32, Mary called Mati 17, Ian 17, Anna 12, Charity called Pull 10, Lucy 6, John 4, Walter 4, Thomas 2, Fanny

D.L. CLAYTON .... pg 218, 30 Nov 1854, sales

Ben sold at Newtown on 26 Dec 1854 to J.H. KEMP

Isaac WOOD .... pg 227, 27 Nov 1853, will

nephew Joseph TAPE? to free Jacob, now 10, at age 21; man Simon to be freed

Judith K. PRITCHARD .... pg 229, 30 Sept 1848, will

girl Susan to be emancipated

Jesse COMEGYS .... pg 230, 27 Mar 1855, inv & appr

boy to serve 5 years

Richard WELLS .... pg 235, 1 Jan 1848 – 1 Jan 1852, estate acct

Negro Fountaine

Jared William CARSON ....
.... pg 237, 12 Nov 1852 - 27 Dec 1853, estate acct

Jonas, Milly, John, Stephen

Martha Rebecca CARSON .... pg 240, 1 Jan 1854 – 1 Jan 1855, gdn acct

Fanny

John MARKER .... pg 241, 5 Apr 1855, inv & appr

Lucy & her child (not to be sold); girl Margaret (not to be sold); man Allen sentenced to be sold & transported from the Commonwealth

Joanna MYERS .... pg 246, 1 Apr 1855, will

woman Evelina to daughter Rachel Ann SHRYOCK; man Thornton to sons Stephen M. MYERS & William A. MYERS

Robert HARRISON .... pg 247, 10 Feb 1855, inv & appr

man 25, woman 21

Henry RICHARDS .... pg 250, 20 Dec 1853, inv & appr

Tom, Thornton, Butler, Peter, Willison; Lucy bequeathed to Mrs. LONG, Phoeba's children Bet & Harry, Phoeba & 2 children, Met & 2 children, Oscar, Oliver, Abel; Allen, John by will to J.R. RICHARDS, Ellen, Susan; Tim by will to M.E. SMITH; Louisa

Mrs. Lydia RICHARDS .... pg 252, 21 Dec 1853, inv & appr

Tom, Thornton, Butler, Rachael, Charlotte & child, Hannah, old Fanny

Edmund PAGETT .... pg 255, 27 May 1851 – 27 May 1854, estate acct

Malack, Alexander, Mary

Joanna G. MYRES .... pg 258, 9 June 1855, inv & appr

Evelina 28 & child George Edward 3 months, Thornton 26

Isaac WOOD .... pg 260, 11 Aapr 1855, inv & appr

man Simon emancipated by the will; boy Jefferson to be free at age 21

Mary B. WILSON .... pg 281, 18 Aug 1855, will

man Reuben, Lelena & child, old Fanny to sisters Jane McCLORY and Ann S. WILSON; Harriet age 15 to sisters Jane McCLORY and Ann S. WILSON, trustees for niece Sarah Jane WILSON

Helen C. GALLOWAY .... pg 288, 25 July 1842, will

all slaves to be emancipated: Milly Williams & her children Martha, Catherine, Eliza, Henrietta, Richard, Mary, & Margaret Ellen Williams; Judy Brown, George William Brown, Samuel Brown, & Fanny Brown children of Caty Brown dec'd; Samuel Armstrong, Fanny Barton & her child George William, Sarah Blackburn & her children Dennis & Louisa Blackburn, Fanny Blackburn & her child Susan, and any future children or slaves

227

Monday Robinson ....pg 370, 2 Feb 1849, will

his children are to be emancipated: Sally Robinson, Charles Robinson, Archibald Robinson, & John Robinson

Thomas A. TIDBALL ....pg 371, 15 Nov 1852, will

slaves are not to be sold

....pg 372, 20 Feb 1856, codicil

Winny & her children & grandchildren to wife Susan W. TIDBALL

Henry MYERS .... pg 373, 2 June 1856? in court, inv & appr

Aaron (Bettie), Moses (William), George (William), James (Bettie), Amy & 2 children (Mary), Bekiy?, Hannah (Bettie), Martha (Bettie)

Joanna G. MYERS .... pg 385, 5 June 1855 – 1 Jan 1856, estate acct

child sold; Thornton

Jared CARSON .... pg 386, 1 Jan – 18 Nov 1855, estate acct

Milly, John, Stephen

Robert C. BERKLEY .... pg 387, 30 Jan 1854 – 12 Apr 1856, estate acct

John sold

Henry MYERS .... pg 389, 14 Feb 1856, sales

Mose, George to W.H. MYERS; man Aaron, woman Hannah, boy James, girl Martha to Betty B. MYERS; Amy & 2 children to Mary MYERS

John GILKESON .... pg 393, 14 Mar 1856, inv & appr

Mary (Lena) & child, Letty & child, Lucius 9, Joseph 7, Ellen 5, Frances 3; woman Frances 85

Robert HARRISON .... pg 433, 26 Feb 1855, sales

woman to James CATHER; man to Robert SMITH

Reuben TRIPLETT .... pg 435, 6 May 1852, will

boy Sandy to son Jeremiah D. TRIPLETT

Solomon S. HARMON..............pg 439, 23 Oct 1855, inv & appr

man James, boy George

Simon CARSON .... pg 450, 10 Apr 1841, will

servants to wife Martha CARSON who is to emancipate male slaves at age 30, women at age 25, male children at age 21 & females age 18; any children who own slaves to follow the request; Hiram & Lee were willed to me by Henry JACKSON until they become 21

Amelia or Emma L. HERSKEL..
..................pg 460, 21 Oct 1853 – 1 June 1855, gdn acct

woman & child

William KERR...............pg 465, 3 June 1854 – 1 Mar 1856, estate acct

Frederick

Reuben TRIPLETT.....................pg 469, 3 Oct 1856, slave div

Peyton to Mandley TRIPLETT; Edmund, Harrison to Uriel TRIPLETT; Adilainde, Sarah to Mrs. Susan BROWN; Emily to Mrs. Harriet ONEIL; Tom to Leonard TRIPLETT; Hercules, Fanny to James TRIPLETT son of Martin; Elizabeth, Eliza to Nimrod TRIPLETT; William to Bushrod TRIPLETT; Henry, Dinah to Jeremiah D. TRIPLETT

Simon CARSON ....pg 483, 9 Sept 1856, inv & appr

Stephen, Mary, Lucinda, Caroline & child, Louisa, Ellen, Hester, Belle, Selah, Amanda, Matilda, Lucy, Sam, Enos, Lewis, Betty?

Mary FISER ....pg 490, 14 Nov 1854 – 31 Oct 1855, estate acct

Henry

WILL BOOK 25
1856 - 1859

Mrs. Sarah DEAHL...............pg 22, 8 Sept 1856, depositions

....pg 25

by David W. BARTON: Jim; a woman died after her master; boy child born since the appraisment

.....................................pg 28, 6 May 1851 – 1 Oct 1855, receipts

Jim; Jim's control passed to William & Barton under the Deed of Trust on 10 Apr 1851; boy George was born 17 May 1848 & came to the estate after the death of David DEAHL; his mother was a slave of the husband's estate & died 1 Aug 1848

Benjamin BRISON.............................pg 51, 7 Aug 1856, will

girl Louisa to be free at the death of wife Mary BRISON

William BYWATERS.......................... pg 52, 1 Sept 1856, distributees

Richard, Matilda, Taylor, sold to Miss A.W. BYWATERS; Judy to Nathaniel CARTMELL; Henry, Lucy to Mary Ann BAKER; Stephen to Rebecca PERRILL; Joseph, William, Caroline to A.W. BYWATERS; George to Thomas W. SMITH; Charles to Elizabeth DUNCAN; Lucy SMITH's children: Thomas W. SMITH, George L. SMITH, Robert B. SMITH, Samuel P. SMITH, Pauline E. SMITH, & William SMITH

.... pg 54, 1 Sept 1856, settlement

Miss Asseneth BYWATERS;, Elizabeth PERRILL, George L. SMITH, Pauline E. SMITH, William SMITH, Elizabeth DUNCAN, H.H. BAKER & wife

Mrs. Ann BYWATERS....... pg 60, 1 May 1855 – 1 Sept 1856, estate acct

Richard, Matilda, Caroline

Henry F. SCHENK............................. pg 68, 27 July 1856, sales

boy Sandy to J.B. SHOWALTER; boy Alfred to G.A. WHITE; woman Lucinda to Edward N. SANDERS; woman Lucinda re-sold at Court House in Winchester

Simon CARSON .... pg 74, 24 Dec 1856, distribution of slaves

Mary, Enos, Betsy to Elisha W. CARSON; Stephen, Lucinda, Belle to Simon CARSON Jr.; Lewis to the heirs of John CARSON; Hester to William CARSON; Amanda to Mrs. Ann S. McLEOD; Louisa, Lucy to Mrs. Jane R. McKAY; Matilda, Sam to the heirs of Robert R. CARSON; Ellen, Selah to M. Reubin CARSON only child of Jared W. CARSON dec'd; Caroline & her child Thomas Allen to James H. CARSON

William STEPHENSON .... pg 76, 14 Dec 1853, will

all slaves to wife & at her death divided between sons John & Henry STEPHENSON

Henry F. SCHENK .... pg 80, 10 July 1856, inv & appr

boys Alfred, Elias, Sandy, girl Lucinda

Roberta P. BURWELL .... pg 97, 7 Jan 185_, will

servants are to be freed

Henry RICHARDS .... pg 98, 3 Dec 1853 – 1 Jan 1857, estate acct

Oscar, 2 women & infants, Ellen & child, Oliver, Ostear, Peter, William, Susan, Louisa & child

Henry SEEVERS .... pg 105, 16 Sept 185_, will

negroes to be rented out until sold

S.S. HARMAN .... pg 113, 23 Oct 1835, a inv & appr

man Jim, boy George

Miss Helen C. GALLOWAY ....
.... pg 118, Oct 1855 – 13 Jan 1857, estate acct

cash of Henry Holmes hire of his wife, George, Sam, Richard, Mary Jane, Henrietta, Emily, Margaret, George Williams, John, Marshal, Milly Williams, Sam, Julia Holmes, Fanny Tidball, Dennis?

emancipated by testatrix: Milly Williams, George W. Brown, Samuel Brown, Julia Holmes, Henrietta Williams, Fanny Tidball, Martha Williams

232

Isaac RICHARDS .... pg 202, 1 Feb 1856 – 1 Apr 1857, estate acct

Peter

Edward R. MUSE..............pg 208, 22 Mar 1856 – 1 Apr 1857, estate acct

Adam, Susan, Phil, Henry, Jane, Rose

Reuben TRIPLETT .... pg 216, 12 July 1856, inv & appr

Adelade & child Sarah, Betsy 22 & child Eliza 2, Fanny 51, Dinah 75, man Hookless 48, Peyton 8, Harrison 13, William 18, Edmund 68, Emily

A.J. GRUBB...................................... pg 219, 13 Nov 1856, sales

woman & 2 children to Jacob RIDGEWAY

Solomon HARMAN............. pg 228, 3 Oct 1855 – 7 Oct 1856, estate acct

boy

Henry SEEVERS.................................. pg 233, 30 June 1857, inv & appr

Sam 45, Harry 41, Arch 36, Walker 34, Lish 16

Thomas BRYARLY.......... pg 235, 4 June 1845 – 1 May 1857, estate acct

woman, girl, Lucy, Nat, Black Mary, Joshua, John, Jordan, Sarah, Mary Massie, Mary Williams, Priscilla

....pg 242, commissioner's note

"...the property devised by the testator is slave Priscilla, who is superannated & is necessarily a charge upon the estate..."

Mrs. A.E. TUCKER ....pg 246, 1 Feb 1855 – 15 Feb 1857, estate acct

Catty

Joseph B. HACKNEY......pg 248, 18 Mar 1853 - 1 Mar 1857, estate acct

woman Louisa

Ludwell C.J. CHIPLEY.......................pg 254, 2 Aug 1857 in court, appr

girl, man Frank

.... pg 256, 3 Aug 1857, sales

girl Ann to Elijah McDOWELL; man Frank to Mrs. Jane R. CHIPLEY

Munday ROBINSON .... pg 266, 3 Apr 1856, inv & appr

Polly, Louisa, Harriet, Manurva, Lucy, Billy, Milly, Lucy, Munday, Fanny, Charles, Archy, Sally, Caroline, John, John

Meredith H. JOLLIFFE .... pg 267, 9 May 1857, ap inv & appr pr

woman's child

.... pg 271, 3 Aug 1857 in court, sales

Mary & child to Margaret H. JOLLIFFE

Jared W. CARSON .... pg 282, 1 Jan 1856 – 1 Jan 1857, estate acct

Milly; John to time of freedom

Miss M.R. CARSON .... pg 283, 12 Jan 1856 – 1 Jan 1857, gdn acct

Fanny

Robert AFFLICK .... pg 284, 1 Aug 1844 – 9 June 1856, estate acct

Jerry

Mundy ROBERTSON .... pg 296, 26 Mary 1856- 1 Feb 1857, estate acct

Harriet, William, Bill, Charles, Archy, John, Milly

Jonathan Taylor, a colored man,,............ pg 306, 25 Apr 1857, inv & appr

William A. CARTER .... pg 312, 11 Aapr 1857, will

servants to be kept by the family

T.A. TIDBALL .... pg 318, 19 June 1856 - 1 May 1857, estate acct

Maria & her children Rachael & Shirley to Robert STEEL; Smith to J.E. TYSON; Harriet & infant to George CREMER; Winney, Jonathan to A.W. McDONALD; girl boarded by Shirley LOVETT; Rebecca, Lewis, Daniel to John LOUTHAN; Maria & her 2 children Rachael & Shirley, to Robert STEEL; Maria's children John, Laura & Mary to Robert STEEL?; old Maria to Mrs. S.W. TIDBALL

Isaac WILLIAMSON .... pg 325, 16 Feb 1856, inv & appr

girl

Isaac WILLIAMSON .... pg 326, 30 Nov 1857, sales

girl Jane to M.B. CARTMELL

Miss Virginia KERR ....pg 327, 17 Nov 1857, inv & appr

Mary 22, alias Mary Hall, in the possession of Dr. Lewis A. MILLER

Mary MILLER .... pg 351, 28 June 1816, will

boy Obed, girl Mary to daughter Sarah Ann MILLER

Edmund PAGETT .... pg 359, 1 Feb 1856 – 1 Jan 1857, estate acct

Malack

Philip SWANN ....pg 362, 11 Nov 1857, will

girl Sarah to wife; girl Judy to daughter Mary; girl Rebecca to daughter
Corneliann; old John & his wife Mary, old Grandison to son Francis &
if he decides not to take them they are to be sold; boy John to be sold

John GILKESON ....pg 366, 1 may 1856 - 1 Oct 1857, estate acct

Joseph sold, taken back, resold

Thomas BROWNING ....pg 369, 6 Sept 1852 – 1 Oct 1856, estate acct

runaway slave; slaves advertised

Mrs. Sarah DEAHL ....pg 375, 1 Oct 1856 – 1 Jan 1858, Trustee acct

Jim

Susan CARPENTER .... pg 393, 1 Jan 1852, Statement B

appraised value of slaves; Elisha W. CARSON's share: Mary, Enos,
Betsey; Simon CARSON Jr.'s share: Stephen, Lucinda, Belle; John
CARSON's share: Lewis; William CARSON's share: Hester; Mrs.
Ann S. McLEOD's share: Amanda; Mrs. Jane R. McKAY's share:
Louisa, Lucy; Robert R. CARSON's heir's share: Matilda, Sam; Jared
W. CARSON's heir's share: Ellen, Selah; James H. CARSON's share:
Caroline & her child Thomas Allen

Henry P. WARD .... pg 405, 20 Mar 1853 - 1 June 1858, Trustee acct

woman Nancy sold

Jared W. CARSON ....pg 409, 1 Jan 1857 - 1 Jan 1858, estate acct

Stephen, Milly

Miss M. Rebecca CARSON ....pg 410, 17 Jan 1857 - 1 Jan 1858, gdn acct

Fanny

Israel WILDESON .... pg 418, 29 May 1857, inv & appr

Charles, Barbara & her 2 children, James

Mrs. Mary MILLER .... pg 424, 8 Jan 1858, inv & appr

Mariah & child, William, Abraham, Harriet & 2 children, Moses, Jack; each person has two appraisals – one if a slave for life and one if free at age 30

C.J. CHIPLEY .... pg 430, 27 Sept 1856 - 1 Mar 1858, estate acct

2 slaves sold; Frank sold

Edward R. MUSE .... pg 452, 6 Apr 1857 – 1 Apr 1858, estate acct

Aaron, Philip, Jane, Henry

Henry WISECARVER .... pg 472, 11 May 1858, inv & appr

man Elisha

....pg 479, 31 May 1858 in court, sales

man Elisha

Miss Virginia E. MUSE ....pg 483, 9 Apr 1857 – 15 Mar 1858, gdn acct

amount to equilize division of slaves

Elisha W. CARSON .... pg 499, 27 Mar 1854 - 1 Jan 1858, Trustee acct

Mary, Enos, Betsy

Peyton Washington .... pg 502, 17 Apr 1857, will

wife Lydia to be free at his death

237

Stephen PRITCHARD ....pg 504, 16 Feb 1858, will

boy William, Marthy & her child to son Stephen Cornelius PRITCHARD now in his possession; Molly, Judith & child, boy Alfred to wife Mary PRITCHARD

Mahlon L. LOVETT .... pg 506, 28 June 1858, will

"...the children...when that age is attained and then an equal share in the whole residue of my estate at that time remaining for their use Negroes inluuded."; man Bob to be sold

Robert M. CARSON ....pg 508, 5 Oct 1857 - 1 July 1858, estate acct

Stephen sold; Belle, Lucinda

Isaac B. COLE.............................pg 522, 8 Sept 1858, inv & appr

woman Mariah

William A. CARTER ....pg 525, 9 Nov 1857, inv & appr

men Miles, Henry, Dolphin, David, Jim Thompson, Jim Smith, boys Peyton, George, man John, women Jane Cooper, woman Caroline, girl Sarah Jane, boy Lee, girl Harriett, Kate & child, woman Eddy

Mrs. Ann E. TUCKER .... pg 544, 28 Feb 1857 – 1 Jan 1858, estate acct

Judy died

Eliza B. CAMPBELL.......pg 546, 31 May 1854 - 1 June 1857, estate acct

Celsy kept by N.M. CARTMELL; paid commissioner for division of servants; Bill, Maria, Barbara, Mary

George D. HARRISON...............pg 551, 6 Dec 1858 in court, inv & appr

Sallie 60, John 37, Flora 35, Millie 33, Levi 28, Jane 26, Polly 24, Frank 28, Neil 22, George 15, Louisa 13, Bill 14, Charles 10, Sarah 9, Henry 8, Betty 7, Jim 6, Lee 6, Scott 4, Wesly 3, Susan 3, Edward 18 months, John 18 months, Charlott 18 months

Thomas B. CAMPBELL .... pg 552, 15 Jan 1858, will

girl Emily 8 to daughter Sarah Catharine

Thomas B. CAMPBELL .... pg 553, 1 Feb 1858, 1st codicil

wife to have any servants for her use, the remainder to be divided among the parties by valuation

....pg 553, 21 July 1858, 2nd codicil

since daughter Sarah Catharine is now dec'd, girl Emily is no longer her share

Isaac B. COLE .... pg 554, 26 Aug 1858, sales

woman Maria to Mrs. COLE

Thomas B. CAMPBELL ....pg 564, 18 Nov 1858, inv & appr

man Isaac, women Judah, Fanny, boys George, Robert, Jacob, girls Sally, Emily

John GOFF ....pg 580, 13 Feb 1858, will

Milly & her children to wife Mary & at her death Milly is to be emancipated & any of her children age 21, those children who are younger to serve until age 21

Felix ROBERTS...................................pg 582, 5 Feb 1857, will

all slaves to be emancipated 4 years from the date of his death

John GILKESON .... pg 69, 12 Aug 1857, Report of Debt

Letty kept by Robert B. HOLIDAY, his claim

Nimrod TRUSSELL .... pg 79, 3 May 1859, inv & appr

man Isreal

Henry RICHARDS .... pg 90, Jan 1857 – 12 Jan 18159, estate acct

Ellen & child; man Abner sold; Susan, Louisa & child, Elen & child, Peter, William, Oscar; boy William to HARMON

William D. GILKESON ....

.... pg 99, 30 July 1858 – 25 Sept 1859, trust acct

Winney to Harriet BAKER

Benjamin W. JEFFERSON ....

.... pg 107, 28 Oct 1857 – 1 Dec 1858, estate acct

Anana?, Ann

Thomas Allen TIDBALL ....

.... pg 115, 1 May 1857 - 1 May 1859, estate acct

2 young servants sold at public sale

.... pg 118, 1 May 1857 - 1 May 1859, separate estate acct

"one half of Mrs. TIDBALLs purchase of property at appraisement exclusive of Maria"; 2 young servants sold at public sale

.... pg 120, 1 May 1857 - 1 Jan 1859, separate estate acct

Bill of Sale for 2 servants

Israel WILKINSON ....pg 139, 14 May 1857 - 1 June 1859, estate acct

Charles sold to J.W. WILKINSON; Barbara & her 2 children, James sold to Jacob F. LARRICK

Susan GROVE .... pg 147, 27 Nov 1858, will

all negroes to be emancipated

Joseph B. HACKNEY .... pg 150, 29 June 18159, will

woman Polly to wife Rebecca Jane on the condition she will not be sold & at Rebecca Jane's death, if still living, to son William; the remaining servants to be divided among children William & Mary Elizabeth & are not to be sold

George W. HAMMOND..................pg 154, 1 Aug 1859, inv & appr

Ben, Fanny & 2 children, old Mima

Mary R. SHEPHERD..................pg 156, 19 Sept 1859, inv & appr

man Henry

Thomas MURPHY.......... pg 156, 6 Apr 1858 – 20 May 1859, estate acct

boy

David HOLLINGSWORTH..................pg 158, 22 Sept 1859, will

servants to be hired out to pay debts after which man Nick may choose to be free, if not to go to son Jonah Isaac HOLLINGSWORTH together with Phil & Georgeanna; Kitty & her son John Henry to daughter Mary Ellen HOLLINGSWORTH; Henrietta & her 3 minor children to daughter Ann Virginia HOLLINGSWORTH

Hester I. GLASS ....pg 159, 23 July 1853, will

man Henry to be set free after serving the full year

Sarah KENNAN ....pg 162, 21 Aug 1852, will

negroes in trust to Isaac RUSSELL for son David STUBBLEFIELD & daughter Mrs. Martha KIGER & to remain with Isaac RUSSELL, never to live with her children or their spouses & to be free if all children die before age 21

.... pg 163, 16 Aug 1859, codicil

Simon age 6, called Sye & the son of Martha, to William G. RUSSELL in trust for daughter-in-law Meriam STUBBLEFIELD the wife of son David STUBBLEFIELD & at her death to son David STUBBLEFIELD

Sylvester Jordan, a free colored man..................pg 165, 18 Mar 1856, will

aggrement made with Lewis & William Jordan; children: Lewis, Sarah wife of Berry Reed, Hiram, Lucinda, & Baylor (dec'd)

Mary McLEOD ....pg 168, 2 Sept 1859, inv & appr

Mahala 30 & her infant son Edward 7 months, John 2, Amanda 5, Harriet 7, Strother 14, William 13, Marshall 12, Charles 9

Mrs. Mary MILLER ....pg 181, 5 Oct 1859, estate acct

Abed & Mary received by Miss Sarah Ann MILLER; Maria & child, William, Abram, Harriet & 2 children, Moses, Jack appraised

.... pg 183, 3 Oct 1859 in court, distribution

Maria & child, William to Thomas C. MILLER; Harriet & her 2 children to Reuben S. LONG & wife; Jack to Miss Sarah Ann MILLER; Moses to John M. MILLER

Orphans of John WRIGHT .... pg 197, 1857 - 1 Aug 1858, gdn acct

John kept by Sarah WRIGHT for 1 year

James P. RIELY ....pg 202, 6 Oct 1859, inv & appr

old Becky, Becky Jane, Sarah, Lawson, Eliza, Arabella & child, Charles, Alcy, Lewis, Winny, Edward, Susan, Fanny, Bazil, Amanda, John, Jack, George, Daniel

William KERR .... pg 204, 23 Oct 1859, 2nd distribution

Frederick; Mary taken by Virginia KERR; infants Benjamin, Margaret, Robert kept by the executor; Peggy

Philip SWANN .... pg 218, 1 Mar 1858 - 1 Sept 1859, estate acct

boy sold; John, Grandison

David HOLLINGSWORTH ....pg 238, 5 Mar 1860 in court, inv & appr

Henrietta & her 3 children, Kitty & child John, Phil, Nick, Georgianna

John RICHARDS ....pg 289, 29 Sept 1859, will

man George, his wife Flora, & their child Hannah to wife Sara RICHARDS

James A. RICHARDS .... pg 305, 2 Mar 1860, inv & appr

man Harrison

John RICHARDS .... pg 305, 19 Apr 1860, inv & appr

boys Jackson, Thornton, girls Mary, Jane, Hannah, Betsy, women Celey, Flora, man George

Stephen PRITCHARD .... pg 320, 3 Dec 1858 – 1 Sept 1859, estate acct

servant kept by James JAITOR

Annis Randolph alias Lovett .... pg 331, 15 Mar 1860, will

"...my Step Son Cyrus Lovett at present the Servant of Mrs. Abby B. HOPKINS...the emancipation of said Cyrus..."

Simon CARSON .... pg 347, 1 Jan 1860, estate acct

Martha E. TAYLOR's hire of Belle, Lucinda

Elisha W. CARSON. .... pg 352, 1 Jan 1859 -1 Jan 1860, Trustee acct

Mary, Enos, Betsy

Robert M. CARSON .... pg 354, 1 Jan 18159 – 1 Jan 1860, estate acct

Lucinda, Belle

M. Rebecca CARSON .... pg 355, 1 Jan 1859 – 1 Jan 1860, gdn acct

Stephen

Thomas Allen TIDBALL ....
.... pg 358, 1 May 1859 – 1 May 1860, estate acct

servants

Mary R. SHEPHERD .... pg 365, 7 July 1859 - 15 Aug 1860, estate acct

Henry sold

Elisha W. CARSON .... pg 366, 5 Sept 1860, inv & appr

Mary, Betsey, Enos

Henry F. SCHENCK .... pg 388, 22 July 1856 - 1 Nov 1858, estate acct

L.F.Y. GRIM redeemed slave held under bill of sale; negro resold; slaves sold; loss on resale on Lucinda to N. SAMUELS

Rebecca JOLLIFF .... pg 430, 5 May 1860, will

Eliza Allen, a free woman who has lived with Rebecca JOLLIFF from her childhood, to have land in trust of son Joseph for her separate use and from control of her husband

Sarah GRIFFIN .... pg 436, 17 Jan 1859 – 1 Jan 1861, estate acct

Rachel

Jacob SENSENEY .... pg 448, 27 Feb 1860, will

choice of 2 negroes to wife Catharine; negroes to be hired out & but divided between wife & 4 children

John MOUNTZ of Georgetown, D.C. .... pg 462, 5 July 1855, will

Isaac to son Joseph or Jose; Ephraim, Susannah & all her children to daughter Elizabeth C. CRAMER

Beverly R. JONES .... pg 465, 15 Jan 1857 - 1 Jan 1861, Trustee acct

Catharine, servant sold to William A. CARTER's estate; Tom sold to Adolph WHITE; Eliza sold to E. WALKINS; girl sold to William G. KEGER; servant, Robert

Philip SWANN .... pg 471, 1 Apr 1861 in court, distributions

servants taken by Francis SWANN; Judy taken by Miss Mary E. SWANN; Rebecca taken by Miss Cornelia SWANN

Ann SWANN .... pg 474, 9 Jun 1859 - 1 June 1860, estate acct

woman Sarah sold

Mahlon S. LOVETT .... pg 476, 9 Aug 1858 – 1 Aug 1860, estate acct

servant, Harriet; Robert sold

Casper RINKER .... pg 484, 22 Jan 1861, will

boy John

George BRINKER .... pg 491, 19 Apr 1854, will

all negreos to wife Elizabeth that came by her marriage; Hester, Harry? to son Benjamin; girl Elisa Ann, in the possession of George M. BRINKER, to son Abraham

Joseph Milton BAKER...................... pg 494, 16 May 1860, will

woman Eliza to wife Edminia S.

David HOLLINGSWORTH................... pg 510, 28 Feb 1861, estate acct

Phil

Jacob SENSENEY ....pg 517, 7 Feb 1861, inv & appr

Mary 40, James 26, Ben 27, __ 25?, Lucy 35, Sarah 17 & her infant child 28 months, Jane 12, ___ 5

Mrs. Sarah DRAKE....................pg 523, 1 Feb 1859 – Feb 1861, gdn acct

Jim to Caspar CO___

Elijah SHULL .... pg 526, 3 June 186_, inv & appr

John 8, Charles 5

George BREAKER ....pg 540, 1 Oct 1861, inv & appr

Harry 75, Hester 16, Eliza Ann 9

William A. CARTER .... pg 566, 18 Oct 1857 - 1 Jan 1861, estate acct

Elisha?, Hally sold

David HOLLINGSWORTH Jr...
.... pg 577, 15 Oct 1863- 12 Apr 1864, estate acct

cash of James BOWLS' Estate hire of negro

Phebe GOLD .... pg 579, __ Apr 1857, will

man Armstead

Sarah Thompson................... pg 585, 8 Dec 180, will

boy Jim to be free at the age of 23, niece Rachael Ann LUPTON? to ___ his wages?; woman Rachael's guardian to be niece Rachael Ann LUPTON?

WILL BOOK 27
1862 - 1865

James BOWLES...pg 1, 4 Oct 1862, will

all negroes to wife

William WOOD ....pg 5, Sept? 1856, will

slaves not to be sold

Joseph KEAN.. pg 14, 24 June 1863, will

"Erlena Orrick and her children Robert Orrick, Emily Orrick, Maria Orrick, & Charles Orrick shall be free but Robert is to attend to me as long as I may live."

David W. BARTON... pg 15, 1 June 1861, will

Lavinia, Susan (or Sucky), Jim, John, little girls Mary & Nancy in residence in town; Dan, Sam, George, Plump, Henry?, Frederick, old Isaac, Polly, Bella at Springdale; Jim, Washington Albert, Brooke? besides these Levina has a child; number of slaves 18 old & young

Joseph NEILL ....pg 21, 22 Feb 1858, will

"The balance of funds...in the purchase... emancipation and removal to some free state of this union all the healthy & able boddied slaves male & female grown and small – the crippled & old ones excepted? which belong to the estate of my Brother Lewis NEILL...together with all the increase since..."

William MILLER.. pg 27, 24 Apr 1862, will

John, Will?, Joseph, Branson, Charles, Buck, Eliza, Mary, Sarah to wife Henrietta Amelia

.... pg 30, 7 Oct 1865, codicil

slaves to be free after the death of wife H.A. MILLER: Joe, Sarah, Mary, Eliza, Charley, John

Joseph M. BAKER Jr...........pg 35, 6 Feb 1862 - 15 July 1863, estate acct

negroe hired from J.R. TUCKER; Eliza to Mrs.? MAGALL?

J.M. BAKER ....pg 53, Oct 1862 in court, inv & appr

boy Presley

William MILLER .... pg 81, 1863, appr property

2 negro houses on Braddock St; 5 negro houses on Washington St

Branch JORDAN .... pg 95, 6 Apr 1864, will

servants to be free at age 25

Thomas GLASS .... pg 165, 5 Feb 1862 in court, inv & appr

Harrison, Mary, Turner?, Phil, Bob, John, Delpha, Salley, Charles, Alice, Press, Andy, Page, Ann

.... pg 187, 18 Dec 1861 – 2 Sept 1865, estate acct

Abner, Harrison, Negro Tom

Thomas CLEVENGER ..... pg 231, 13 Dec 1862 - 1 Nov 1865, estate acct

woman

Elizabeth KNIGHT .... pg 235, 29 May 1863, will

old Robert Forge to receive money managed by David W. BARTON, executor

James H. CAMPBELL .... pg 257, 10 Mar 1862, inv & appr

Elsey, Charlotte, Mary, Ann, Charles, John; old woman Hannah to be kept for life

.... pg 262, __ Dec 1865, sales

Charlotte, Charles to Josiah COOPER; John to John QUIGLEY?

Elisha W. CARSON............. pg 12, 9 Aug 1860 – 1 Jan 1862, estate acct

Mary, Enos, Betsy

Robert M. CARSON .... pg 16, 3 Sept 1860 – 1 Jan 1861, estate acct

servants sold

Simon CARSON .... pg 20, 3 Sept 1860 – 14 Mar 1861, estate acct

hire of Bell, Lucinda; deduct share of expenses of their sale

Archibald LARRICK .... pg 35, 18 Nov 1861, inv & appr

woman Hannah

Elisha W. CARSON............ pg 60, 15 Nov 1859 – 1 Jan 1861, estate acct

Mary, Enos, Betsy

Warner W. KOWN.................................... pg 87, 19/20 Oct 1865, sales

*A. Green purchased hay stack; cow

*A. Green (col'd) failed to comply with ___ of sale & property resold
1 Jan 1866

Elijah SHULL .... pg 130, 19 Mar 1861 – 1 June 1866, estate acct

negro

William HENING .... pg 201, 28 Jan 1862 - 4 Oct 1866, estate acct

servant died

Susan P. CARTER ....pg 214, 10 Feb 1853, will

woman & all her children to niece Mary Susan PITMAN daughter of
brother Joseph PITMAN; man Bower to chose his master

Jonas CHAMBERLIN...................................... pg 215, 18 Dec 1866, will

George Mason to be furnished with a house, victuals, & clothes as long
as he may desire to remain & assist wife Elizabeth B. CHAMBERLIN

James S. CLARK .... pg 252, 18 Dec 1860 - 1 Jan 1864, estate acct

boy, girl sold

Nimrod TRUSSELL .... pg 307, May – 25 June 1860, estate acct

Israel sold

John HOFF .... pg 336, 8 Mar 1859 – 7 July 1867, estate acct

servant

Isaac RICHARD .... pg 340, 1 May 1857 – 1 Jan 1863, estate acct

Servant Peter

Henry MYERS .... pg 360, 1 Jan 1856 – 5 Sept 1859, estate acct

George; Betsy boarded one week, died

Mary W. MAGILL .... pg 369, 30 Jan 1857, will

Sally to daughter Sarah, Letty to daughter Mary, Jim to son Alfred, Evelina to daughter Virginia; John, Bob, Louisa & her future increase to children Sarah, Mary, & Alfred; woman Louisa to Executor in trust for husband & children

Casper RINKER, Sr. .... pg 399, 21 May 1961, inv & appr

man

.... pg 401, 28 May 1868, sales

Josiah RINKIN hire of negro

Francis B. JONES .... pg 408, 6 Dec 1862 – 4 Sept 1867, estate acct

Tom, Kitty, & family to G.A. WHITE

Anna M. JONES .... pg 426, Feb 1860 – Nov 1865, gdn acct

servant Lydia to New Orleans?

James B. RIELY .... pg 436, 4 Nov 1850 – 1 Jan 1866, estate acct

slaves sold; servant to Mrs. A.E. TIDBALL; man to Robert WOOD; servant died

INDEX

Albert, 140, 160, 181, 193, 249
ALBERT: Adam, 52
Albert Harley, 83
Albin, 119
Alce, 24, 39, 41, 117
Alcey, 140
Alcy, 218, 244
ALDRIDGE: Adam, 70, 74; Robert, 28
Alec, 24
Alex, 221
Alexander, 78, 84, 88, 126, 130, 158, 188, 199, 212, 213, 219, 226
ALEXANDER: Elizabeth, 28; John, 124, 137; Maj. Morgan, 22; Mary, 160; Morgan, 23, 24; Samuel, 219; Sarah, 27, 100, 105; William, 160, 162
Aley, 206
ALFORD: John, 2; Priscilla, 2
Alfred, 50, 52, 56, 70, 75, 76, 81, 82, 100, 105, 106, 107, 118, 121, 126, 128, 130, 146, 147, 150, 152, 158, 191, 197, 204, 231, 232, 238
Alia, 35
Alia_, 169
Alice, 2, 24, 35, 40, 46, 92, 94, 103, 109, 111, 113, 116, 121, 123, 126, 127, 137, 149, 161, 169, 221, 250
Alick, 83
Alis, 218
Alleck, 27
ALLEMAN: Elizabeth, 45; Jacob, 45
Allen, 44, 218, 225, 226; Eliza, 246
ALLEN: David H., 75; John, 33; Nancy, 140; Robert, 13, 28; Sarah G., 75; William, 147

ALLENSWORTH: Butler, 52; Catharine, 75; Catherine, 73; Henriette, 49; John, 75; Philip, 44; Reuben, 107
Alley, 33, 197
Allford: William, 20
ALLISON, 224; W., 224
Ally, 34, 71, 78, 131
Alped, 87, 88
Alphias, 137
Alse, 101
Amah, 53
Amanda, 150, 177, 182, 183, 199, 211, 229, 232, 236, 241, 244
Ambrose, 9, 76, 84, 87, 88, 101, 149, 150, 160, 177, 191, 196, 203, 224
Ame, 127
Amelia, 77, 118, 120, 137, 183, 187, 191, 194, 207
Ames, 71
Amey, 20, 34, 44, 46
Amie, 178
Aminto, 40
AMISS: Elizabeth, 13; Gabriel, 13
Amistead, 215
Ammanda, 149
Amnias, 173
Amos, 47, 48, 77, 78, 170, 203, 217
Ampel, 113
Ampy, 44, 138
Amy, 26, 33, 43, 64, 74, 87, 92, 149, 150, 151, 156, 168, 179, 217, 228
Anana, 242
Anderson: Clar, 253
ANDERSON: Abraham, 49, 52; Bartholomew, 3; Elizabeth, 1; Gizzle, 118; Grizzella G.,

206; Jacob, 156; Joseph, 113, 150; Nathan, 161; Thomas, 1
Andrew, 10, 34, 38, 41, 52, 55, 56, 74, 87, 102, 108, 113, 121, 127, 149, 173, 192
Andy, 195, 250
Angelina, 101
Angellah, 101
Angus, 10
Ann, 13, 37, 40, 56, 57, 64, 81, 85, 88, 102, 121, 124, 125, 126, 131, 137, 139, 147, 148, 149, 160, 164, 168, 177, 179, 182, 186, 190, 193, 196, 199, 201, 215, 217, 222, 223, 234, 241, 242, 250
Anna, 51, 63, 64, 79, 106, 108, 122, 125, 150, 153, 173, 194, 202, 221, 225
Anna Sa___, 158
Anna Semerica, 159
Annaca, 38, 41
Anne, 28, 29, 62, 103, 194
Anne Mariah, 137
Annear Nancy, 196
Annetta, 214
ANNIN: Daniel, 62
Anthony, 16, 56, 57, 63, 77, 86, 103, 105, 108, 114, 124, 125, 137, 138, 157, 159, 175, 208, 209
Antinett, 217
Antony, 68, 158
Antzelly, 80
APPOLD: Susan C., 182
Arabella, 244
Araminta, 93
Aranah, 88
Arch, 71, 234
ARCHDEACON: Dr. Michael, 34; Elizabeth, 34
Archy, 45, 67, 85, 178, 182, 235
Areanna, 78

Arena, 118, 173
Arenia, 80, 129
Ariana, 89, 104, 123, 124, 129
Arianna, 217
Armanias, 114
Armestead, 209, 215
Armested, 121
Armistead, 131, 137, 138, 141, 149, 150
Armisted, 69, 160
Armstead, 44, 68, 82, 91, 122, 190, 191, 247; George, 114; John, 114
Armstrong: Samuel, 226
ARMSTRONG: George, 63; John, 63
Arnod, 205
Aron, 56, 69
Arthur, 27, 108, 139
ARTHUR: Hetty Z., 180, 185, 187; Joseph, 187
Asa, 137
Asaneth, 223
Ash, 34; Francis J., 185; Mrs., 185
ASH: Capt. Francis, 111; Dolly, 60; Francis, 119, 129, 136, 157, 159, 185; Francis T., 119; George, 89, 120, 137, 143, 149, 152, 169, 173, 178, 181, 184, 188; George B., 119; George H., 184, 190; George Henry, 158, 163; Littleton, 60; Mary Sophia, 158, 163, 193; Pamely, 60; Peggy, 60; Urial, 60; William T., 119
Ashalinda, 92
ASHBY: Alfred D., 71; Buckner, 50; Enoch R., 126; Jane, 132; John, 132; Judith, 132; Judy, 50; Leannah, 71; Lewis, 50, 52, 132, 191;

Baron, 77
Barshaba, 137
Bartlett, 223
BARTLETT: Elizabeth, 105; Henry, 132; W., 121
Bartly, 182
Barton: Fanny, 226
BARTON: D.W., 169, 185; David W., 176, 231, 249, 250; Dr. Robert B., 176; James G., 85; Martha, 176; Martha Virginia, 176; Mary, 85; Richard P., 83, 97; Thomas W., 176; Undril, 37
BATCHELOR: John, 25
BATHALL: William, 4
BAUGUS: Henry, 1; Richard, 1; Robert, 1; Winefred, 1
BAYARLY: Elizabeth L.G., 119; Robert, 119
Bayles, 129
Bayless, 157
BAYLESS: Sophia, 192
Baylis, 119
BAYLIS: John W., 118; Thomas, 102
Baylor, 243
Bayly, 40, 185
Bazil, 244
BAZZEL: Elizabeth, 153
Be__, 187
BEALL: Ely, 212; Margery, 47, 72
BEALOR: Joseph, 59; Lucretia, 59; Polly, 59
BEAN: Hannah, 87; James, 62, 154; Magdaline, 219; Mordecai, 73; Mordicai, 68, 219
Beard: Sarah, 10
BEARD: Jacob, 53
Beatty, 151

BEATTY: Henry, 186, 188; Maj., 41
Becca, 142
Beck, 25, 36, 56, 69, 75, 77, 87, 91, 119, 129, 143, 153, 165
Beckey, 41, 107, 193
BECKLEY: Charles, 102; Elizabeth, 102; Mr., 114
BECKWITH: Jennings, 60; Richard B., 67; Richard M., 60
BECKWORTH: Richard, 70
Becky, 38, 46, 63, 73, 81, 87, 122, 129, 157, 160, 162, 198, 208, 244
Becky Jane, 244
BECSON: Dulcibella, 146; Edward, 146
BEDINGER: Henry, 14; Magdalen, 14
BEELER: Charles, 7; Frederick, 7, 8; George, 7; Joseph, 59; Lucretia, 59; Polly, 59
Beggy, 103
BEKCLEY: Charles, 114
Bekiy, 228
Beksmith: Jesse, 195
BELFIELD: Mary B., 88
Bell, 219, 221, 222, 251; Samuel, 205; Sawney, 205
BELL: Ann, 19; George, 122; Harry, 122; James, 73; John, 19, 20, 179; John N., 194; Julia, 222; Samuel, 53, 211; Squire, 122; Strother, 222
BELL Jr.: Thomas, 70
Bella, 83, 249
Belle, 229, 232, 236, 238, 245
Ben, 5, 16, 17, 19, 20, 23, 24, 25, 28, 29, 30, 33, 37, 39, 41, 44, 45, 46, 50, 53, 56, 60, 62, 67, 69, 70, 75, 76, 77, 84, 85, 87, 101, 110, 120, 123, 125, 132,

135, 137, 141, 145, 147, 150, 153, 156, 169, 173, 175, 177, 180, 187, 194, 202, 208, 212, 213, 215, 225, 227, 243, 247
Benah, 162
BENCKLEY: Susan, 102
Benjamin, 28, 47, 52, 59, 68, 82, 92, 93, 103, 127, 129, 141, 145, 149, 169, 197, 206, 212, 215, 244, 253
Benn, 20
Bennet, 204, 211
Bennett, 207
BENNETT: James, 72
Berella, 181
Berkeley, 56
BERKELEY: Dr. Robert, 79; Edmond, 163; Edmund, 99; Elizabeth W., 99; Frances A.T., 163; Frances Ann Tasker, 99; Julia, 99, 163; Landon, 132; Lewis, 117, 124; Lucy H., 163; Lucy M., 99; Robert, 99, 124; Samuel, 150; Sophia C., 99, 163
BERKELY: B., 62; Elizabeth W., 98; Frances Ann Tasker, 99; Julia, 98, 227; Lucy Mary, 99; Sophia Carter, 98
BERKHAMER: Henry, 148
Berkley, 29
BERKLEY, 155; Benjamin, 176; Elizabeth, 163; Elizabeth W., 227; Julia, 132, 227; Reuben, 62; Robert, 163; Robert C., 221, 228
BERNETT: James, 93
BERRY: Benjamin, 22; Caty, 76; Edwin, 61; Enoch, 61; George, 56; Hulda, 88; Joseph, 76; Maria, 61; Matilda, 61; Samuel, 76;

Thomas, 76, 81, 82, 87; William, 76; Winney, 61
BERRY Jr.: Joseph, 169
Berthe__, 94
Bery, 216
BESLIN: Isaac, 102
Bess, 7, 17, 24
Bet, 7, 8, 30, 51, 69, 175, 226
Bets, 48, 97
Betsey, 39, 63, 70, 84, 91, 94, 101, 104, 108, 117, 124, 127, 129, 135, 139, 175, 184, 236, 245
Betsey Ann, 162
Betsy, 18, 41, 69, 73, 78, 79, 84, 87, 88, 123, 124, 129, 138, 164, 179, 189, 198, 203, 204, 206, 207, 208, 211, 213, 232, 233, 234, 237, 241, 245, 251, 252
Betsy Ann, 143, 153
Bett, 19, 36, 39, 63
Bettie, 228; Aaron, 228; Hannah, 228; James, 228; Martha, 228
Betty, 24, 27, 29, 30, 33, 34, 35, 36, 37, 39, 40, 44, 56, 60, 62, 64, 67, 68, 73, 74, 78, 79, 86, 87, 95, 96, 114, 122, 123, 125, 138, 141, 144, 148, 151, 154, 155, 157, 160, 173, 175, 179, 202, 206, 217, 218, 221, 224, 227, 229, 238
BETTY: Major, 53
Bety, 111
Betz, 48
Beverly, 57, 79, 91, 104, 118, 119, 128, 169
Bill, 13, 16, 26, 27, 29, 36, 37, 46, 49, 52, 59, 72, 74, 75, 77, 81, 82, 87, 91, 92, 93, 101, 103, 111, 112, 114, 116, 120, 121, 123, 125, 133, 137, 138,

149, 158, 175, 179, 192, 194,
197, 203, 205, 208, 211, 212,
213, 214, 215, 216, 217, 218,
235, 238
Billey, 38, 51, 93
Billy, 35, 40, 41, 46, 50, 69, 73,
75, 77, 79, 83, 87, 95, 102,
103, 104, 124, 141, 148, 151,
179, 195, 211, 235, 241
Bina, 40
Binah, 41, 53
Biny, 164, 168
BIRCHELL: John, 102
Bishop, 116
BISON: B., 186
Black, 217
Black Mary, 234
BLACKBOURN: John, 4
Blackburn: Dennis, 226; Fanny,
226; Louisa, 226; Sarah, 226;
Susan, 226
BLACKBURN: Samuel, 18
BLACKEMAN: Marquis Q.,
120
Blacksmith: Jack, 206
Blackwell, 111
Blake, 70
BLAKEMAN: J.N., 127;
Thomas, 117
BLAKEMORE: Alice McKirn
Quinney, 218; Eliza, 218,
219; George, 168; George N.,
185; Marquis Q., 95;
Penelope J., 157; T.L., 219;
Thomas, 124
BLANK: Christian, 14
BLUNDELE, 34
Boats_x_ein, 13
Boatswain, 114
Bob, 15, 18, 19, 20, 21, 24, 27,
28, 30, 33, 34, 37, 38, 41, 43,
46, 50, 52, 55, 56, 65, 67, 70,
71, 77, 87, 88, 95, 101, 102,

107, 114, 117, 120, 122, 123,
124, 127, 129, 131, 138, 147,
149, 150, 152, 157, 159, 160,
162, 171, 172, 173, 175, 179,
190, 191, 198, 203, 205, 238,
250, 252
Bobb, 16, 29, 78
BOND: William, 41, 82
BONHAM: Ann, 64; Daniel S.,
159
Booler: Henry, 1
BOOTH: Mordechai, 26;
William A., 26
BOOTH Sr.: William, 26
BORDON: Benjamin, 1
Boson, 43
BOSTEYAN: Adam, 171
BOSTEYON: Adam, 149, 160,
161
BOSTYON: Adam, 197
BOSWELL: George, 147
BOURN: William, 149
BOURNE: William, 141
Bowen: Billy, 102
BOWEN: Henry, 23, 25; Jacob,
23; John, 23; Mead, 74;
Thornton, 125
Bower, 251
BOWERS: Harrigen, 211;
Harrison, 206; Morton, 124
BOWIN: William, 137
BOWLES: James, 249; John,
117, 124, 143
BOWLS: James, 247
BOWMAN: Abraham, 26;
George, 9, 10, 14, 26; Isaac,
26; Joseph, 26; Mary, 9
BOYD: Abraham, 107; John,
107; Mary A., 130; Nancy,
51; Robert, 107, 109; Samuel,
27, 39; Thomas T., 130
BOYER: J.C., 204
BRABSON: Maria, 212

BUCKNER: Frances, 119; Horace, 119; Otway G., 119
Bundy: Tom, 87
Buoy, 195
Burch: David, 11
BURCHELL: John, 106, 124
Burdet, 48
BURGESS: Harriet A., 212; James H., 212
BURNE: John, 22
Burrell: Nathaniel, 253
Burwell, 218
BURWELL: Anna, 65, 69; Ariana, 74; Carter, 65; Dr. Lewis, 108; Dudley, 148, 159; Edwin B., 142, 153, 167, 171; Frances Housden, 65; Frances Howden, 69; Lewis, 121, 139; Nathaniel, 107, 184; Phillip, 164, 168; Robert C., 67; Roberta P., 232; W., 123; William N., 87, 96, 111, 125, 141, 160, 168
Bush, 212
BUSH: Elizabeth, 196; Henry, 26; John, 91; M.C., 196; Philip, 63; Polly, 63; S.E., 196; Vance, 104, 112, 116, 117, 134, 139
BUSH Jr.: Philip, 91
BUSHELL: John, 117
Bushrod, 149
BUSHROD: Mildred, 24
Butler, 226
BUTLER: Lawrence, 60; Major Lawrence, 62
Butt, 62
BYERS, 215
BYNON__: Joseph, 199
BYRD: Charles C., 162; Charles Carter, 94; Elizabeth Hill, 94; Francis Otway, 94; Mary, 94; Mary A., 104, 112, 164;

Richard Evelyn, 94; Thomas T., 112, 164; Thomas Taylor, 94; W., 123
BYWATER: William, 201
BYWATERS: A.W., 231; Ann, 223, 231; Asaneth, 223; Asenath, 197; Asseneth, 231; Miss A.W., 231; William, 197, 231

C_aal, 38
Ca_ty, 208
CABLE: Daniel, 150; John, 139
CADWALLADER: Rees, 22; Ruth, 15
Caesar, 30, 93
Cain, 81
CALAMESE: William, 15
CALDWALL: Andrew, 5
CALMES: Betsey, 76; Fielding Gibbs, 15; George, 15, 20; Isabella Elliche, 15; Mariam, 15; Marquis, 4, 15, 20; Miriam, 20; Mrs. William, 15; Spencer Neavel, 15; William, 15, 20
CALVERT: Richard, 13
Calvin, 177
Camar: Emily Susan, 156; Margaret, 156
CAMPBELL: Eliza B., 238; Elizabeth, 59; Franklin, 179; James H., 250; James Harrison, 179; John, 53, 56, 59, 76; Laban F., 194; R.M., 185; Rebecca, 218; Thomas, 56, 59, 87, 238; Thomas B., 239; William, 179, 184
CAN: Cornelius B., 142; Isaac L., 142; Joseph S., 142; Mary E., 142; Richard, 142; Richard B., 142
CANGH__: John, 203

263

Carey, 123
CARNEGY: William, 91, 93
Caroline, 56, 70, 77, 81, 112,
116, 127, 128, 143, 149, 150,
162, 164, 173, 176, 177, 178,
182, 184, 190, 197, 201, 203,
205, 218, 223, 224, 227, 229,
231, 232, 235, 236, 238, 241
CARPENTER: Susan, 236
CARROL: Joseph, 24
CARSON: Elisha W., 232, 236,
237, 241, 245, 251; James H.,
232, 236; James Harrison,
118; Jared, 228; Jared W.,
214, 216, 232, 235, 236, 237,
241; Jared William, 213, 225;
John, 232, 236; M. Rebecca,
237, 241, 245; M. Reubin,
232; Martha, 229; Martha R.,
241; Martha Rebecca, 205,
223, 225; Miss M.R., 235;
Mr., 53; Robert M., 238, 245,
251; Robert R., 232, 236;
Simon, 158, 229, 232, 233,
245, 251; William, 232, 236
CARSON Jr.: James H., 169;
Martha Rebecca, 221; Simon,
232, 236
Carstine, 173
Carston, 180
Carstun: Mary, 175
Carter, 79, 124, 149, 150, 175,
208, 213; John, 221
CARTER: Ann, 39; Elizabeth
N., 156; James, 39, 40, 84, 85,
109; John, 74, 95, 195, 198;
Joseph, 202; Joseph K., 159,
168; Joseph R., 156; Joseph
W., 147, 152, 156, 158, 170;
Lucinda, 109; Susan P., 251;
William, 84, 85, 150; William
A., 146, 203, 235, 238, 246,
247

CARTER Jr.: William, 150
Cartine, 223
CARTMELL: Dorothy H., 2;
Dr. Solomon, 71; Edward, 2;
Eliza, 179; M.B., 184, 227,
236; Martin, 76; N.M., 238;
Nathaniel, 76, 107, 109, 136,
231; Sarah, 69, 76, 107
CARTMILL: M.B., 223;
Mankin, 194; Mordicai B.,
194; Nathan, 5; Thomas K.,
194
CARTMILL, Sr.: Nathaniel, 34
Casar, 36
Casas, 35
Cashanner, 92
Cass, 74
Cassa, 56
Cassee, 84
Cassy, 56
CASTLEMAN: Alfred, 150; D.,
127; David, 120; James, 109,
124, 125, 138; John, 117, 120,
124; Thomas, 75, 105, 160;
William, 152
CASTLEMAN Jr.: William, 150
Casy, 124
Cate, 1, 21, 26, 33, 36, 40, 74,
81, 85, 88, 93, 153, 202, 204
Cate Jr., 202
Catey, 111
Catharine, 118, 127, 138, 149,
150, 169, 208, 212, 246
CATHER: Daniel, 202; David,
117, 124, 150, 169, 177, 187;
James, 169, 228; Thomas,
152, 156; W., 218
Catherine, 16, 69, 72, 89, 111,
119, 143, 184, 213, 223, 225,
226, 227
CATLETT: Alexander, 110;
Alley, 49; David, 50;
Elizabeth, 158; Eljah, 49;

264

George, 44, 50; Henrietta, 146, 158; Henry, 50, 130, 158; James, 44, 49; Jesse, 50; John, 49, 74, 110, 115, 120, 128; John A., 110; Louisa, 49; Marian, 158; Mary, 50, 158; Matilda, 49; Nimrod, 44; Patsey, 49; Peter, 74; Polly, 49; Rachel, 74; Robert, 44, 45, 50, 74; Sarah, 159; Susan, 159

CATLETT Jr.: J., 120

CATLETT Sr.: James, 37

Cato, 15, 16, 29, 36

CATTELL: John, 105

CATTLET: Mary, 19

CATTLETT: Anny, 28; Henry, 28; John, 105; Mary F., 105; Peter, 28

CATTLETT Jr.: Peter, 20

Cattrerine, ix, 206

Catty, 234

Caty, 26, 44, 68, 69, 84, 88, 101, 172, 209, 226

CAULEY: Daniel M., 154

Cealey, 102

Ceally, 82

Ceasar, 44, 141

Ceaser, 103, 184

Cece, 26

Celah, 100

Celey, 245

Celia, 51, 85, 111, 137, 203, 205

Celina, 165

CELSER: Mathias, 7

Celsy, 238

Cesar, 2, 29, 40, 47, 51, 84, 138

Cezar, 39

CHAMBERLIN: Elizabeth B., 251; Jonas, 251

Chance, 204, 211

Chancey, 87

Chancy, 149

CHAPMAN: Capt. Thomas, 37; Robert H., 158

Charity, 52, 56, 70, 76, 83, 96, 129, 147, 149, 160, 173, 207, 217, 225

Charles, 10, 15, 16, 19, 23, 26, 27, 29, 30, 36, 43, 46, 48, 59, 62, 63, 64, 67, 68, 70, 71, 74, 80, 85, 87, 93, 100, 101, 102, 105, 108, 110, 111, 113, 115, 118, 119, 120, 122, 124, 125, 129, 130, 132, 133, 135, 138, 139, 140, 143, 146, 147, 149, 150, 151, 154, 156, 159, 160, 161, 163, 164, 168, 170, 171, 175, 176, 178, 180, 184, 185, 190, 191, 195, 196, 197, 198, 201, 202, 203, 204, 205, 206, 207, 208, 211, 212, 213, 214, 216, 231, 235, 237, 238, 241, 242, 244, 247, 249, 250

Charles Jr., 36

Charles Sr., 36

Charlet, 61

Charlette, 136

Charley, 96, 249

Charlot, 192

Charlott, 53, 129, 173, 238

Charlotte, 33, 36, 47, 55, 59, 62, 74, 82, 87, 93, 98, 102, 110, 118, 129, 137, 145, 151, 152, 168, 179, 180, 181, 183, 184, 187, 191, 193, 194, 195, 200, 207, 218, 226, 227, 250, *See*

Charly, 173, 203

CHENOWETH: Catharine, 45; John W., 186; Sarah Matilda, 186; William, 45

CHERRY: Thomas, 7

CHERRY, Sr.: Thomas T., 5

China, 122, 129

Chinman, 206

266

Cuffy, 117, 148
CUGLER: Robert, 171
CUMBLETON: Solomon, 112
CUNNINGHAM: Ann, 10;
Eleanor, 10; Elizabeth, 10;
George, 10; James, 10; Jane,
10; Robert, 10; William, 10
Cupid, 27, 34, 36, 51
CURTWELL: Martin, 102
Custer, 122
Cy, 109
Cymon, 175, 184
Cyntha, 97
Cynthia, 33, 46, 49, 82, 207, 211
Cyrus, 36, 38, 51, 64, 93, 103,
111, 198, 204, 207, 211, 215

D_mmo_d, 70
Daffney, 71
Dafney, 129, 147
DAINGERFIELD: Mrs.
C.M.B., 84
Daisy, 123
Dale, 177
DAMIER: David, 159
Dan, 25, 93, 102, 137, 249
Dandridge, 205
Dangerfield, 173
DANGERFIELD: John E., 161;
LeRoy, 88; LeRoy P., 88;
William, 88
Daniel, 15, 16, 17, 19, 20, 23,
24, 25, 29, 30, 34, 35, 36, 39,
41, 43, 47, 48, 51, 52, 53, 56,
59, 62, 67, 68, 69, 70, 71, 72,
79, 81, 83, 87, 88, 92, 93, 94,
95, 96, 97, 102, 103, 104, 106,
107, 108, 109, 111, 113, 114,
116, 119, 121, 122, 125, 126,
128, 129, 130, 131, 140, 148,
158, 161, 163, 164, 168, 170,
173, 177, 182, 183, 190, 197,

203, 205, 209, 212, 235, 244,
253
DANIELS: Taylor L., 178
Dann, 28
DANNER: J., 130
DANVER: Jacob, 217
Daphney, 22, 33, 89, 173
Daphny, 63
Darcus, 56, 62, 130
Darius, 48
Darkey, 116
Darkus, 40
DARLINGTON: Edmund
Shackleford, 180; Meredith,
23
Dasy, 138
Dave, 48, 50, 138, 209, 211,
212, 218, 221, 222
Davey, 93
David, 11, 16, 19, 30, 33, 44, 48,
52, 53, 56, 69, 73, 74, 78, 79,
81, 83, 84, 85, 91, 93, 98, 105,
109, 111, 112, 116, 117, 119,
130, 131, 133, 135, 137, 141,
152, 159, 169, 177, 181, 188,
192, 194, 196, 201, 204, 212,
216, 217, 238
Davis, 174, 191
DAVIS: Baalis, 105, 109, 111;
Capt. James, 78; David, 27,
28, 175; Eliza, 121, 142;
Gabriel H., 175, 182; James,
77, 81; James S., 133; John,
14; John C., 157; Julia, 132;
Julia A., 133, 205; Leonard
Y., 149; Margaret, 27, 105;
Mary, 175; S., 105; Sally, 97;
Sally I., 77; Sarah I., 131, 132;
Stephen, 75; Susannah, 157;
William, 78, 105, 133
DAVISON: Alexander N., 213;
E.J., 150

Davy, 24, 27, 29, 30, 35, 36, 47, 52, 63, 82, 88, 91, 107, 135, 142, 157, 203
DAWSON: Ben, 107; David, 1
DEACON: George, 8
DEADRICK: Elizabeth F., 88
DEAHL: David, 231; Sarah, 231, 236, 241
DEALE: James, 38
Dean: Richard, 5
DEARLY: Peter, 14
DEARY: Jacob, 130, 139
Debborah, 18
Debby, 29, 30
Deborah, 93
DEDERICK: David, 9; Elizabeth, 9; Mary, 9; Susannah, 9
DeHAVAN: Erna, 250
Deley, 13
Delf, 39, 41
Delia, 47, 93
Delila, 218
Della, 173
Delpha, 121, 250
Delphey, 123
Delphia, 76, 142
Delphy, 114, 124
DENEALE: John E., 109; Matilda, 109; Mrs., 74
DENEALE Jr.: George, 68, 74, 86
Denis, 40
DENNEY: Walter, 89
Dennis, 40, 48, 71, 81, 85, 111, 118, 126, 133, 146, 158, 191, 198, 232
Denny, 112
DENNY: Walter, 78; William, 221
DENT: Thomas, 79, 199
Dercas, 67
DERICK: David, 9

DERMAN: Ann, 61; Betsy, 61; John, 61; Mary, 61; Peter, 61, 63
Deskin, 128
DEVLON: Captain John, 8
DEWDALL: Jane, 187
Diana, 119
Dianah, 162
Dianna, 33, 40
Diannah, 160
Dice, 39, 41, 71, 102
Dick, 7, 10, 21, 24, 27, 28, 29, 39, 40, 41, 44, 45, 46, 50, 59, 63, 67, 71, 73, 77, 87, 88, 93, 107, 111, 119, 125, 138, 140, 141, 142, 151, 153, 154, 161, 162, 163, 173, 175, 176, 191, 195, 197, 205, 212, 214
Dicky, 123, 129
Dilley, 101
Dina, 83, 158
Dinah, 10, 16, 17, 19, 34, 36, 39, 41, 44, 56, 60, 74, 75, 86, 88, 92, 93, 98, 130, 135, 138, 141, 149, 150, 164, 229, 234
Dinces, 40
DINGES: Daniel, 172; David, 162
Dini, 19
Dinis, 40
Dinnah, 199
DIXSON, 97
Doctor, 208
DODDS: Solomon, 139
Dole, 138
Doll, 13, 27, 39, 41, 63, 93, 101, 123
Dolley, 45
Dolly, 44, 91, 124, 141, 160, 181, 191, 208
Dolphin, 238
DONALDSON: John, 37, 41
Dora, 207

Dorcas, 30, 68, 204
Dorcey, 207
Dorcus, 176
DORMISE: Michael, 83
Dorsey, 143
DORSEY: Joshua, 18
Doss, 215
DOUGHERTY: E., 130; Ezekiel, 121
Dove: Jim, 141
DOVEY, 97
DOWDALL: Jane, 95; Maxwell, 95, 134, 145, 187
Dowdell, 126, 127
DOWELL, 156
Doyle, 111
DOYLE: Edward, 45
DRAGGO: Benjamin, 39
DRAKE: John, 106, 118; Phebe, 118; Sarah, 247
Draper: Billy, 108
Driver: Jack, 121
Drucelia, 70
Drucilla, 178
Drury, 56
Druscilla, 183
Drusy, 124
DUCHWALL: Rebecca, 171
DUCKWALL: John, 169; Joseph, 179, 183, 186, 188, 191; Rebecca, 175, 179
Duke, 87, 172
DUNBAR: Dr. Robert, 92; Robert, 73
DUNCAN: Elizabeth, 223, 231; Thomas, 223
DYSORE: John, 179

Eadine, 54
Eady, 79
Ealse, 16
Eancy, 219

EARHART: Marg, 50; Philip, 48, 50
EARLE: Archibald, 109; Elias, 164, 170; Esaias, 109, 121, 122; Esais, 102; James B., 121; John B., 109; Maj. John D., 172; Maria B., 168; Sally, 122; Samuel, 13
EARLES Jr.: Sam, 4
Earnest, 164
Easter, 24, 26, 37, 39, 41, 51, 54, 78, 81, 85, 102, 179, 201, 221, 222
Easther, 70
EASTON: Anne, 16; Richard, 16
Eddy, 71, 238
EDDY: William, 162
Edman, 148
Edmon, 106
Edmond, 41, 47, 101, 179, 204, 207
EDMONDSON Jr.: Thomas, 23
Edmund, 38, 48, 74, 98, 122, 129, 173, 229, 234
Edna, 221
Edney, 221
Edny, 222
Edwan, 179
Edward, 4, 57, 104, 112, 122, 136, 143, 148, 153, 164, 177, 182, 185, 204, 207, 208, 238, 244
Edwin, 59, 179, 183
Edy, 46, 135, 179
EL__: Fanny, 107
Elby, 73
Eleanor, 122, 129
Eleck, 73
Elee, 241
Elen, 242
Eli, 168

270

Elias, **88**, 109, 129, 159, 162, 167, 173, 175, 221, 232
Elick, 57
Elie, 111
Elija, 142, 153, 215, 233
Elijah, 69, 76, 143, 175, 179, 185, 194, 213
Elinor, 125
Elisa, 128
Elisa Ann, 246
Elisabeth, 14
Elisha, 114, 237, 247
Eliza, 52, 61, 79, 81, 83, 84, 85, 86, **88**, 89, 102, 106, 118, 119, 126, 130, 131, 132, 133, 137, 143, 151, 158, 159, 162, 164, 167, 170, 171, 173, 177, 178, 179, 184, 185, 189, 190, 194, 197, 202, 203, 205, 208, 212, 213, 219, 223, 226, 229, 234, 244, 246, 247,249
Eliza Ann, 247
Elizabeth, 79, 92, 115, 125, 143, 149, 150, 169, 175, 188, 194, 196, 201, 203, 206, 211, 216, 229
Ellen, 51, 96, 114, 149, 160, 186, 218, 226, 228, 229, 232, 236, 241, 242
Ellick, 46, 63, 64, 89, 108, 222
ELLIOTT: B., 79
Ellison, 118
ELLSEA: John, 93
ELLZEY: John, 81; William, 77
Elon, 150
Else, 132
Elsey, 250
Ely, 150
Emalina, 152
Emaly, 87
Emanuel, 106, 118, 128, 152, 206
Emely, 77, 92

Emile, 83
Emily, 52, 61, 70, 83, 87, **88**, 89, 91, 100, 105, 106, 116, 123, 126, 130, 139, 141, 143, 148, 149, 151, 153, 158, 159, 160, 161, 162, 164, 168, 169, 173, 175, 191, 195, 196, 203, 206, 208, 213, 218, 221, 224, 225, 227, 229, 232, 234, 238, 239, 249
Emma, 93, 97, 104, 199
EMMETT: Jane, 222; Jane B., 222, 227; Maria Catherine, 222
Emmy Liza, 103
ENDERS: Jacob, 157; Mrs., 172
ENGLE: Samuel, 149
Enoch, 50, 52, 81, 158, 172
Enock, 101
Enos, 229, 232, 236, 237, 241, 245, 251
Ephraim, 84, 101, 246
Erlena, 249
Essea, 94
Essex, 95, 187
Ester, 17, 54
Esther, 9, 16, 18, 34, 35, 38, 40, 44, 47, 61, 62, 64, 91, 102, 107, 109, 111, 121, 123, 125, 129, 139, 140, 142, 153, 167, 171, 176, 184, 187, 197
Ethalinda, 103, 126, 127
Euordo, 179
Evalina, 149, 191
Evan, 179
Evans, 136, 178; Randell, 135
EVANS: David, 195; Elizabeth, 41
Eve, 29, 30, 87, 192, 193
Evelina, 78, 81, 83, 85, 87, **88**, 96, 109, 121, 129, 143, 149, 150, 186, 188, 195, 198, 226, 252

Eveline, 89, 91, 97, 103, 104, 116, 125, 130, 137, 157, 159, 233
Evelyn, 125, 153
EVERHART: Jacob, 79
EYSLERS: D., 178

Fa_me_, 79
Faddy, 33, 45, 63, 65
Fagan: Barney, 59
Fairfax, 43, 91, 118, 135, 161
FAIRFAX: Bryan, 21; Hannah, 35; Thomas Lord, 21
Faithey, 70
Faithy, 120
FALKERSON: Amealia, 131; Henry Jackson, 131; Thomas Willy, 131
FALLS: Frances M., 179
Famy, 72
Fan, 27, 29, 30, 96, 102
Fanender, 143
Fann, 77, 130
Fanncy, 117
Fanney, 108, 130
Fanny, 13, 14, 16, 19, 35, 36, 43, 45, 46, 51, 53, 54, 59, 63, 64, 67, 68, 74, 75, 76, 78, 79, 81, 83, 84, 85, 86, 87, 91, 93, 96, 97, 98, 101, 102, 105, 106, 107, 108, 116, 120, 121, 123, 128, 130, 135, 136, 139, 141, 149, 150, 151, 152, 160, 172, 175, 181, 186, 191, 193, 194, 195, 202, 203, 206, 207, 208, 209, 217, 218, 221, 223, 225, 226, 229, 232, 234, 235, 237, 239, 241, 243, 244
Fanny Ann, 149
Fathy, 95
FAUNTLEROY: Dangerfield, 99; David, 211; Elizabeth, 92,

99; John, 98; Laurence B., 98; Robert, 99; Robert H., 98
FAUNTLROY: Joseph, 73
FAUQUARY: Walter, 117
FAW: Mary Ann, 77; Mrs, 77; Samuel, 77
Federic, 129
Federick, 147
FEGINS: John, 62
Felicia, 132, 133, 143
Fenmore, 10
Fentin, 158
FENTON: Enoch, 47, 48, 97; Hannah, 97
Fergurson: Philip, 130
FERGUSON: Hugh, 21
FERNLEY: William, 1
Ferris: Peter, 195
Fick, 67, 70
FICKLIN: James D., 206; James G., 102, 203
Fida, 29, 30
Fiday, 142
Fidy, 153
Fielden, 145
Fielding, 70, 106, 142, 143, 197
Fill, 96
Fillah, 91
Filles, 37
Fillis, 48, 55, 162
Fini, 150
FISER: Mary, 227, 229
FISH: Elizabeth, 131
Fisher, 179
FISHER: Elizabeth B., 106; Joseph, 177, 187
FITZHUGH: William H., 113
FIZER: Mary, 224, 225
Flanegan: James, 208
Flank, 175
Flannegan, 227
FLEECE: W.J., 222

Flood, 73, 75, 77, 81, 87, 91, 116, 133, 146
Flora, 16, 23, 27, 47, 48, 53, 56, 70, 84, 93, 101, 108, 209, 219, 238, 244
FLORES: Frederick, 94
Florinda, 73, 92, 105, 174
FOISTER: Jane, 140
FOLEY: William, 54
Forester, 16
Forge: Robert, 250
FORSTER: Jane H., 147
Forten, 130
Fortin, 146
Fortune, 11, 26, 27, 40, 50, 53, 64
FOSTER: James, 141
Fountain: Rebecca, 181
Fountaine, 225
Fran Betty, 10
Frances, 25, 35, 40, 73, 92, 105, 114, 175, 177, 183, 187, 188, 190, 191, 205, 208, 218, 228
Francis, 27, 124, 160, 178, 182, 191, 196, 205, 217
Frank, 20, 27, 36, 37, 39, 48, 52, 62, 63, 68, 73, 83, 84, 86, 87, 91, 92, 97, 102, 107, 109, 111, 117, 119, 125, 130, 136, 140, 148, 149, 150, 152, 156, 159, 164, 167, 170, 175, 178, 181, 185, 188, 189, 193, 202, 203, 204, 205, 217, 218, 224, 234, 237, 238
FRANK: Henry, 118
Franke, 108
Frankey, 108
Franklin, 175
FRANKS: Edward, 100; Henry, 100; July Ann, 100; Strauther, 100
Franky, 101, 102, 114, 122, 123, 124, 125, 129, 130, 194, 207

FRASHER: John H., 190; Mary, 190; Noah, 131, 190, 196
Fred, 124
Frederic, 219
Frederick, 13, 43, 67, 74, 76, 81, 82, 85, 88, 93, 95, 107, 121, 122, 123, 124, 128, 173, 175, 177, 182, 202, 203, 204, 206, 207, 215, 229, 244, 249
Free: John, 68
Free Jack, 39
Freelove, 224
FRENCH: Shapleigh, 187, 197
Fridy, 162
FRIEND: Israel, 2, 3
FROST: G., 127; Griffin, 126; William, 41, 45
FRYE: Jacob, 182, 188; James, 182; Joseph, 50; Judith, 182; Martha, 182; Mordecai B., 182
FUGATE: Edward, 21
FUNKHOUSER: Isaac, 137
FUNSTEN: Ann, 170, 188, 191; Oliver, 118
FUNSTON: Ann, 127, 146, 181; Anna, 175; David, 128; Eliza, 146; Elizabeth, 139; Emily, 146; Margaret, 108, 139, 146, 153, 159; Maria, 139, 146; Mrs., 120; Oliver, 108, 120, 128, 131
Furey: Abraham, 14
FURGUISON: Hugh, 2
Furlong, 168, 170
FURR: Abraham, 62
FURSTON: Eliza, 126; Emily, 122; Margaret, 122; Maria, 122; Oliver, 122

G___, 116

273

Gabriel, 39, 41, 49, 51, 70, 74, 89, 94, 104, 105, 114, 126, 137, 160, 173, 208
Gaby, 22
GALLOWAY: Helen C., 189, 226, 227, 232; James B., 189; Margaret, 189, 191; Richard S., 189
GAMBLE: Joseph, 157
GANT: Isaac N., 118, 135; John, 127
GARDENER: Elizabeth, 9; John, 9
GARDNER: Peter, 150; Samuel, 126
GARRISON: Ephraim, 80, 113
Garrow, 33
Gean, 18
Gebney: Margaret, 17
Geffree, 7
Geleka, 83
General, 69, 83
George, 5, 13, 14, 15, 16, 19, 24, 26, 27, 35, 38, 39, 40, 41, 43, 44, 45, 50, 51, 52, 53, 54, 56, 59, 62, 65, 67, 68, 69, 71, 72, 73, 75, 76, 78, 79, 85, 87, 88, 92, 93, 95, 100, 101, 102, 104, 105, 106, 107, 108, 110, 112, 117, 118, 120, 121, 122, 123, 124, 125, 126, 127, 128, 130, 136, 138, 139, 140, 143, 146, 148, 149, 159, 160, 161, 165, 168, 170, 171, 172, 173, 174, 176, 177, 179, 180, 184, 188, 191, 194, 195, 196, 197, 198, 201, 203, 204, 205, 206, 207, 208, 209, 211, 215, 216, 221, 222, 224, 225, 227, 228, 229, 231, 232, 238, 239, 241, 244, 245, 249, 251, 252, 253
GEORGE: William, 186
George Edward, 141, 226

George Jr, 29
George Sr, 29
George William, 226
Georgeanna, 243
Georgeylina, 108
Georgianna, 87, 244
GETTES: George, 200
Gibb, 30
GIBBONS: Jacob, 162
GIBBS, 23; Charles, 115, 130; William, 23
GIFFEN: John, 212; Sarah, 212
GIFFIN: John, 187
Giffy, 171
Gil, 78
Gilbert, 40, 44, 69, 76, 95, 108, 109, 123, 124, 134, 136, 145, 153, 187
Gilbird, 39, 41
GILDARD, 49; Francis, 26
GILKESON: John, 26, 33, 105, 132, 228, 236, 242; Sarah, 24; William, 179; William D., 242
GILLASPY: Patrick, 1
GILMER: A.E., 224
Gin, 67
Gincy, 69
Ginny, 64, 147, 149
GLASCOCK: French, 92
Glascoe, 50
Glasgow, 56, 91
GLASS: Ann, 84, 117; Ann McCalister, 84; David, 16; Eliza Wilson, 84; Elizabeth, 19, 33, 86, 203, 204; Elizabeth M., 86; Emmeline Marshall, 84; Hester I., 243; Hester Sophia, 84; J.V., 139; James, 86; James McCalister, 84; James V., 62, 102, 216, 223; Jas V., 158; Jos, 170; Joseph, 33, 84, 91, 96, 117,

118, 136, 148, 159, 170, 178; Peggy, 37; Rev Joseph, 136; Rev. Joseph, 185, 189; Robert, 33, 37, 70, 78, 193, 203; Robert D., 197, 204; Rutha, 37; Sally, 37; Samuel, 33; Sarah Ann, 84; Sidney _inesby, 84; Susan Emily, 84; Susanna, 37; Thomas, 86, 152, 203, 250

GLASSCOCK: Benjamin, 116, 140; French F., 165

GLENN: William, 10, 54

Gloria, 131

Gloster, 29

Gloston, 91

Gloucester, 30

Glover: Richard, 59

Godfrey, 46, 67, 79, 96, 119, 181

GOFF: John, 239

GOLD: Daniel, 97, 215; Phebe, 247; Washington, 117

GOLD, Sr.: John, 96, 97

GORE: Joshua, 192, 194, 197, 204, 209, 222, 223; Margery D., 218

GOSNEY: Jane, 37

Grace, 29, 30, 38, 39, 41, 65, 75, 76, 78, 80, 92, 169, 179, 187

Gracy, 173

Gramah Amah, 53

GRAMMER: Mr., 97

Grandison, 236, 244

Grason: Sam, 108

GRAVES: Charles, 69, 71; Elizabeth, 69

GRAY: Anna, 108; Enos M., 137; Robert, 108

GRAYSON: Col. William, 30; Dr. Robert O., 102; William, 27, 29

Green: A., 251; Gabriel, 70

GREEN: Ann, 36, 153; Elizabeth, 153; Irene P., 218; James, 153; Lane, 153; Mary, 138; Mary Ann, 138; Moses, 40, 153; Richard, 153; Whitson, 82; Winnifred, 74

Green__, 46

GREENFIELD: John, 10

Grey, 36

Griff, 44

GRIFFIN: Sarah, 246

GRIGLAR: Christopher, 88

GRIM: L.F.Y., 245

GROVE: David, 97; Grove, 242; Henry, 103; Susan, 209

GROVE, Sr.: John, 209

GROVERMAN: William, 38

GRUBB: A.J., 233, 234; Caterania, 207; Stephen, 207, 214; Thomas, 135; Westly, 186

GRUBBS: Caterania, 203; Stephen, 201, 203; Thomas, 132, 170; Westly, 186

GUNNELL: Elizabeth, 128, 142; Henry, 128; William, 128

Gustavus, 179

Guy, 1

Gye, 17

HACKLEY: Benjamin, 23

HACKNEY: Joseph B., 234, 242

HADDON: John, 106

HADDOX: John, 126

HAGAN: James, 22

Hagar, 30

Hager, 29

HAINES: Joshua, 4

HALFPENNY: Robert, 15

Hall: Mary, 236

HALL: Bennett, 87; Caleb B., 233; Caroline L., 160; Catharine, 160; Christian, 171; Edward E., 160; Elisha J., 160; Elizabeth L., 160; Frances N., 233; George W., 160; James, 38; James B., 102, 219; James Bennett, 87; James W., 160, 233; Margaret, 233; Marthy E., 233; Nancy, 87; Nancy V., 233; Richard, 83; Sally, 87; Susan J., 160; William, 8

Hally, 247

Ham, 47, 93

HAM: Peter, 53

Hamar: Richard, 4

HAMILTON: Charles, 82; John, 82, 101, 156; Miriam, 109; Robert, 78; Ruth, 82; Thomas, 82; William, 109; Wilson, 102

HAMMAND: Charles, 55

HAMMOND: Charles, 55; George W., 243

Hamore: Richard, 5

Hampshire, 44

Hampson, 177

Hampton, 45, 50, 59, 76, 87, 104, 130, 164, 169, 181, 193

HAMPTON: George, 19; John, 56; Mary, 86; Mrs., 59

HAMTON: Charles Chester Coulson, 19; Frances, 19; George, 19; Joseph, 19; Judith, 19; Margarett, 19; Mary, 19; Sary, 19

Hanah, 43, 50, 143

HAND: Robert, 109; Sarah, 109; Thomas, 109; William, 109, 111, 125

Haney, 24, 117, 221

HANEY: Molly, 55

HANING: Mary, 18

Hanna, 35, 136

Hannah, 3, 4, 10, 15, 16, 17, 18, 20, 23, 25, 27, 29, 30, 36, 37, 38, 40, 41, 44, 48, 49, 50, 52, 53, 55, 56, 60, 63, 67, 68, 69, 70, 75, 77, 82, 83, 86, 87, 89, 91, 93, 102, 103, 105, 106, 108, 109, 114, 116, 118, 121, 122, 129, 132, 133, 139, 149, 150, 152, 158, 159, 164, 165, 168, 171, 173, 175, 178, 179, 184, 188, 193, 194, 197, 198, 201, 203, 204, 206, 207, 208, 209, 211, 218, 219, 223, 226, 228, 244, 245, 250, 251

Hannah Susan, 216

Hanner, 40, 53, 71

Hanney, 35

Hannibal, 108

Hanny, 43, 121

Hanover, 122

Hansford, 168

Hanson, 48

HANY: Maria, 91

Happy, 142

HARDESTY: Mary, 60; Polly, 60

Harey, 71

HARFORD: William, 20

Hariet, 227

Hariett, 100

HARMAN: S.S., 232; Solomon, 136, 234

HARMON, 242; Solomon, 149; Solomon S., 229

Harr, 186

Harriet, 52, 61, 63, 70, 78, 82, 83, 85, 88, 100, 101, 111, 112, 116, 117, 143, 146, 147, 149, 150, 160, 161, 162, 164, 169, 171, 172, 173, 192, 194, 195, 205, 208, 209, 212, 214, 216,

218, 225, 226, 235, 237, 244, 246
Harriett, 56, 64, 71, 86, 119, 128, 142, 173, 186, 208, 212, 238
Harriot__, 195
Harriott, 129
Harris, 130
HARRIS: Benjamin, 109, 110, 112; Fulton I., 109; Jesse, 113; John B., 109, 112, 148, 155; William H., 109, 112, 128
Harrison, 71, 86, 112, 117, 125, 128, 129, 133, 142, 173, 193, 195, 197, 214, 224, 229, 234, 244, 250; Thomas, 151
HARRISON: Elizabeth, 62; George D., 79, 238; Mary, 62; Mary Anne, 62; Robert, 226, 228
Harrt, 160
Harry, 1, 8, 9, 10, 16, 21, 23, 24, 27, 28, 29, 30, 34, 35, 36, 37, 38, 39, 40, 41, 43, 44, 46, 47, 50, 52, 53, 54, 56, 59, 61, 62, 67, 68, 70, 71, 73, 74, 79, 87, 89, 93, 96, 97, 98, 101, 104, 105, 108, 109, 113, 115, 123, 124, 129, 130, 132, 138, 139, 141, 145, 146, 149, 151, 152, 153, 162, 164, 167, 172, 173, 179, 183, 184, 185, 186, 188, 190, 191, 204, 207, 209, 213, 222, 226, 234, 246, 247
HART: Daniel, 1; Edward, 150
Harvey, 211, 212, 214
Harvy, 62
HARVY: Benjamin, 86
Hary, 160, 201
HASKILL: Anne Elizabeth, 194; Emilia Susan, 194; John,

194; John White, 194; Sarah, 194; Susan, 194
HATHAWAY: Francis, 137; Sarah, 137
HATLEY: Catharine, 37; John, 37
Hattey, 209
Hawe: William, 4
HAWKING: Joseph, 14
HAWKINS: Joseph, 14; R., 182
HAY: Dr., 130; John, 150
Hayden: John, 216
HAYDEN: Dr. John, 150
Hayes, 97
HAYMAKER: Susan, 189
Haynie, 105
HAYNIE: Griffin, 55; Presley, 54, 55
HEADLEY: W.O., 203
HEATH: William, 2
HEDGE: Joseph, 120
HEDGES: John R., 69
HEILSEL: Catherine, 68
HEIM: Leonard, 1
HEISKELL: Emily S., 218; John, 102, Polly, 68
HEIST: John S., 241
Helen, 35
HELM: Ann B., 162; Capt. William, 39; Catharine, 93; Catherine, 81; Frances, 81, 85; Helen M., 93; M., 162; Margaret, 18, 67; Maria, 81, 93, 104, 114, 207; Meredith, 1, 47, 93, 103; Mrs. F., 61; Nancy, 103; P.N., 162; Strother, 47; Strother M., 111; Thomas, 18, 39; William, 30, 103, 138, 142, 153, 162
HELM Jr.: Meredith, 3, 39
Hence, 97
HENDERSON: Jesse, 62

HENDREN: Robert, 109; Sarah, 109, 143
HENDRICK: Job S., 202, 203
HENING: William, 148, 251
HENKELL: Sarah, 196
Henney, 108
HENNING: Robert, 18; William, 186
Henny, 22, 36, 50, 79, 104, 112, 131, 191, 213, 241
Henory, 71
Henrey, 116
Henrieta, 158
Henriett Ann, 141
Henrietta, 84, 86, 89, 159, 203, 206, 217, 226, 232, 243, 244
Henry, 24, 29, 44, 45, 47, 48, 52, 71, 78, 79, 81, 82, 83, 85, 87, 88, 89, 94, 101, 105, 108, 110, 111, 118, 119, 120, 121, 125, 126, 127, 129, 132, 133, 134, 135, 137, 138, 139, 141, 142, 143, 146, 149, 153, 157, 159, 162, 164, 165, 168, 171, 172, 177, 180, 181, 182, 183, 185, 189, 190, 193, 194, 197, 198, 201, 202, 203, 204, 205, 207, 208, 211, 216, 218, 224, 225, 227, 229, 231, 233, 234, 237, 238, 243, 245, 249
HENRY: B.H., 137; Betsey, 36; Bryant Hampson, 136; Daniel, 54, 55; Enoch, 137; Rebecca, 136; William Vannester, 136
Henson, 48, 143
Hercules, 23, 229
HERSKEL: Amelia, 229; Emma L., 229
HESS: Abraham, 125, 139, 188; Mary Ann, 188; Nancy, 139
Hester, 34, 71, 88, 111, 142, 229, 232, 236, 246, 247

Het, 69
HETERICK: Mary Ried, 185; Mrs., 196; Robert, 185, 186, 191
HETRICK: Mr. R., 61
Hetty, 25, 69, 76, 77, 165, 208, 218, 224, 227
Hezakiah, 173
HICKMAN: Isaac, 20
HICKS: Amelia, 173; John, 173; Levi, 168, 171, 173; Mary, 173
Highland, 206
Hilbind, 160
HILL: Louisa, 186, 217; Rees, 23, 217
Hilyard, 140
Hiram, 70, 159, 218, 229, 243
HITE, 23; Ann, 174; Ann T., 212, 213, 216; C.B., 194; Cornelius B., 195, 201; Dr., 213; Eleanor, 26; Henry, 203; Isaac, 26, 34, 36, 37, 174, 175, 224; Isaac F., 213; J.M., 124; James M., 125, 146; Joseph, 14; Madison, 102, 144; Susan C., 203; W.M., 224
HITE Jr.: Isaac, 34
Hitt, 46
HITT: Jacob, 137
Hitty, 114
HO___D: William, 204
HOFF: Elizabeth, 130, 139; John, 78, 252; Lewis, 156; Mary, 130
HOGAN: Lettia N., 61; Martin, 146
HOGE: Agnes, 35; James, 35, 36
HOLDMAN: Daniel, 13
HOLIDAY: James, 136; Robert B., 242
HOLKER: John, 96

HOLLINGSWORTH: Ann Virginia, 243; David, 192, 195, 243, 244, 247; Eleanor, 192; Isaac, 192, 195; Isaac M., 195; Isaac Milton, 192; Isaiah, 102; J., 136; John, 192, 195; Jonah Isaac, 243; Joseph P., 192; Mary Ellen, 243
HOLLINGSWORTH Jr.: David, 247
HOLME: Elizabeth, 107
Holmes: Henry, 232; Julia, 232
HOLMES: Andrew Hunter, 43; Col. Joseph, 34; David, 34, 51, 156, 170; Davis, 152; Eliza, 34; Elizabeth, 43; Gertrude, 34, 51; Hugh, 34, 126; Hunter, 34, 51; Joseph, 34, 36, 44, 51; Judge, 51; Mrs., 34; Nancy, 34, 43; Rebecca, 34, 43, 51; William, 143, 156
HOLMES Jr.: Joseph, 43
Holter: Moses, 209
HOLTZMAN: Frederick, 120
HOLYDAY, 173
Hom, 123
Hood, 69
HOOF: Elizabeth, 130; Mary, 130
HOOK: Thomas, 174
Hookless, 234
HOOPER: Joseph, 85; Nicholas, 178
HOOVER: Charity, 68; Henry, 68, 69, 110; John, 68; Philip, 68, 183, 186
Hopewell, 29, 30
HOPEWELL: William, 83
HOPKINS: Abby B., 245; Harriet, 167; John, 121, 151, 161

Horace, 86, 120, 142, 159, 197, 203, 204, 207
Hotten, 87
HOTZENPELER: Stephen, 17
Howard, 157, 168, 201
HOWARD, 99; John, 20; Patrick, 187
HULET: Charles, 171, 172
Hull: Abraham, 118
HUME: James, 77
Humphrey, 16, 73, 104, 116, 121, 123, 139, 215
HUMPHREY, 139; John, 22; Ralph, 2; Sary, 22; Thomas G., 150
Humphry, 73, 147, 209
HUMSTED: T., 173
HUNSUCKER: Jacob, 142
Hunter: Peter, 5; Thomas, 208
HUNTER, 43; Henry, 39
HUNTSBERRY: Conrad, 117, 124, 179, 182, 183, 185
HURST: Rebecca, 73; William, 67, 73
HUTCHIN: Francis, 89
HUTCHINGS: Francis, 97, 104; Mrs., 97
HUTCHINS, 34
HUTCHINSON: Lemuel, 124
Huton, 24
Hyram, 158

Ian, 225
Immanuel, 118
INGLETON: Judith, 38
Ira, 135
Ireland, 164, 175, 184, 189
IRELAND: Frances, 52; James, 53; Mrs., 52; Samuel, 52
Isaac, 16, 17, 24, 29, 30, 36, 43, 44, 45, 48, 50, 52, 54, 67, 73, 74, 78, 81, 83, 84, 88, 89, 95, 97, 103, 108, 119, 123, 124,

81, 86, 88, 92, 100, 105, 111, 112, 114, 116, 125, 126, 127, 128, 130, 135, 142, 143, 149, 150, 158, 159, 160, 161, 163, 177, 179, 193, 194, 195, 197, 199, 203, 205, 206, 208, 211, 218, 224, 227, 234, 236, 237, 238, 241, 245, 247

JANES: Henry, 131, 136; Willy, 131

Janey, 30, 83, 116, 157

Janney, 33, 101, 106, 126, 160

Janney Ann, 150

Janny, 35, 69, 94, 136, 141

Jansy, 56

Jany, 56, 133

Jarad, 186

Jared, 141, 173, 175, 197, 217

Jarret, 115

Jarry, 136

Jary, 111

Jason, 222

Jasper, 92, 119, 149

Jean, 8, 13, 18

Jeanny, 69

Jeena, 17

Jeff, 39, 41, 116, 139, 147, 203, 215

Jefferson, 79, 87, 162, 180, 181, 226

JEFFERSON: Ann Elizabeth, 216; Benjamin W., 216, 242; Lucy Ellen, 216; Lucy Ellen S., 216

Jeffery, 14, 102

Jeffre, 13

Jeffrey, 129

Jeffry, 114, 119, 121

Jem, 7, 68, 194

Jemima, 143

Jemina, 40

Jeminia, 118

Jen, 20

Jene, 19

Jeney, 191

Jenkins, 60

JENKINS: Stephen, 185; William, 124, 125, 137

Jenney, 135

Jennings: Bery, 216

Jenny, 15, 17, 29, 33, 34, 39, 43, 46, 52, 63, 64, 67, 71, 73, 79, 87, 91, 94, 105, 122, 124, 126, 129, 131, 138, 146, 162, 164, 168, 172, 184, 185, 194, 207

Jeny, 75, 130, 173, 189

Jerey, 74

Jerome, 168

Jerrard, 138

Jerry, 27, 28, 30, 39, 41, 43, 47, 75, 87, 88, 93, 95, 97, 137, 140, 143, 151, 152, 156, 158, 169, 170, 175, 181, 184, 191

Jery, 27

Jess, 76, 142

Jesse, 13, 27, 48, 68, 76, 83, 86, 97, 100, 142, 153, 154, 156, 167, 170, 171, 185, 187, 195, 209, 218, 219, 221, 222

Jessy, 69, 94, 125

Jim, 24, 26, 27, 29, 38, 45, 54, 55, 56, 69, 70, 75, 87, 91, 96, 101, 102, 108, 114, 117, 119, 122, 123, 127, 129, 136, 138, 141, 143, 147, 148, 152, 156, 157, 159, 162, 164, 167, 168, 170, 172, 175, 177, 178, 179, 184, 185, 188, 189, 194, 197, 200, 201, 202, 206, 207, 208, 212, 213, 218, 222, 223, 224, 227, 231, 232, 236, 238, 241, 247, 249, 252

Jinncy, 143

Jinney, 64

Jinney Ann, 108

Jinny, 50, 71, 197

281

282

JORDAN: B., 183; Branch, 168, 182, 183, 198, 250; Thomas, 72
Jordon, 137
Jos, 118, 142, 152
Joseine, 116
Joseph, 34, 36, 40, 54, 55, 61, 68, 74, 84, 87, 91, 92, 101, 103, 105, 112, 114, 117, 121, 137, 139, 149, 150, 153, 173, 174, 181, 187, 191, 193, 194, 197, 198, 199, 201, 207, 218, 221, 228, 231, 236, 249
Joseph Reuben, 151
Joseph W. Augustus, 218
Josephine, 233
Joshua, 29, 56, 85, 92, 97, 143, 234
Josiah, 177
Juber, 87
Juboy, 76
Juda, 69, 87, 147, 175, 194
Judah, 24, 63, 64, 137, 239
Judath, 76
Juddy, 33
Jude, 15, 16, 20, 27, 34, 35, 39, 41, 47, 49, 62, 68, 70, 110, 201, 222
Judea, 103
Judia, 197
Judith, 25, 44, 202, 219, 238
Judy, 23, 24, 35, 36, 41, 46, 48, 51, 54, 64, 77, 78, 93, 102, 105, 108, 122, 123, 124, 125, 126, 129, 139, 143, 150, 173, 181, 186, 188, 194, 196, 203, 204, 206, 207, 208, 211, 223, 224, 225, 226, 231, 236, 238, 246
Jul, 47
Jula, 102
Juleous, 24

Julia, 84, 107, 114, 125, 139, 222, 232
Julia Ann, 217, 225
Julian, 72, 194
Juliana, 146
Julianna, 186
Juliet, 27, 88, 89, 113, 164, 167, 181, 193
JULIET: Mary Ann, 40
Juliet Ann, 83
Juliss, 51
Julius, 24, 44
July Ann, 103
JUMP: George, 17, 20

Kalph, 64
Kate, 1, 17, 18, 20, 28, 29, 30, 45, 47, 71, 79, 97, 109, 130, 211, 238
Katilda, 125
Katina, 36
Katy, 26, 67, 122, 124, 129, 174
KAUFMAN: M.R., 222
KEAN: Joseph, 249
KECKLEY: Benjamin, 211, 212
KEEDING: Eliza, 215; Peter, 215
KEELER: Joseph, 112
KEGER: Jacob, 143; William G., 246
KEMP, 204; J.H., 225; Sally, 41; Sarah, 42
KEN: Rebecca I., 202
KENDERICK: Benjamin, 130; Elizabeth, 130
KENDRCK: John, 137
KENDRICK: Benjamin, 137, 144; Benjiman, 178; John, 137; Sam, 137
KENNAN: Sarah, 243
Kennedy, 87
KENNEDY: Hugh, 103, 117; Jesse, 103; Washington, 103

KENNERLY: Thomas, 92, 114
KENNON: Thomas, 111
KENNON, Sr.: Thomas, 101
KERCHEVAL: Elijah, 153;
Jane, 76; John, 26; Matilda,
76; Thomas B., 76;
Winnifred, 26
KERCHWOOD: Elijah, 52
KERFOOT: Ann, 127; George,
20, 124; George S., 117; John,
160; Margaret, 73; Nancy,
127; Samuel, 20, 71; William,
20, 59
KERFOTT: Mary Tate, 28
KERMAN: Sally, 76
KERN: Mary, 195; Nicholas,
195, 200, 201
KERNS: Adam, 233
KERR: Virginia, 236, 244;
William, 214, 215, 229, 244,
253
Kesia, 129
Ket, 175
KEYES: Gershom, 8; Ruth, 8
KEYS: Gresham, 11
KIBBLE: Thompson, 132
KICKLEY: Benjamin, 214;
Benjamin F., 214; Josiah,
214; Mary, 214; Mary Jane,
214
KIGER: Amelia, 49; Jacob, 141;
Jane, 219; Joseph, 49; Louisa,
49; Mariah, 49; Martha, 243;
Patsey, 49; Susan, 49;
Thomas, 49; Thomas W., 219
KING: Joseph, 49, 50, 52
KINNEY: Ann, 207
Kip, 63
Kisiah, 137
Kissey, 173
Kissy, 193
Kit, 43, 93, 105, 110, 125
Kitt, 182

Kittey, 95
Kitty, 28, 34, 36, 43, 46, 47, 48,
51, 77, 78, 81, 84, 85, 104,
109, 111, 116, 119, 120, 126,
129, 131, 134, 160, 161, 172,
188, 191, 196, 197, 199, 206,
209, 218, 243, 244, 252
Kitty Ann, 218
KIZER: Amilia, 52; George, 50
Kiziah, 122
Kizzey, 97
Kizzy, 124
KLINE: A.W., 222
KNIGHT: Elizabeth, 250;
James, 25
KOWN: Warner W., 251
KOWNSLAR: Conrad, 117, 150
KYGER: Mrs., 75

L__, 159, 168
L___, 141
LACY: Henry, 219; James R.,
219
Lancaster, 126
Landen, 212
LANE: G.S., 103; Isaac, 29;
Joseph, 150; William, 137
Laney, 74
Lang, 127
LANGDON: Joseph, 13
LANGHORN: William, 111
Langley, 184
Langly, 175
LANICK: George, 145; Joseph,
204; Mary, 219
LANIE: Jabez, 156
Lanny, 39
LARICK: Jacob F., 224
Larina, 158
Larkin, 168, 170
LARNE: Clary, 56; James, 56,
57

LARRICK: Archibald, 251; Caper, 23; J.B., 217; Jacob B., 214; Jacob F., 242; John, 55; Margaret, 55; Rebecca, 214, 217
Larry, 120, 121
Larue: Samuel, 22
LARUE: Alfred L.P., 175; Francis C., 175; Jabez, 103; Jaby, 126; James W., 175; Jane, 39; John D., 175; Margaret, 175; Phebe, 46; Robert A.I., 175; Samuel, 102
LATHSOUR: Abner, 44
Laticia, 24
LAUCK: Peter, 62, 185, 187
LAUDER: George, 52
Laura, 88, 121, 235
Lavenia Jr, 208
Lavina, 81, 83, 173
Lavinah, 129
Lavinia, 191, 208, 249
Law: William, 104
Laws: William, 164
Lawson, 130, 158, 244
Le_, 205
Leah, 23, 73, 103
Leana, 93
Leana Jr., 143
Leanah, 103
Leanna, 124, 202
Leannah, 153, 162
Leannah Jr., 143
Lec, 93
Ledey, 29
Lee, 97, 106, 107, 158, 162, 164, 195, 215, 229, 238; Jim, 172; Sam, 45
LEE: Claraline, 47; Daniel, 156, 161
LEETCH: Jeremiah, 38
LEFEVER: John, 140

LEFEVRE: John, 158; Lewis, 158
Leg, 191
Legrand, 159
LEGRAND: Mrs., 34; Nash, 51
LEHEN: John, 18; Spencer, 18
LEHEW: Catlett, 110; John, 18, 19
LEHUR: Nancy, 49
LEITH: George, 10; John, 25
Lelena, 226
Lelia, 125, 138
Leman, 15
Lemmon, 34, 36, 51, 97, 114, 130, 158
Lemon, 15, 16, 17, 20, 21, 97
Len, 162
Lena, 228
Leona, 47
Leonadas, 125
Leonidas, 139, 140
Leroy, 198
Let, 50, 53, 126, 215
Letice, 15
Leticke, 43
Letitla, 81, 85, 104
Lett, 15
Lette, 27
Lettie, 54, 101
Letty, 30, 35, 43, 45, 54, 64, 65, 74, 75, 83, 86, 87, 121, 127, 130, 222, 228, 242, 252
Leven, 107
Levi, 105, 120, 121, 143, 152, 159, 238
Levin, 93
Levina, 56, 209, 249
Levinah, 36
Levingston, 34, 36
Levinia, 30
Levy, 103
LEVY: Joseph, 212

287

Ma__ch, 46
Mabriel, 46
MacDONALD: Mary, 26, 27
MACKIE: Catharine, 27;
Edward, 28; Polly, 28
MACKY: Dr., 30; John, 93, 113;
Rebecca, 139, 140
MADDEN: Jacob, 53, 63, 94,
95; Jane, 82; Mabra, 49;
Samuel, 138, 139
MADDEN Jr.: Mabra, 205
MADDEN Sr.: Mabra, 205
MADDEN, Sr.: Mabra, 49
Madison, 128
MAGALL: Mrs., 249
Mage, 135
MAGILE: Archibald, 172
MAGILL: Archibald, 82, 89,
153, 162; Charles, 112;
Charles L., 211; Evelina
Tucker, 224; John S., 194; L,
172; Mary, 112; Mary B.,
211; Mary Elizabeth, 197;
Mary W., 252
MAGRUDER: Eleanor, 181,
193
Mahala, 137, 149, 150, 203, 204,
244
Mahale, 209
Mahaly, 201
MAHAN: Sarah, 40; Timothy
W., 40
MAHANEY: Lewis, 112
Major, 5, 103
Major Kudgoe, 92
Malack, 199, 226, 236
Malah, 193
Malinda, 89, 160, 218
Mall, 182, 183
Mance, 218
MANCK: Michael, 136, 151,
161; Michale, 149
Mandly, 201

Manley, 203
Manlia, 137
Mansfield, 92, 103
Manuel, 56, 152, 175, 198
Manurva, 235
Maranda, 207
Marcia, 83
Marcus, 137, 168, 175, 194
Margaret, 17, 52, 59, 110, 126,
128, 129, 134, 141, 143, 173,
175, 191, 194, 207, 208, 212,
215, 217, 223, 225, 232, 244
Margaret Ann, 215
Margaret Ellen, 226
Margate, 137
Marge, 105
Margery, 37, 91
Margory, 36
Maria, 24, 46, 52, 64, 69, 78, 81,
83, 87, 88, 89, 92, 103, 108,
109, 110, 112, 113, 114, 116,
124, 125, 126, 128, 130, 131,
132, 133, 137, 138, 139, 146,
147, 148, 153, 162, 164, 167,
168, 172, 173, 174, 175, 184,
185, 187, 188, 190, 191, 194,
197, 203, 205, 207, 208, 211,
212, 215, 233, 235, 238, 239,
242, 244, 249
Mariah, 24, 38, 41, 53, 56, 71,
76, 78, 85, 94, 95, 105, 117,
126, 135, 213, 215, 216, 218,
222, 237, 238
Mariah F., 218
Marian, 221
Marie, 70
Mariel, 128
Marinda, 202, 204
MARK: Alexander, 198, 199;
M__, 199; Samuel, 199
Markam, 209
MARKER: Alpheus, 223;
Cornelius B., 223; Jacob A.,

288

223; John, 223, 225; John H.,
223; Reuben, 223; Sarah, 223
MARQUIS: Betty, 34; John, 31,
33, 34, 39; Nelly, 34
Marrion, 136
Mars, 87
Marshal, 150, 232
Marshall, 106, 148, 244; John,
211
MARSHALL: Elizabeth, 92, 94;
Fanny, 82; James, 82; Mary
Keith, 82; Thomas, 82
Martan: William, 76
MARTEN: Samuel, 150
Martha, 79, 105, 110, 197, 198,
202, 206, 207, 209, 213, 218,
221, 222, 226, 228, 232, 243
Martha Ann, 134, 149, 150
Marthy, 238
Martin, 82, 184, 196
MARTIN: Ann, 85; Charlotte,
56; Donny, 21; George, 3;
James S., 101; Lewis B., 112;
Philip, 195; Phillip, 21;
Richard, 85; Samuel, 150;
Sarah, 186; Thomas Bryan,
21
Mary, 13, 30, 35, 37, 40, 46, 49,
50, 51, 53, 54, 56, 59, 61, 63,
64, 69, 70, 71, 72, 73, 74, 75,
76, 77, 79, 82, 83, 87, 88, 89,
92, 97, 101, 102, 103, 105,
106, 112, 114, 116, 117, 118,
119, 121, 122, 124, 125, 126,
128, 130, 131, 132, 133, 134,
135, 136, 137, 138, 140, 141,
143, 147, 149, 150, 151, 152,
153, 160, 161, 162, 164, 172,
175, 177, 179, 181, 182, 183,
184, 187, 189, 190, 191, 192,
193, 194, 195, 197, 199, 200,
202, 204, 205, 207, 208, 209,
211, 212, 213, 214, 215, 217,
218, 221, 222, 223, 224, 225,
226, 227, 228, 229, 232, 234,
235, 236, 237, 238, 241, 244,
245, 247, 249, 250, 251, 253
Mary Ann, 59, 83, 84, 91, 117,
119, 129, 138, 139, 141, 151,
162, 164, 209
Mary Eliza, 201, 203
Mary Elizabeth, 179
Mary Jane, 153, 232
Maryan, 36
MASEN: J.W., 211; Seth, 211
Masia, 53
Mason: George, 251; Robert,
158, 202
MASON: Armistead T., 78;
James M., 124; James W.,
125, 202, 207; Maj., 162;
Seth, 202, 204, 207
MASON Jr.: Seth, 204
Masse, 149
Massie, 150; Mary, 234
MASSIE: Benjamin M., 206;
John B., 208; Mildred, 208;
Sidney, 208
MASTIN: Charlotte, 49;
Richard, 79
Mat, 95, 122
MATHEWS: Joseph, 5
Mathilda, 137
Mati, 225
Matilda, 27, 47, 56, 76, 88, 109,
110, 136, 139, 140, 146, 160,
162, 164, 168, 173, 181, 191,
193, 195, 201, 223, 229, 231,
232, 236, 241
Matilda Jr., 143
Matildia, 69
Matildy, 71
Matlock, 213
Matt, 10, 56, 123, 124, 129, 130,
177
Matthew, 75, 109, 125, 139, 140

MATTOX: Nelly, 118; Robert, 118, 128, 134, 139
Matty, 152
May, 168, 191
MAYHEW: John, 157
Mayor, 43
Mazy, 178, 182
McALISTER: Alice, 117
McALLISTER: Alice, 121; John, 111
McCALISTER: Alice, 124
McCANDLASS: Robert, 177
McCANDLESS: R.P., 183; Robert, 93, 182, 183; Robert P., 182, 183
McCell_: Samuel, 8
McCLORY: Jane, 226
McCOMRICK: Margaret, 86; Samuel, 86
McCONNELL: Abraham, 13
McCONNICK: Charles, 142; Isaac, 141, 142; Lucy, 142; Thomas, 141
McCOOL: Cassandra, 199
McCORMICK, 138; Andrew, 10; Ann, 10, 207; Armistead T.M., 193; B., 193; Brockenbrough, 193; Bushrod, 157; D., 127; Dawson, 172, 174, 180; Edward, 207; Frances, 150; George, 115; Isaac, 98, 113, 127, 167; James, 10; John, 10; Lucy, 167, 176; Maza, 167; Otway, 183; P__, 172; Province, 157, 167; Samuel, 89, 98, 113, 115, 174; Thomas, 114, 115; Thomas W., 193; William, 10, 107, 115, 207
McCORMICK Jr.: Thomas, 113
McCORMISH: George, 125; Otway, 182

McCORWAN: Thomas, 115
McCOWAN: Thomas, 103, 111
McCOWIN: Thomas, 104
McCRU__: Mary, 8
McDANALD: Mary J., 218
McDANIEL: James, 132
McDONALD: A.W., 235; Angus, 19; Anna, 19; Arche, 26; Archibald, 26; Benjamin, 110, 119; Daniel, 196; James, 135; Mary, 26; Massey, 110
McDOUGLE: Peter, 26
McDOW: E., 227
McDOWELL: Elijah, 234
McGINNIS: Edward, 140
McGOVERN: Joseph, 178, 179
McGUIRE: David Holmes, 121; Dr., 183; E.D., 139; Edward, 51, 121, 125, 139, 154; Edward D., 121; H.H., 211; Milicent, 51
McGUIRE, Sr: Edward, 51
McHENRY: Baranaby, 2
McILHANY: Taliaferro M., 95
McINTOSH: Sarah Virginia, 189
McIvoy: James, 15
McKAY: Harriet, 205; Jane R., 232, 236
McKE__: Warren, 204
McKEARN: Hugh H., 77; Hugh Henry, 55
McKNIGHT: John, 150
McKOWN: Ann Amelia, 216, 225; Francis Samuel Silver, 216; Lucy Ann, 216; Warner, 216
McLEOD: Ann S., 232, 236; Mary, 244; Thornton, 112; William, 130
McLINN: Samuel, 206; Sarah, 206

McMURRAY: John, 100; Mary, 134, 147; Peter, 100
McMURRY: Peter, 114
McNAMARA: John S., 72
McNEILL: William C., 200
McPHERSON: Nathaniel, 61, 63, 72
Meade: Mary, 116
MEADE: D., 153; David, 127; Drayton G., 190, 213; Harriet, 190; Harriet G., 213; Lucy, 149, 189; Lucy F., 116, 127, 213; Mary, 64; R.K., 184; Richard K., 127, 164, 175; Susan, 113, 116, 127, 149; William, 189
Meary, 191
MEEM: Frances, 39
Meg, 53, 213
Melford, 16
MELTON: Alexander, 68
Mely, 71
MERCER: Margaret, 152
Meriah, 106
Merial, 118
Met, 226
METZGER: Daniel, 217, 233
MEYERS: Joseph, 150
Michael, 73, 98, 109, 122, 124, 129, 138, 169, 179, 207
Michel, 111
MICHLIN: Joseph, 42
MIDDLETON: Sarah, 47
Mike, 69, 75, 81, 87, 91, 112, 143, 202, 221
Mildred, 50, 105
Miles, 46, 87, 95, 130, 184, 238
Milford, 23, 113, 116, 139
Milfred, 76
Mill, 19, 39, 41, 44, 110
Milla, 15
Mille, 23
Millee, 24

MILLER: Abraham, 192; Alexander, 168; Catharine R., 168, 180; Dr. Lewis A., 236; Elizabeth, 168; Godfried, 46; H.A., 249; Henrietta Amelia, 249; Ja__ D., 142; Jacob, 8; John C., 174; John M., 194, 244; Joseph, 217, 218; Mary, 217, 236, 237, 244; Rebecca, 192; Sarah Ann, 236, 244; Thomas C., 244; William, 101, 141, 143, 197, 249, 250
Milley, 15, 16, 19, 26, 45, 52, 95, 101, 105, 121, 204
Millie, 238
Milly, 10, 17, 20, 22, 26, 27, 28, 29, 34, 36, 43, 46, 47, 48, 50, 51, 52, 59, 60, 61, 63, 68, 69, 74, 76, 78, 79, 82, 83, 87, 89, 93, 102, 105, 108, 109, 112, 116, 117, 122, 124, 128, 129, 130, 136, 141, 143, 148, 149, 150, 151, 155, 158, 160, 162, 173, 174, 175, 178, 181, 182, 184, 194, 195, 207, 213, 216, 217, 225, 226, 228, 232, 235, 237, 239, 241
Milo, 207
MILTON: John, 30, 95
Mima, 36, 54, 77, 82, 127, 136, 153, 187, 243
Mime, 18, 39, 41
Mimery, 83
Mimia, 197
Mimy, 82
Mina, 69, 92
Ming, 222
Mingo, 35, 36, 84, 91, 92, 102, 103, 117, 136, 148, 159, 170, 178, 185, 189
Minney, 143
Minny, 141, 173
Minta, 29, 30, 52

Mintee, 24
Minty, 68, 116
Miranda, 203, 205
MITCHALL: William, 4
MITCHEL: Nancy, 63; William, 63
MITCHELL: Carey, 41; Cary, 39; Charles G., 147; Henry, 93, 106, 107; James, 129, 147, 173; John C., 76; Thomas, 165, 169, 176, 182; William, 81
MITTON: Eben, 115
Mo__,, 141
MOFFETT: John, 40, 41, 53
Mol, 7
Moll, 13, 18, 20, 25, 27, 83, 123
Molley, 45, 102, 143
Molly, 34, 35, 36, 37, 38, 41, 46, 49, 53, 63, 64, 67, 78, 79, 84, 91, 94, 102, 104, 105, 114, 115, 117, 119, 122, 124, 125, 129, 130, 136, 139, 148, 170, 172, 173, 174, 175, 178, 179, 180, 185, 189, 198, 205, 238
Monimia, 181
MONROE: Catharine, 106; Eliza, 106; John, 106; Thomas, 106; William, 106, 132
MONROE Jr.: William, 106
MONTGOMERY: R., 174; Robert, 171
Mony, 29
MOORE: Catharine, 79; Henry, 67; James, 107, 120, 138; Maria, 91; Reuben, 51
More, 217
Morgan, 91, 160, 191; Henry, 168; Olive, 11; Rebecca, 181
MORGAN: Benjamin, 148; Drusilah, 5; Elizabeth, 148; John, 148, 173; Richard, 79

MORRIS: George H., 125
Mortimer, 87, 151
Mos, 63, 168
Mose, 228
MOSELY: Martha D., 222
Moses, 14, 18, 19, 27, 28, 34, 39, 43, 45, 47, 56, 57, 61, 62, 64, 68, 69, 73, 74, 75, 76, 91, 92, 93, 112, 117, 119, 120, 121, 122, 127, 135, 142, 143, 146, 150, 156, 165, 169, 176, 177, 179, 181, 182, 195, 196, 198, 208, 209, 218, 228, 237, 244
Mossie: Nat, 172
Mosy, 56
MOUNTZ: John, 246
MOYERS: Jacob, 47
Mumpha, 94
MUMPHRY: Daniel, 150
Munday, 235
MURPHEY: Thomas, 82
MURPHY, 243; Darby, 10
MURRAY: Cyrus, 55; Cyrus W., 51, 54, 55; George, 30, 36, 51, 54, 55; Jane, 30, 51; Mary I., 138; Polly, 51, 54; Polly R., 30
MUSE: Edward, 201, 202; Edward R., 227, 234, 237; Elizabeth, 201; Emily, 201; Frances, 201; John, 63, 67, 70, 72, 109, 201; John N., 205; Joseph R., 205; Julia Ann, 201; Lucinda, 201; Martha, 201, 203; Martha E., 205; Mary Ann, 201; Mrs. E.B., 205; Rob B., 205; Robert, 201, 203, 205; Susan, 109; Susannah, 72; Virginia E., 237; Warner, 109
MUSGROVE: John, 2
MYERS: Betty B., 228; Henry, 228, 252; Joanna, 226, 233;

108, 120, 124, 125, 138, 153, 163, 180; William Byrd, 170
PAGE Jr: Joseph, 129
PAGETT: Edmond, 192, 193, 199, 213; Edmund, 226, 236; Jane, 192
PAINTER: John, 125; Peter, 9
Paisey, 28
Palace, 149, 150
Pallas, 27
Pamela, 199
Pampy, 216
Paracutis, 168
Park: John, 67
Parker, 55, 122, 129; Lucy, 197
PARKER: John, 147; R.E., 150; Richard C., 83; Sally, 83; Sarah, 83; Thomas, 30, 78
PARKHAM: Rebecca R., 202
PARKINS: Alfred, 192, 195; Eliza, 192; H., 211; Isaac, 15, 40; Joseph, 211; Nathan, 141
PASH: William, 72
Pat, 14, 24, 47, 49, 50, 52, 107, 123, 138, 170, 187
Patience, 26, 28, 76
Paton, 77
Patrick, 27, 78, 105, 151, 152
Patsey, 102, 208
Patsy, 69, 83, 128, 199, 208, 212, 223
Patt, 56, 129
Pattis, 29
Patty, 35, 63, 64, 70, 72, 77, 78, 84, 88, 102, 108, 114, 115, 137, 160, 182, 186, 192, 195, 197, 222, 223, 224
Paul, 207
PAYNE: George, 160, 196; Moses, 55; Sarah, 196; William, 137
Payton, 143
PEACHY: Leroy, 135

PEARIS: George, 3
PECK: Polly, 88; Samuel, 88
Peg, 15, 26, 27, 47, 48, 53, 71, 102, 107
Pegg, 7, 16, 17, 20, 52, 76, 102, 114
Peggy, 26, 40, 52, 56, 69, 76, 102, 110, 116, 122, 123, 124, 129, 139, 149, 150, 154, 175, 191, 194, 215
Peghe, 2
Pegpee, 2
PELTER: George, 102, 205, 211
PEMBERTON: Eljiah, 4; George, 4; Margaret, 4
PENDLETON: Edmund, 82; Edward, 102; Elizabeth, 82
Penny, 108, 122, 124
Perkins: Thomas, 16
Pero, 72
PERRILL: Elizabeth, 231; Rebecca, 231; Zebulon, 223
Perry, 87
PERRY: Ignatius, 56; Thomas, 137
Persey, 129
Pete, 152, 159, 165, 173
Peter, 3, 5, 10, 18, 19, 22, 23, 27, 28, 29, 30, 33, 34, 35, 38, 39, 40, 41, 43, 44, 45, 49, 50, 52, 53, 56, 57, 59, 60, 61, 62, 70, 73, 74, 79, 80, 83, 84, 86, 89, 95, 102, 105, 107, 114, 115, 118, 120, 121, 123, 124, 125, 130, 151, 153, 158, 163, 164, 167, 168, 194, 195, 198, 199, 208, 212, 214, 215, 222, 223, 226, 232, 234, 242, 252
PETERS: Elizabeth, 3; Otho, 4
Peyton, 73, 77, 92, 146, 181, 193, 205, 229, 234, 238

PEYTON: John, 48; Mrs., 48, 61; Mrs. Henry, 20; Susan, 140
Pez, 52
Phebe, 10, 26, 33, 34, 44, 79, 84, 86, 106, 135, 136, 137, 149, 151, 190, 200, 221
Pheby, 52, 102
Pheh, 198
PHELPS: Elisha, 72
Phil, 24, 27, 38, 41, 44, 67, 70, 74, 83, 85, 102, 108, 112, 114, 123, 157, 164, 172, 175, 186, 188, 192, 195, 234, 243, 244, 247, 250
Philas, 40
Philip, 70, 105, 117, 119, 130, 154, 162, 173, 204, 207, 211, 227, 237
Philips: William, 17
Philis, 29, 45, 47, 52, 103, 104
Phill, 24, 39, 41, 44, 46, 51, 52, 62, 67, 71, 77, 124, 130, 160
Phillip, 97, 98, 107, 165
PHILLIPS: Jonah, 218
Phillis, 7, 18, 20, 27, 29, 30, 43, 50, 53, 54, 68, 74, 84, 86, 94, 97, 188
Phlake, 218
Phoeba, 226
Phoebe, 80, 218, 222
Picket, 41
Pierce, 241
PIERCE: Charles, 4; Peter M., 100
PIFER: Ephraim, 193
PINE: Sagamus, 117
Pirnitta, 216
PITMAN: Andrew, 192; C.A., 216; John W., 178; Joseph, 251; Philip, 215, 216; Susan, 251
PITMAN Jr.: John, 59

PLANK: Christian, 16
Planter, 53, 56
Pleasant, 82
Pleasants, 47, 48, 89, 114
Plummer, 59, 87
Plump, 249
Poindexter, 84, 188
POLAND: John, 75
POLK: Duvall, 172; Mary A., 172; Robert W., 172; Susan N., 172
Poll, 4, 15, 36, 50, 82, 97, 122
Pollard: Amelia, 207; Charlotte, 174, 207; Francis, 174; Franky, 207; James, 174, 207; Mary, 174, 207; Thomas, 174; William, 174, 207
POLLARD: Chattin, 14; Doggord, 14; Elijah, 14, 52; Frances, 15; James, 67; Joseph, 14, 45; Manna, 14; William, 14; William Frances, 15
Polley, 149
Polly, 26, 46, 49, 50, 54, 56, 60, 73, 79, 81, 83, 85, 98, 103, 118, 123, 149, 160, 162, 172, 189, 193, 202, 235, 238, 242, 249
Polly Ann, 153
Pomp, 71
Pompay, 86
Pompey, 4, 56, 85, 114
Pompoy, 152
Pomprey, 4
Pompy, 71
Pona, 111
Pony, 225
POOL: Daniel, 62
Poss: John, 195
Potter: Betsey, 94, 104; Richard, 104, 164; Thomas, 104, 130; Tom, 164

POWELL: Alfred H., 115, 116, 151, 152, 158; Leven M., 152
POWERS: C.W., 222; Charles William, 221; Daniel, 92, 102, 219, 221, 222; David, 102; Elizabeth, 65; J.W., 222; James, 64; John, 46, 65, 92; John W., 221; Joseph, 221; Martin, 65; Mary, 221, 222; Nancy, 91, 92; Sally, 57; Thomas, 60, 61, 92; William, 221; Yancy, 91
Presley, 30, 128, 147, 151, 156, 160, 250
Presly, 87, 150
Press, 250
Prestley, 121
Preston, 125
Pretty, 88
PRICE: John, 138, 182, 183, 188; Samuel, 20
PRICHARD: Margaret Eskridge, 77; Stephen, 76
Pricilla, 94, 116, 143
Priscella, 70
Priscilla, 27, 82, 87, 108, 175, 177, 182, 234
Priss, 224
Prissilla, 10
PRITCHARD: Betsy Kanner, 77; Judith K., 225; Judith Kanner, 77; Mary, 238; Stephen, 77, 97, 143, 194, 238, 245; Stephen Cornelius, 238; Susannah James, 77
Providence, 36, 109, 111, 143
Pru, 111
Prudence, 44
Pull, 225
Punch, 73
Purah, 45
PURVIS: Cassandra, 77, 78, 79
Putman, 153

Putnam, 142
Putnum, 167

QUIGLEY: John, 250
Quigly, 164
QUIGLY: Dr., 150
Quiller, 148

Rachael, 36, 43, 45, 83, 88, 91, 93, 114, 122, 123, 124, 150, 182, 226, 235, 247
Rachal, 29
Rachel, 11, 26, 30, 33, 52, 53, 54, 56, 57, 68, 69, 79, 80, 81, 82, 84, 87, 93, 101, 102, 106, 107, 111, 117, 119, 132, 133, 142, 149, 150, 151, 159, 164, 170, 173, 178, 185, 186, 188, 189, 208, 212, 218, 246
Rachell, 62
RAILEY: Farrill, 5
Ralph, 44, 79, 88, 93, 94, 104, 118, 123, 124, 130, 135, 138, 141, 143, 153, 162, 177, 182
RAMEY: John, 94, 98, 223; Mary A., 223
RAMY: John, 55
Randall, 105, 115, 179
Randel, 53
Randell, 135
Randle, 70, 118, 120
Randolph, 94, 122, 129, 184; Annis, 245
RANKER: Casper, 216
RANKINS: Col. Robert, 76; Peggy, 76
Ransone: Charlotte, 86; Peter, 86
Rape: Peter, 3
Rawdy, 53
Rawleigh, 27
Rawley, 50

RAYNOLDS: Frances C., 170; George, 170, 171, 174, 181, 183, 187, 191, 194; George H., 170; Jane, 129, 135
READ: John, 61; Samuel, 61
Rebecca, 73, 78, 79, 81, 101, 110, 112, 145, 163, 169, 174, 181, 198, 216, 217, 235, 236, 246
Rebecca Jr., 217
Rebeckah, 50
Rebuen, 199
REDMAN: Benjamin L., 184; Benjamin S., 165, 176; Frederick B., 165; J., 133; John, 132, 133; John M., 190; Mary Catharine, 176; Mary Catherine, 165; Mrs., 126; Nancy, 127; R.S., 103; Richard L., 126, 127; Richard S., 92, 103; Stewart, 154; Thomas, 7
REDMON: Benjamin L., 133; Catherine B., 132; Frederick B., 133; John Milton, 133; Thomas Jett, 133
REDMOND: Catharine, 155; Frederick B., 155; John N., 155; Thomas Jett, 155
Reed: Berry, 243
REED: Ann, 21; Edward, 18; Hannah, 137; Jacob, 112, 134, 145; John, 61; William, 3
Reeth, 71
Reuben, 21, 36, 37, 43, 45, 52, 61, 74, 78, 79, 81, 82, 85, 88, 91, 105, 130, 143, 149, 150, 160, 161, 175, 206, 208, 209, 224, 226
Reubin, 13, 70, 105, 115, 117
REYNOLDS: George, 207
RHODES: R., 121
Rhody, 95, 185

RICE: Samuel, 15
Richard, 4, 5, 37, 40, 59, 64, 73, 75, 77, 78, 92, 97, 101, 102, 103, 104, 105, 115, 118, 125, 129, 130, 140, 151, 164, 168, 173, 175, 201, 223, 226, 231, 232
RICHARD: Isaac, 252
RICHARDS: Capt. Henry, 30; Henry, 29, 204, 218, 226, 232, 242; Isaac, 222, 234; J.R., 226; James A., 244; James R., 218, 219; Jane, 29; Jememiah, 150; John, 29, 162, 244, 245; Joseph, 204; Lydia, 226; Moses R., 219; Sara, 244
RICHARDSON: James, 97; John, 102, 107, 162, 178; William, 84, 96
Richmond, 22, 27, 142
Ricky, 145
RIDGEWAY: Jacob, 234
RIDGWAY: Richard, 61
RIELY: James B., 252; James P., 244
RILEY: James, 62
RINKEN: Caspar, 194
RINKER: Casper, 45, 246; Mary, 45
RINKER, Sr.: Casper, 252
RINKIN: Josiah, 252
Rippon, 227
RISER: Robert O., 50
RISLER: George, 139
RISSLER: George, 138
RITCHIE: Dr., 147
RITEN__: John William, 209
RITENOUR: Joseph, 148
RITTER: James, 113; Mathius, 168
ROACH: Robert, 41
ROADS: Elizabeth, 172
Rob, 18, 21, 69

Robbin, 39, 41, 87, 113
Roben, 27
ROBERDEAU: Daniel, 34, 35;
Gen. Daniel, 34, 38; Jane, 34,
35; Mrs., 38
ROBERSTON: Elizabeth, 136;
William, 136
Robert, 29, 44, 51, 53, 59, 64,
69, 77, 84, 91, 92, 94, 97, 101,
104, 105, 108, 110, 111, 114,
117, 118, 120, 125, 126, 136,
137, 138, 143, 145, 148, 151,
158, 159, 164, 168, 173, 175,
181, 188, 194, 197, 201, 202,
205, 208, 215, 218, 239, 244,
246, 249, 250
ROBERTS: Elizabeth, 8, 23;
Felix, 239; John, 183; Joseph,
5; Ph., 104; Philagathus, 93;
Thomas, 183, 189; William, 9
ROBERTS, Sr.: William, 8
ROBERTSON: Muncy, 235
Robin, 16, 23, 24, 35, 62, 64, 74,
76, 88, 118, 122, 124, 129,
130, 131, 169, 183, 208, 212
Robinson: Archibald, 228;
Charles, 228; Frank, 181;
John, 228; Monday, 228;
Sally, 228
ROBINSON: Johnathan, 181;
Lyles R., 162, 164, 168; Mrs.
France, 222; Munday, 235
Robison, 218
RODES: Lewis, 74
Rodger, 59
Rody, 180
Roger, 86, 87, 96
ROGERS: John, 45; Mary, 45
ROMINE: Adison, 134;
Elizabeth, 134; Lydia, 134;
Mahaley, 134; Peter, 53;
Reuben, 126, 134
Rommey, 178

Rosanna, 227
Rosannah, 25, 33
Rose, 1, 16, 19, 20, 22, 24, 26,
33, 37, 78, 79, 81, 95, 102,
107, 108, 110, 112, 120, 128,
130, 131, 143, 158, 172, 197,
201, 207, 227, 234
Rosella, 67
ROSENBURGER: Jacob, 73
Rosetta, 216
ROSS: David, 22, 48; Frances,
21; George, 21
ROTHEL: Clibborn, 16
Rou, 22
ROUT: John, 68, 69
ROWSE: Mrs., 53
Roy, 218
Roze, 37
Rozetta, 197
Ruben, 72, 73
Rubin, 169, 195
RUSSEL: Margaret, 214
Russell, 168
RUSSELL: Christiana, 195;
Elizabeth, 163; I.G., 212;
Isaac, 243; John, 163, 167,
182; Margaret, 211; William,
18; William G., 243
RUST: A., 132; Benedict, 112,
126, 133, 144, 146; Elizabeth,
72; Hannah M., 203; Jane M.,
144; John, 51, 92; Marshall,
133, 190; Matthew, 141, 143,
146; Petert, 72; Robert, 203;
Roger, 132; Thomas, 79
RUST Sr.: Benedict, 111
Ruston: Elisabeth, 14
Ruth, 13, 22, 87, 97, 108, 124,
149, 150
Ruthy, 48, 164
RUTTER: Stephen, 117, 124

S__ERS: Edward, 24

Sadde_, 3
Sal, 4, 7, 13, 29, 30, 48, 62
Salena, 61
Sall, 10, 13, 25, 26, 27, 28, 29,
  36, 38, 50, 56, 60, 93
Salley, 106, 126, 129, 250
Sallie, 238
Sally, 20, 38, 40, 41, 46, 52, 53,
  61, 63, 69, 76, 83, 84, 89, 91,
  93, 95, 102, 108, 116, 117,
  122, 123, 124, 126, 129, 138,
  141, 143, 147, 148, 156, 159,
  161, 162, 164, 170, 171, 172,
  173, 175, 178, 180, 181, 188,
  193, 209, 213, 218, 233, 235,
  239, 252
Sally Ann, 102, 109, 209
Sam, 19, 20, 22, 23, 26, 27, 28,
  29, 30, 34, 35, 40, 43, 45, 48,
  49, 53, 54, 55, 56, 63, 67, 68,
  70, 71, 73, 74, 78, 79, 81, 85,
  87, 93, 95, 97, 101, 115, 116,
  118, 120, 125, 128, 129, 132,
  137, 147, 149, 151, 160, 163,
  164, 168, 175, 177, 182, 191,
  213, 229,232, 234, 236, 249
Sama, 207
Samantha, 74, 98
Sambo, 34, 36
Samey, 211
SAMPLE: Samuel, 25; William,
  25
Sampson, 16, 27, 52, 60, 68, 74,
  86, 105
Samuel, 8, 16, 36, 48, 50, 56, 59,
  69, 83, 94, 104, 105, 109, 119,
  128, 147, 150, 157, 172, 195,
  201, 205, 226, 232
SAMUELS: N., 245
SANDERS: Edward N., 231
Sandy, 131, 143, 202, 204, 208,
  228, 231, 232
Sanford, 169

SANFORD: Ann, 81; John P.,
  81; Robert, 81, 93
SANKS: Zachariah, 192, 195,
  199
Sarah, 5, 10, 16, 20, 22, 24, 27,
  29, 35, 36, 40, 41, 45, 46, 50,
  62, 64, 67, 68, 69, 70, 71, 73,
  74, 78, 79, 81, 84, 85, 86, 88,
  89, 91, 92, 100, 101, 102, 103,
  107, 109, 112, 114, 117, 121,
  122, 123, 124, 125, 129, 132,
  133, 136, 137, 139, 141, 142,
  146, 148,149, 151, 152, 153,
  155, 159, 161, 162, 165, 169,
  172, 173, 176, 177, 180, 181,
  183, 192, 193, 194, 195, 196,
  197, 201, 203, 206, 207, 221,
  222, 226, 229, 234, 236, 238,
  243, 244, 246, 247, 249
Sarah Ann, 78, 208
Sarah Catharine, 151
Sarah Catherine, 136
Sarah Frances, 219
Sarah Jane, 141, 227, 238
Sary, 13
Saul, 98
Sauney, 209
SAVAGE: Joseph, 69
Save, 37
SAVICK: Henry, 73; Jacob, 73
SAWERS: D., 54
Sawney, 54, 87, 124, 151, 205
Sawny, 54, 173
SAWYER: George, 124
SAYERS: George, 117
SCAGGS: Isaac, 145
SCARFF: John, 55
SCHENCK: Henry F., 245
SCHENK: Henry F., 231, 232
SCHULL: Lucy, 196
Scig_, 136
Scipio, 46, 140
Scissio, 27

301

Sidner, 128
Sidney, 47, 50, 54, 106, 111, 120, 144, 146, 147, 169, 186, 195, 212
Sie, 105
Silla, 34, 162, 180, 185
Sillah, 25, 56, 98
Siller, 60, 68
Sillow, 61
Silva, 61, 62, 63
Silvah, 50
Silvee, 20
SILVER: Frances, 217, 223; Francis, 188, 216; James, 109; Zephaniah, 216
Silvester, 52, 57
Silvey, 43
Silvia, 4, 15
Silvie, 15
Silvy, 51, 149
Simeon, 103
Simon, 21, 27, 36, 37, 50, 71, 79, 85, 149, 164, 175, 183, 184, 187, 194, 207, 225, 226, 243
SIMPSON: Samuel, 112, 114
SIMRALL: James, 39; Sarah, 39; William F., 39
Sina, 14, 158
Sinah, 27, 36, 48, 51, 73, 87, 130, 168, 180
SINGLETON: Gen. James, 102; James, 101; John, 71; Mrs., 110; W.G., 198
Sipio, 152
Sippio, 51
Sirus, 71
SLACK: William B., 192
Sly, 7
Sly_e, 17
Smith, 55, 77, 209, 235; Ben, 208; Jim, 238; Rebecca, 17; Robert, 205

SMITH: Andrew, 65; Augustine, 126, 127; Bartholomew, 75, 76, 99, 115, 116, 139, 147; Charles, 17; Crizer W., 206; Dr. Philip, 117; E., 115, 147; Edward, 110, 115; Elizabeth, 8, 110, 115; George, 54; George L., 231; Henry, 139; Jere, 34; Jeremiah, 33; John, 1, 150; Jonathan, 168; Joseph, 150; Joseph D., 86; Lewis, 127, 145; Lewis A., 127; Lucy, 223, 231; M.E., 226; Margaret, 219; Margaret E., 218; Michael, 139; Nathen, 53; Patrick, 201; Paul, 94, 149, 150; Pauline E., 231; Philip, 117, 125; Robert, 228; Robert B., 231; Samuel, 34; Samuel P., 231; Sarah, 201; Stephen F., 206; T., 103, 127; Thomas, 94; Thomas W., 231; Walter A., 86; William, 206, 207, 213, 223, 231; William R., 86
SNAP, 137
SNAPP: Joseph, 101, 155, 167; Mrs. H., 155
SNICKERS: Edward, 24, 27; William, 27
SNYDER: D., 115
Sofy, 71, 107
Soloman, 41
Solomon, 16, 26, 30, 39, 40, 52, 54, 62, 72, 78, 79, 89, 93, 97, 101, 102, 104, 107, 113, 115, 123, 125, 129, 130, 138, 141, 153, 157, 163, 170, 173, 180, 181
Sonny, 71
Sopha, 156
Sophah, 103

Sophia, 43, 128, 145, 170, 195
Sophy, 56, 178, 182
Soul, 59
SOUTHAN: John, 173
SOUTHARN: George, 64
SOWERS: Catharina, 87; D.,
132; Daniel, 69, 73, 77, 87,
112, 133; Daniel W., 146;
David, 81, 104; Elija Ann,
140; Eliza A., 87; Eliza Ann,
133; G.K., 132; Jacob, 86, 88,
92; James, 76; James H., 171;
John, 68, 111; Mrs., 73;
William, 117, 160
SOWERS Jr: Daniel, 116
SOWERS Jr.: Daniel, 72, 75, 91
Spencer, 87, 131, 142, 149, 151,
153, 167, 208; Charlotte, 181
SPENGLER, 41; Ann, 157;
Philip C., 173, 175; Sol S.,
156
SPENGLER Jr.: Anthony, 157
SPERRY: Mary, 215; Peter,
198, 199; Thomas, 159
SPINGLER: Samuel M., 178
Squire, 47, 93, 122, 125, 180
STANTHOPE: John, 128;
Nancy, 128
Stape, 89
STARET: Samuel, 150
STEEL: Robert, 235; Susan, 103
Stephen, 24, 97, 136, 179, 190,
199, 201, 213, 225, 228, 229,
231, 232, 236, 237, 238, 241,
245
STEPHEN: Alexander, 9;
Laurence, 17
STEPHENS: B.M., 212; Brian
M., 205, 212; Bryan M., 59,
171; Caroline, 212; Catharine,
187; Emma, 212; Laurence,
17; Lewis, 145; Mary, 17, 26,
79, 93, 148, 151, 159

STEPHENSON: D., 222; Hena,
8; Henry, 232; John, 8, 130,
232; Richard, 8; William,
114, 150, 158, 232
STEPHERSON: Mrs., 182, 183
Stepney, 120
Stepto, 119
Steptoe, 209
Stern: L., 216
Steve, 98
STEWART: Charles C., 198
STICKLEY, 120
STIGLER: David, 79
STILLMAN: J.M., 128
STIPE: Henry, 193, 197, 201;
Tabitha, 193
STONE: Jacob, 127; William,
167
STRANG: Reuben, 139
Strange: Thomas, 124
STRANGE: Reuben, 140
STRIBLING: Elizabeth, 28;
Francis, 78, 93, 105, 112, 171;
John, 53; Magmus, 171;
Nancy, 171; Sally, 101;
Sarah, 146; Sarah E.T., 100;
Sarah Elizabeth Taliaferro,
83; Sigismund, 78, 88, 101,
114; Sigismund E., 125;
Taliaferro, 23, 24; Taliferro,
16, 101, 125; Thomas, 101;
William, 30, 35, 38
STRIBLING Sr.: Francis, 89,
125
STRIKLER: David, 137
STRINGFELLOW: Mrs., 184
Strother, 184, 244
STROTHER, 209; Charles, 105;
Elizabeth, 121; Enoch, 121;
George, 122; James, 121, 122,
148; John, 121; William, 122
STROUP: William, 8

Benjamin, 71; Bennett, 70, 71; Bus, 150; Bushrod, 99, 102, 125, 149, 150, 205, 211; Catherine G., 75; Charlotte, 85; Charlotte B., 96; Ebin, 135, 147, 149; Elvin, 86; Griffin, 50, 75, 127, 150; James, 150; John, 19, 50, 59, 63, 85; John B., 75, 102; John C., 96; Mandly, 117; Marly, 124; Martha E., 245; Mary, 60, 75, 131; Mary H., 59; Mrs., 150; Sarah E., 233; Sarah N., 218; Septimus, 63; W., 122; William, 74, 150

TAYLOR Sr.: William, 71
TEEMAN: Jonathan, 1
Teller, 170, 178
Temp, 36
Temple: Charlotte, 145
TEMPLEMAN: Nathaniel, 121
Tenar, 67, 108, 139
Terry, 35, 217
Thance, 44
THENA: George, 44
THI___: Gabriel, 121
THO_TAS: George, 24
Thomas, 48, 53, 68, 94, 95, 104, 114, 116, 124, 129, 130, 137, 141, 151, 158, 160, 162, 168, 174, 179, 181, 187, 191, 194, 199, 201, 207, 208, 209, 218, 225; John, 181
THOMAS: Dr., 161; Sarah, 91; Townsend W., 126; William, 142
Thomas Allen, 232, 236
Thomason, 191
THOMPKINS: Jane, 222
Thompson, 219; Jim, 238; Samuel, 172; Sarah, 247
THOMPSON: Isabella, 193
Thoms, 183

Thorn, 62
Thornten, 208
Thornton, 29, 68, 78, 79, 92, 94, 98, 108, 109, 111, 112, 114, 121, 123, 126, 129, 133, 143, 146, 149, 150, 169, 173, 175, 179, 180, 202, 204, 207, 218, 226, 228, 233, 245
THORNTON: John S., 76
Thortum, 50
THRASHER: Richard, 9
THROCKMORTON: Albion, 35, 46; Amelia, 85; Catharine, 46; Hannah, 46, 64; Judith, 36; Kitty, 64; Mildred, 46; W., 19; William, 61; William T., 85, 86
Thruston: Jack, 173
Tibbs: Eliza, 2
Tidball: Fanny, 232
TIDBALL: A.S., 168; James, 61; Mrs., 242; Mrs. A.E., 252; Mrs. S.W., 235; Susan W., 228; T.A., 235; Thomas A., 228; Thomas Allen, 242, 245
Tilden, 69
Tildy, 49, 52
TILGHMAN: Ann B., 222; George, 222
Tillah, 101
Tim, 27, 226
Timathey, 143
TIMBERLAKE: Capt., 136; D., 105; David, 132, 202, 204; Elizabeth, 202; James W., 202; Jane, 202; Richard, 172
Timothy, 197
Titus, 27, 86, 88, 92
Toby, 26, 35, 156
Tody, 208
Tofer, 70
Tolaver, 127
Toliver, 103

Venice, 10, 129, 147
Venis, 143
Venus, 24, 31, 33, 44, 108, 173
Vilet, 39, 41, 142
Vilett, 49
Vina, 121, 164, 175, 190, 213
Vincent, 36, 160, 212, 223
Vincent Jr, 208
Vincent Sr, 208
Vind, 85
Vine, 159
Vinny, 121
Viny, 175
Violet, 49, 85, 149, 150, 162
Violett, 129, 147, 153, 173
Virgil, 95, 161
Virgin, 173
Virginia, 148, 206, 217
Virtue: James, 15
Vole, 15
Von REESEN: Susan C., 182
VONREIZEN: John, 93

WAGGONER: Polly,   92;
    William, 92
Wagoner, 191
WAITE: Obed, 198
Waley: George, 14
Walker, 27, 234
WALKER: Edward, 188; James,
    40, 41, 94; Lewis, 22; Thomas
    B., 74
WALKINS: E., 246
Wall, 56, 182
WALL: George M., 184
Wallace, 81, 93
Wallis, 47
WALLS: George, 117, 124
Walter, 175, 225
WALTER: John, 132; Thomas
    B., 67, 116
WALTERS: Thomas B., 57

WARD: George W., 204; Henry
    P., 236; R.G., 82
WARE: Charles A., 95; Charles
    Alexander, 83; Harriet, 95;
    Harriet M., 91; Harriet Mary
    T., 151; Harriet Mary Tod,
    83; J.W., 101; James, 83, 95,
    100, 151; James William, 83,
    151; Josiah William, 83, 100;
    Lucy Catharine, 83, 150;
    Thomas,   87;   Thomas
    Marshall, 83, 151
Warner, 81, 126, 143, 149, 150,
    174, 206
Warren, 128, 203
Washington, 59, 81, 91, 93, 97,
    106, 107, 118, 119, 136, 159,
    164, 170, 175, 208, 249; John,
    116; Peyton, 237
WASHINGTON: Catherine, 24;
    Elizabeth, 24; Fairfax, 46;
    Hannah, 24, 46; Herbert, 174;
    Mildred, 24; Mrs. John, 24;
    Warner, 24, 35, 135; Whiting,
    46
Wat, 87, 121, 125
WATERS: Jane, 172; Thomas, 5
WATKINS: Isham, 146
WATSON: Eveline, 158, 169;
    James,   136,   148,   149;
    William, 142
Watt, 108, 164
WATTS: David, 16; Judith, 16
Waverly, 177
WAY: Elias, 109; Elijah, 105;
    James, 126, 131; R., 170;
    Thomas, 109
Weaver: John, 103
WEAVER: David,   215;
    Marshee, 183; William, 215
Webb, 23; Esther, 197
Wells: Alfred, 126
WELLS: Mrs., 59; Richard, 225

307

Heritage Books by Sandra Barlau:

Some Slaves of Caroline County, Virginia,
Will Books 19, 29, 30, 31 and 32; and Guardian's Book

Some Slaves of Fauquier County, Virginia
Volume I: Will Books 1–10, 1759–1829
Volume II: Will Books 11–20, 1829–1847
Volume III: Will Books 21–31, 1847–1869
Volume IV: Master Index, Will Books 1–31, 1759–1869

Some Slaves of Frederick County, Virginia, Will Books 1-28, 1743–1868

Some Slaves of Prince William County, Virginia,
Partial Will Books, 1734–1872

Some Slaves of Rappahannock County, Virginia,
Will Books A to D, 1833–1865 and Old Rappahannock County, Virginia,
Will Books 1 and 2, 1664–1682

Some Slaves of Virginia, 1674–1894:
Lost Records Localities Digital Collection of the Library of Virginia

Some Slaves of Virginia:
The Cohabitation Registers of 27 February 1866 from the
Lost Records Localities Digital Collection of the Library of Virginia

Volume I: Augusta County, Buckingham County, Caroline County,
Culpeper County, Floyd County

Volume II: Fluvanna County, Goochland County, Hanover County,
Henry County, Lunenburg County

Volume III: Montgomery County, Prince Edward County, Richmond
County, Roanoke County, Scott County

Volume IV: Smyth County, Surry County, Warren County, Washington
County, Westmoreland County, Wythe County

Volume V: Master Index

Some Slaves of Warren County, Virginia Will Books A, B, C, 1835–1904

Washington, D.C. Slave Owner Petitions, 1862–1863,
Filed under the Act of April 16, 1862 and Other Documents from the
National Archives and Records Administration, Washington D.C.